NEW HORIZONS IN
HISPANIC/LATINO(A)
THEOLOGY

NEW HORIZONS IN HISPANIC/LATINO(A) THEOLOGY

BENJAMÍN VALENTÍN

THE
PILGRIM
PRESS
Cleveland

For each and every preceding Latino(a) theologian and religious scholar,
who has labored to bequeath to our and all future generations
a discursive tradition worthy of recognition.

The Pilgrim Press
700 Prospect Avenue
Cleveland, Ohio 44115-1100
pilgrimpress.com

© 2003 by Benjamín Valentín

All rights reserved. Published 2003

Printed in the United States of America on acid-free paper

08   07   06   05   04   03   5   4   3   2   1

Library of Congress Cataloging-in-Publication Data
New horizons in Hispanic/Latino(a) theology / [edited by] Benjamin Valentin.
    p. cm.
  ISBN 0-8298-1542-2 (pbk. : alk. paper)
  1. Hispanic American theology.   I. Title: New horizons in Hispanic/Latino
theology.   II. Title: New horizons in Hispanic/Latina theology.   III. Valentin,
Benjamin.
BT83.575.N49 2003
230'.089'68073 – dc22

                                                          2003057951

Contents

Acknowledgments   vii

Contributors   ix

Introduction   1

Part I
EXPERIENCES, REPRESENTATION, AND CRITICAL RELIGIOUS DISCOURSE

1. Encountering the Bible in an Age of Diversity and
   Globalization: Teaching toward Intercultural Criticism
   FRANCISCO LOZADA JR.   13

2. Visions of Hope: The Legacy of the Early Church
   ZAIDA MALDONADO PÉREZ   35

3. *Dis*-covering the Silences: A Postcolonial Critique
   of U.S. Religious Historiography
   HJAMIL A. MARTÍNEZ-VÁZQUEZ   50

4. En-Gendered Territory: U.S. Missionaries' Discourse
   in Puerto Rico (1898–1920)
   MAYRA RIVERA RIVERA   79

Part II
CULTURE, POLITICAL THEORY, AND THEOLOGICAL HERMENEUTICS

5. *Oye, ¿Y Ahora Qué?* / Say, Now What? Prospective Lines
   of Development for U.S. Hispanic/Latino(a) Theology
   BENJAMÍN VALENTÍN   101

6. Unearthing the Latino(a) Imagination: Literature and
   Theology, Some Methodological Gestures
   MICHELLE A. GONZÁLEZ   119

7. "Liberation" in the Latino(a) Context: Retrospect and Prospect
   CHRISTOPHER D. TIRRES   138

8. The Fundamental Problematic of U.S. Hispanic Theology
   MANUEL J. MEJIDO   163

Part III
AGENCY, COMMUNITY,
AND RELIGIOUS PRACTICE

9. On Tragic Beauty
   ALEX NAVA   181

10. A Rereading of Latino(a) Pentecostalism
    SAMUEL CRUZ   201

11. Transformative Struggle: The Spirituality of Las Hermanas
    LARA MEDINA   217

12. The Predicament of *Neplanta:* Chicano(a) Religions
    in the Twenty-First Century
    RUDY V. BUSTO   238

Index   251

Acknowledgments

In the role of editor, I have many people to acknowledge and thank as this book appears. First, I am happy to dedicate this book to preceding Latino(a) theologians and religious scholars of what may be called the first and second generations. Their intellectual and political labor has cleared the way for current religious colloquies and for all future theological fields of vision. *¡Gracias a todos!* Personally, I wish to thank Justo González, Daisy Machado, Ada María Isasi-Díaz, Otto Maduro, Fernando Segovia, Luis Rivera Pagán, Harold Recinos, Eldin Villafañe, Milagros Peña, Efraín Agosto, Ana María Díaz-Stevens, Anthony Stevens-Arroyo, and Roberto Pazmiño for manifold support throughout the years. I would like to thank my parents — Rev. Angel M. Valentín and Santa Valentín — for their boundless love, care, and ideal example in life. Special thanks is also due to my beloved siblings — Elieser Valentín and Bethsaida Valentín — for their many-faceted encouragement and esteem. I love you both. I want to extend a special thank-you to my sweetheart, soul mate, and fiancée — Alba Karina Aguirre — for her love, backing, and edifying inspiration. Just as Solomon once proclaimed, I today can enthusiastically say that "I found her whom my soul loves. I held her and would not let her go." I would also like to thank my beloved "brother" and dear friend, Anthony B. Pinn, for his unreserved support, encouragement, guidance, and incomparable friendship over many years. Similarly, I am grateful to Catherine Keller and Gordon D. Kaufman for granting me many-sided nourishment, friendship, valuable prodding, backing, and their edifying regard over the years. Thank you always!

I, and all of the contributors to this book, send out a loud and wholehearted thank-you to the Hispanic Theological Initiative, and all those connected to the HTI, for providing community and multifarious support. This generation, and many future generations of Latino(a) theologians and religious scholars, will be able to conceptualize new theological and/or hermeneutical horizons in large part because of your travail. I especially wish to thank Justo González, Daisy Machado, Zaida Maldonado Pérez, Joanne Rodríguez, Angela Schoepf, and Maria Kennedy for their service and friendship. *¡Gracias siempre!* I thank the faculty, administrators, staff, and students at Andover Newton Theological School for providing me supportive space in which to work.

I would also like to thank all the members, ministerial leaders, and friends of mine at La Congregación León de Juda/The American Baptist Congregation Lion of Judah in Boston and La Iglesia de Dios/The Church of God in New York City for their warm embrace, spiritual nourishment, community, and support. *¡Muchas gracias!*

A hearty thanks is due to my of more recent make extended family — Melissa Valentín, Sylvia Rodríguez, Jackie Rodríguez, Félix "Jr." Meléndez, Bert Rodríguez, and Jorge Burgos — for their acceptance and affection. *¡Qué Dios les bendiga siempre!*

Finally, I want to thank all the folks at The Pilgrim Press for their help in making this book a reality. Particularly, I thank Timothy Stavetieg and George Graham for believing in this project. I am also grateful to Ulrike Guthrie for her thoughtful contributions to the manuscript. And, for sure, I offer a strong and loud thank-you to the folks who contributed essays to this project. Thank you all!

Contributors

Rudy V. Busto is Assistant Professor of Religious Studies at the University of California, Santa Barbara. His research and teaching interests are in Asian American/Pacific Islander and Chicano(a)/Latino(a) religious traditions.

Samuel Cruz earned his Ph.D. in the area of Sociology of Religion at Drew University (Madison, New Jersey). His research and teaching interests are in Latino(a) Pentecostalism and Afro-Caribbean religions. He is Associate Minister at the Fort Washington Collegiate Church (New York City).

Michelle A. González is Assistant Professor of Theological Studies at Loyola Marymount University (Los Angeles). Her research and teaching interests include U.S. and Third World liberation theologies; feminist theologies; and interdisciplinary work in theology and literature. She recently completed a book on the theology and philosophy of seventeenth-century Mexican writer Sor Juana Inés de la Cruz, which will be published by Orbis Books.

Francisco Lozada Jr. is the Chair of the Religious Studies Department and holds the Thomas A. French Chair in Religious Studies at the University of the Incarnate Word (San Antonio, Texas). His specialty is in the area of contemporary biblical hermeneutics. He is the author of *A Literary Reading of John 5: Text as Construction*.

Zaida Maldonado Pérez is Assistant Professor of Theological Studies at Asbury Theological Seminary (Orlando, Florida). Her research interests lie in early Christian history. With Justo González, she is coauthor of *An Introduction to Christian Theology*.

Hjamil A. Martínez-Vázquez earned his Ph.D. in Religious History at the Lutheran School of Theology in Chicago. His interests are in U.S. religious history, philosophy of history, postcolonial theory, and Chicano(a) studies.

Lara Medina is Assistant Professor of Religious Studies at California State University, Northridge, and the author of numerous publications. Her research and teaching interests emphasize the role of Latinas in shaping religious discourse and practice.

Manuel J. Mejido is a Ph.D. candidate in the Ethics and Society Program of the Graduate Division of Religion at Emory University (Atlanta). He is currently a visiting researcher at the Institut Superieur de Philosophie of the Université Catholique de Louvain. Author of numerous articles that analyze Hispanic/Latino(a) religion and theology, his particular interests are the sociology of religion, the sociology of knowledge, and critical theory.

Alex Nava is Assistant Professor of Religious Studies in the Department of Classics at the University of Arizona (Tucson). His research and teaching interests lie in U.S. Hispanic/Latino(a) and Latin American Religion and Theology, and in the study of Native American traditions of the Southwest from the time of the conquest to the present. He is author of *The Mystical-Prophetic Thought of Simone Weil and Gustavo Gutiérrez.*

Mayra Rivera Rivera is a Ph.D. candidate in the Theology and Religious Studies Department at Drew University (Madison, New Jersey). Her research focuses on the potential relatedness of postcolonial feminist theory and contemporary theology, and on the doctrine of divine transcendence.

Christopher Tirres is a Ph.D. candidate in the Department of Religion at the Graduate School of Arts and Sciences at Harvard University (Cambridge, Massachusetts). His areas of interest include North American Hispanic/Latino(a) theology, critical theory (Frankfurt School); and the philosophy of religion.

Benjamín Valentín is Assistant Professor of Theology and Culture at Andover Newton Theological School (Newton Centre, Massachusetts). His research and teaching interests are in contemporary theology and culture, constructive theology, the relation of religion and theology to American public life, and liberation theology. He is author of *Mapping Public Theology: Beyond Culture, Identity, and Difference* and coeditor of *The Ties That Bind: African American and Hispanic American/Latino/a Theologies in Dialogue.*

Introduction

In the introduction to their wonderful book *Recognizing the Latino Resurgence in U.S. Religion,* Ana María Díaz-Stevens and Anthony Stevens-Arroyo begin their historical recovery of the varieties of Latino(a)[1] religious experience by calling attention to a narrative found in the Gospel of Luke 24:13–35. Their superb recapitulation of that biblical story offers a good starting point for this book's introduction. As they summarize it, the chronicle goes like this:

> Two disciples are leaving Jerusalem after the Passion and Death of Jesus, with heads held low as they walk on the road leading out of the city. They meet a stranger, with whom they strike up a conversation as they go along. He seems not to know anything of the events of the past three days, and the disciples spin out their tale. They admit they had hoped that Jesus would restore the Kingdom of Israel to its past glory, which discloses their political views; they relate that they do not believe the account of "some women" that Jesus had risen from the dead, which says mountains about a gender bias. But the stranger proceeds to cite the prophets and the scripture to convince them that they should have anticipated these events rather than be discouraged about them. As the trio approaches the

---

1. The terms "Hispanic" and "Latino" or "Latina" are often used interchangeably within our national context in an attempt to coalesce the varied U.S. experiences and identities of peoples with Spanish-speaking ancestry. I generally use the signifier "Latino/a" to refer to Latinos and Latinas, except in areas where such a gender-conscious designation may prove cumbersome. Although both terms have limitations and are variously problematic, I prefer to use the panethnic umbrella term "Latino/a" rather than "Hispanic," believing that it better embraces all Latin American nationalities, some of which have no ties to Spain. This designation also allows me to refer at once to Latinas and Latinos, without having to repeat or to alternate the use of the gender-specific terms. Nevertheless, when referring to the theological production emanating from the different Latino/a communities, I will generally use the term "Hispanic/Latino(a)." I do this because certain Latino and/or Latina theologians prefer the term "Latino" or "Latina," while others prefer "Hispanic." For a good presentation of the objections that could be raised against both "Hispanic" and "Latino" or "Latina," see Jorge Gracia, *Hispanic/Latino Identity: A Philosophical Perspective* (Malden, Mass.: Blackwell, 2000), esp. 1–26.

1

small town of Emmaus, the two disciples excitedly plead with the stranger to dine with them now that evening has fallen. And when he breaks bread at table with them, they recognize that the stranger is Jesus. He vanishes from their sight before they can recover, and they are left with emotion: Their hearts, they feel, were "burning inside them" as they walked on the road with a man they did not recognize, speaking of events they had not understood.[2]

This narrative provides a fitting analogy from which to speak about U.S. Hispanic/Latino(a) theological and religious scholarship, because Latino(a) theology and religious studies resemble that unacknowledged, unrecognized conversation partner "on the road to Emmaus." Despite the fact that it has existed right alongside other theologies of liberation, and alongside other progressive religious colloquies since at least 1975, Hispanic/Latino(a) theology and Latino(a) religious discourse in general have largely been overlooked in the broader spheres of religious scholarship. This neglect mirrors the lack of recognition that has more generally been tendered to the Latino(a) experience in the broader U.S. society.

Change is in the air, however. Gradually, the inimitable theological expressions and religious interpretations of Latino(a) theologians and religious scholars are beginning to draw the attention of many within the U.S. theological academy and the greater society. Spurred on by the recent interest in the long-ignored reality of Latino/as in the United States, perhaps due to the heightened awareness of the Latino(a) population's increase and the growth in the numbers of Latino(a) scholars, U.S. Hispanic/Latino(a) theology and religious scholarship have recently taken enormous strides both in the proliferation and richness of their distinctive expression. Along with this have come a long-overdue increased visibility and recognition.

Although Latino(a) theological and religious discourse may seem to be a novel elaboration to many in the mainstream of U.S. theology, it is possible to speak of three waves in the articulation of U.S. Hispanic/Latino(a) theology and religion. The initial stage of U.S. Hispanic/Latino(a) theological and religious articulation was founded upon the formative published contributions of a precious few Latino(a) writers such as Virgilio Elizondo, Andrés Guerrero, Justo González, Orlando

---

2. Ana María Díaz-Stevens and Anthony M. Stevens-Arroyo, *Recognizing the Latino Resurgence in U.S. Religion: The Emmaus Paradigm* (Boulder, Colo.: Westview Press, 1998), xvii.

Costas, Allan Figueroa Deck, Anthony Stevens-Arroyo, Ada María Isasi-Díaz, and Yolanda Tarango from 1975 to 1990. In the 1990s Latino(a) theology and religious theory burgeoned, displaying an impressive array of creative theological and hermeneutical innovations founded upon both the continuing contributions of some first-wave Latino(a) thinkers and the emergence of a strong second wave of Latino(a) religious hermeneuts. Thinkers such as María Pilar Aquino, Arturo Bañuelas, Orlando Espín, Ismael García, Roberto Goizueta Jr., Daisy Machado, Roberto Pazmino, Harold Recinos, Jeanette Rodríguez-Holguin, Jean-Pierre Ruiz, Fernando Segovia, and Eldin Villafañe, among others, helped to usher in this second wave of Latino(a) religious scholarship. Along with the pioneering voices of the first wave, these second-wave articulators have helped to set in place Latino(a) theology's distinctive focus on the categories of culture and identity and on the thematic concepts of *mestizaje* (cultural hybridity), popular religion, and *teología en conjunto* (theology done in joint collaboration and in community).

I believe that at present we are beginning to witness a third wave in the articulation of Latino(a) theological thought, and more generally in the theoretical interpretation of the varieties of Latino(a) religious experience, with the initial and distinctive writings of thinkers such as Edwin Aponte, Rudy Busto, Samuel Cruz, Miguel De La Torre, Teresa Delgado, Miguel Díaz, Gastón Espinoza, Michelle González, Leticia Guardiola-Sáenz, Francisco Lozada Jr., Zaida Maldonado Pérez, Loida Martell-Otero, Hjamil Martínez, Lara Medina, Manuel Mejido, Alex Nava, Luis Pedraja, Nancy Pineda-Madrid, Mayra Rivera, Christopher Tirres, and myself, Benjamín Valentín. The work of these more recent authors honors and builds upon the thematic and interpretive foundations put in place by earlier and still-contributing Latino(a) writers. Yet, beyond this, I suggest that the work of some of these authors has begun to promote a critical expansion of the horizons of Latino(a) theology. Whether by expanding on previous categories, by focusing on new themes and motifs, by seeking to fill earlier blind spots, or by casting a critical eye on previous assumptions and/or tendencies, the writings of this third wave of religious scholars provide a window on the continued emergence of, and the new turns and methodological directions being taken in, U.S. Hispanic/Latino(a) theology and religious scholarship.[3]

---

3. For more on the historical and thematic development of Latino(a) theology see my article, "Strangers No More: An Introduction to, and Interpretation of, U.S. Hispanic/Latino(a)

Since 1992, nine anthologies have appeared which are devoted both
to the elaboration and tracing of U.S. Latino(a) theology: (1) *Voces:
Voices from the Hispanic Church* [1992]; (2) *Frontiers of Hispanic Theology in the United States* [1992]; (3) *We Are a People! Initiatives in
Hispanic American Theology* [1992]; (4) *Mestizo Christianity: Theology from the Latino Perspective* [1995]; (5) *Hispanic/Latino Theology:
Challenge and Promise* [1996]; (6) *Teología en Conjunto: A Collaborative Hispanic Protestant Theology* [1997]; (7) *From the Heart of Our
People: Latino/a Explorations in Catholic Systematic Theology* [1999];
(8) *The Ties That Bind: African American and Hispanic American/
Latino/a Theologies in Dialogue* [2001]; and (9) *A Reader in Latina
Feminist Theology: Religion and Justice* [2002].[4] These texts are very
valuable for understanding U.S. Hispanic/Latino(a) theology. Nevertheless, little attention is given in them to the ways in which the voices of
more recent Latino(a) theologians and religious scholars are extending
and in some cases even contesting the boundaries of this germinal theo-
logical/religious discursive tradition. Thus, they do not shed full light on
the waves of articulation found within Hispanic/Latino(a) theology and
religious scholarship and, therefore, on the continuing development of
this field of study. This volume distinctively seeks to provide a sampling
of some of the *new horizons* emerging in U.S. Hispanic/Latino(a) theology and religious scholarship, all while also considering the implications
of these for this still-evolving discursive analogue.

Obviously this book is not a comprehensive guide to U.S. Hispanic/
Latino(a) theology and religious scholarship, its history, thematics, concerns, and list of articulators. Rather, it is an attempt to hint at the
continuing development and progression of this theology and religious

---

Theology," in *The Ties That Bind: African American and Hispanic American/Latino/a Theologies in Dialogue*, ed. Anthony B. Pinn and Benjamín Valentín (New York: Continuum, 2001),
38–53.

4. Justo González, ed., *Voces: Voices from the Hispanic Church* (Nashville: Abingdon
Press, 1992); Allan Figueroa Deck, ed., *Frontiers of Hispanic Theology in the United States*
(Maryknoll, N.Y.: Orbis Books, 1992); Roberto Goizueta, ed., *We Are a People! Initiatives in
Hispanic American Theology* (Philadelphia: Fortress Press, 1992); Arturo Bañuelas, ed., *Mes-
tizo Christianity: Theology from the Latino Perspective* (Maryknoll, N.Y.: Orbis Books, 1995);
Ada María Isasi-Díaz and Fernando Segovia, eds., *Hispanic/Latino Theology: Challenge and
Promise* (Minneapolis: Fortress Press, 1996); José David Rodríguez and Loida Martell-Otero,
eds., *Teología en Conjunto: A Collaborative Hispanic Protestant Theology* (Nashville: West-
minster John Knox Press, 1997); Orlando Espín and Miguel Díaz, eds., *From the Heart of Our
People: Latino/a Explorations in Catholic Systematic Theology* (Maryknoll, N.Y.: Orbis Books,
1999); Pinn and Valentín, eds., *The Ties That Bind,*; *A Reader in Latina Feminist Theology:
Religion and Justice* (Austin: University of Texas Press, 2002).

subfield as it is made manifest within the writings of a select group of third-wave scholars. The thirteen authors represented here do not write on the same topic, nor do they pursue the same issues. Similarly, they do not necessarily converge on matters of methodology or sources, and they do not agree on which questions to ask — much less on the possible answers to these. But the diverse contributions of these writers do reveal how widespread is the development of U.S. Hispanic/Latino(a) theology and religious scholarship. One trait that unites all of the chapters in this book is a longing to contribute to the further unfolding of Latino(a) theology and religious studies. Another hallmark that is shared by these essays is synchronously an interdisciplinary and "de-disciplinizing" sensibility: a desire to navigate across disciplinary lines and an unwillingness to be tied down to a specialty and the imposed restrictions or expectations of a field of study.

Beyond this affective and responsive connection, the articles in this book implicitly if not explicitly reflect a concern with a guiding set of questions:

1. What inadvertency is identifiable in U.S. Hispanic/Latino(a) theology or religious studies?

2. What are the implications of the new thematics, concerns, and/or sources introduced in these essays for matters of theological or religious epistemology in this germinal discursive analogue — that is, for our ways of "understanding" the nature and/or tasks of Latino(a) theology or religious studies?

3. What are the implications of the new thematics, concerns, and/or sources introduced in these essays for matters of methodology in this discursive arena — that is, for our ways of "doing" Latino(a) theology or religious scholarship?

Part 1, "Experiences, Representation, and Critical Religious Discourse," contains four essays that in differing ways offer a fresh (re)reading and treatment of history or textual memory. This section opens with an essay written by Francisco Lozada Jr., titled "Encountering the Bible in an Age of Diversity and Globalization: Teaching toward Intercultural Criticism." The piece is an attempt to challenge teachers in the field of religious studies and, more particularly, in biblical studies to consider a variety of postmodernist and postcolonial pedagogies in the reading and teaching of the Bible in light of our increasingly diverse and "globalized" world. In the second essay of this section, "Visions of Hope: The Legacy of the Early Church," Zaida Maldonado Pérez looks at an underexplored realm of Christian history within Latino(a) theological literature and, in the process, tenders a liberationist (re)reading of the visions and actions of early Christian martyrs. In our search for historical connectedness, she argues, we need also to lay claim to the legacy bequeathed to us by our Christian ancestors: In it we will find a wealth of stories of "caminantes/sojourners" who subverted oppressive political, religious, and social structures through their defiant hope. The third essay, "*Dis*-covering the Silences: A Postcolonial Critique of U.S. Religious Historiography," sets forth Hjamil Martínez's efforts to provide readers with an alternative methodology of deconstructing and reconstructing U.S. religious historiography. His ultimate aim is to expose and confront the colonialist agenda within traditional U.S. religious historiography, and to provide hints of the ways in which new *post*colonial historiographies can be constructed. The final essay in this section, Mayra Rivera's "En-Gendered Territory: U.S. Missionaries' Discourse in Puerto Rico (1898–1920)," is a postcolonial feminist reading of the U.S. missionaries' discourse in Puerto Rico immediately following its invasion in 1898. Focusing on the processes of identification that shaped the missionaries' self-identity, the article traces the intricate relationships that existed between ideas of subordination of women, nature, and darkness in the missionaries' descriptions of themselves, of Puerto Rican *others*, and of the character of the evangelizing mission. Rivera ends her essay by issuing a challenge to Latino(a) theology: Latino(a) theologians can and should not only counter the sociopolitical oppression suffered within their communities, but also offer alternative articulations of traditional doctrines, such as the doctrine of creation, in order to better support the project of liberation in all of its complexity.

Part 2, "Culture, Political Theory, and Theological Hermeneutics," includes five essays that in various ways engage with cultural practice and/or political philosophy and also venture into the realm of discourse analysis. My essay, "*Oye, ¿Y Ahora Qué?* / Say, Now What? Prospective Lines of Development for U.S. Hispanic/Latino(a) Theology," opens this section. The piece heralds Latino(a) theology's focus on the category of culture, on matters of self and collective/group identity, and on a dialogical and collaborative spirit in theological work. It suggests that Latino(a) theologians are now in position to advance these worthy emphases by further incorporating Hispanic/Latino(a) cultural production in their theologies; by problematizing and/or complexifying their emphasis upon a discourse and politics of identity; and by expanding their notion of *teología en conjunto* (i.e., collaborative or joint theology) to include and promote the desirability of transcultural dialogue and coalition building across lines of difference. The second essay in this section, "Unearthing the Latino(a) Imagination: Literature and Theology, Some Methodological Gestures," by Michelle González examines the role of theological aesthetics in the discourse and method of Latino(a) systematic theology through the lens of literature. González proposes literature as a theological source and voice, emphasizing the theological import of literary voices. Building on the work of Swiss theologian Hans Urs von Balthasar, she offers a methodology for the integration of theological aesthetics in Latino(a) theology.

Christopher Tirres puts forward the section's third essay, titled " 'Liberation' in the Latino(a) Context: Retrospect and Prospect." This essay addresses Latino(a) theology's ambiguous use of the term "liberation." Following an analysis of writings by Andrés Guerrero and Roberto Goizueta, Christopher Tirres argues that two ideas of liberation — liberation as resistance and revolution — can often be found within this discursive analogue. In an effort to bring into clearer view the link between resistance and social transformation/revolution, he suggests that the idea of "integral liberation" can offer a useful taxonomic framework for the purposes of connecting the various accents or dimensions of liberation. In closing, Christopher Tirres submits that U.S. Latino(a) theology has tended to interpret liberation by way of an appeal to the idea of resistance. He proposes that much could be gained by more explicit engagement with the Marxian paradigm of "production" and "revolution" in Latino(a) theology. The section's final essay, "The Fundamental Problematic of U.S. Hispanic Theology," is authored by Manuel Mejido. He proposes that U.S. Hispanic theologians are caught between two radically different understandings of theology: theology understood as historical-hermeneutic science and theology understood as a critically oriented science, theology as understood by the dominant European and Anglo-American theological traditions and theology as understood by the Latin American theologies of liberation. Calling attention to the threat of intellectual assimilation, Mejido suggests that it is the task of a new generation of U.S. Hispanic theologians to rethink the base concepts of Latino(a) theology in light of this tension. As both a critically oriented theological hermeneutic of liberation and a set of scholarly practices that reflectively resist assimilation, he argues, Hispanic theology can claim its proper ground only by regarding itself as the theological articulation of a Latino(a) history of *mestizaje* — in short, as the theological rendering of a fragmented life and history.

Part 3, "Agency, Community, and Religious Practice," contains four essays that by different means explore Latino(a) religious experience, action, and creativity. In this section's first essay, "On Tragic Beauty," Alex Nava takes on the challenge that evil and suffering pose to aesthetical theologies. Adeptly weaving together a narrative and reflective style, he challenges us to search into a tragic sensibility and to wrestle with divine ambiguity in the face of tragedy. In view of the absurdity of unjust suffering, Nava's essay rehearses us in the practice of a lament of survival, resistance, and hope; a poetics of love; and a faith that motivates us to believe that the hidden God is there — "invisibly present in the desolate circumstances of life." Samuel Cruz presents this section's second essay: "A Rereading of Latino(a) Pentecostalism," a significant contribution to the study of Pentecostalism. Contrary to popular perception and much prior literature on the subject, Samuel Cruz argues that Latino(a) Pentecostalism is much more than a "pie in the sky" religious movement and that it is actually much more grounded in the concrete social, cultural, and political reality of Hispanic communities than other liberal and conservative Protestant traditions.

The third essay in this final section, "Transformative Struggle: The Spirituality of Las Hermanas," is put forward by Lara Medina. The essay assists in filling the vacuum of scholarly studies on the agency of Latinas by analyzing the religious discourse and practice of Las Hermanas, a thirty-year-old national religious-political feminist organization of Latina Roman Catholics. Lara Medina submits that for three decades Las Hermanas has provided a counter-discourse to the patriarchy and Eurocentrism of the U.S. Roman Catholic Church by creating an alternative space for Latina Catholics to express a feminist spirituality and theology. Furthermore, she suggests that the history of this organization offers both a model for how Latinas live in the intersection of the sacred and the political and also a holistic epistemology that could enrich Latino(a) religiosity and theology. In the book's final essay, "The Predicament of *Neplanta:* Chicano(a) Religions in the Twenty-First Century," Rudy Busto explores forms of Chicano(a) religious expression that may be seen as "extrachurch." That is, he looks into modes of religion that transcend the boundaries of church life, going far beyond mass and sacrament, text or ritual. Busto suggests that these may be read as "Neplanta Religion," as religious expression that points to the negotiation and pursuit of religiosity beyond the "predicate" of what normatively constitutes religion or Chicano(a) cultures. Moreover, he submits that in these epic spaces of extrachurch Chicano(a) religious expression there exists the potential to move and breathe new life and interpretations into ancient stories and knowledge away from the censoring pens of "scholars" and theological authority. These also pay homage, Busto offers, to a world that — despite the corrosive powers of the modern and postmodern predicaments — has managed to survive.

These articles convey varied perspectives, concerns, and interests, and they most definitely also communicate distinct approaches to their topics. This heterogeneity, however, is not something that I or the contributors to this book deem a cause of concern about inconsonance or disconnectedness. On the contrary, the diversity conveyed in this volume is something we intentionally sought both to ensure and to celebrate. We were interested to see what new and diverse entries might be brought to bear on the analysis and formulation of U.S. Latino(a) theology and religious studies. Taken together, the essays collected here herald the realization and possibility of these scholarly subfields. Together they long to call attention to new intonations and horizons in U.S. Hispanic/Latino(a) theology and religious studies. This volume, then, attempts to provide a portal through which these *voices* and *horizons* might be synchronously conceived, celebrated, accessed, and expanded.

PART I

Experiences, Representation, and Critical Religious Discourse

1

Encountering the Bible in an Age of Diversity and Globalization

Teaching toward Intercultural Criticism

FRANCISCO LOZADA JR.

INTRODUCTION

Teaching biblical studies in this age of diversity and globalization is like crossing a geographical or cultural border, physically as well as electronically, for the very first time.[1] One never knows what to expect. This uncertainty, whether it is approached with trepidation or anticipation, challenges one to reexamine not only the world of the other, but also one's own world — particularly one's own identity in relation to sameness and difference. It also forces one to analyze one's own pedagogical discourse and practices, which are the focus of this chapter. In other words, as someone who has committed himself to the study of the Bible and ancient Jewish texts, encountering diverse identities in the text as well as outside it is a daily event in the classroom. This chapter aims to reflect critically upon how I construct my own pedagogical discourse and practices in relationship to identity and ancient texts. The goal here is not to argue for one approach, but rather to try to start a conversation on how pedagogical discourses and practices about ancient texts are transmitted in the classroom as well as on international soils. The proper place to begin is with my own approach.

This is a revised version of an essay that appeared on-line in *Religious Studies News/SBL Edition* 1, no. 1 (August 1, 2000), under the title, "Ethnic Identity in the Classroom." See *www.sbl-site.org/Newsletter/08_2000*.

1. For a very good understanding of the role of technology and the teaching of religion see Richard S. Ascough, "Designing for Online Distance Education: Putting Pedagogy before Technology," *Teaching Theology and Religion* 5, no. 1 (February 2002): 17–29.

Central to my critical reflection on pedagogy is the question of who stands to benefit from my particular discourses and practices and who does not. In other words, the assumptions and principles one employs in training students how to read and study texts must be critically scrutinized. What assists me in engaging the assumptions and principles of my pedagogy is intercultural criticism, which several Latino(a) biblical scholars and theologians have constructed and developed in recent years.[2] This chapter not only intends to build on this research; it also attempts to make a contribution to the contextualization of teaching — an area that needs addressing in the field of Latino(a) religion or theology.[3] It is a modest effort to begin a conversation regarding how to go about using or implementing intercultural criticism in the classroom.

The predominant version of intercultural criticism within the field of biblical studies is a strategy of reading that takes seriously three dimensions of the interpretative process: text, readers, and readings. First, with regard to the text, the focus is on the text as a literary, ideological, and rhetorical product: literary in the sense of its artistic dimension, namely,

---

2. Fernando F. Segovia has written much on the topic of intercultural criticism, see "Toward Intercultural Criticism: A Reading Strategy from the Diaspora," in *Reading from This Place,* vol. 2, *Social Location and Biblical Interpretation in the United States,* ed. Fernando F. Segovia and Mary Ann Tolbert (Minneapolis: Fortress, 1995), 303–30, and "Reading-Across: Intercultural Criticism and Textual Posture," in *Interpreting beyond Borders,* The Bible and Postcolonialism 3, ed. Fernando F. Segovia (Sheffield, U.K.: Sheffield Academic Press, 2000): 59–83. For an example of the application of the approach see Jean-Pierre Ruiz, "Cardinal Francisco Ximénez de Cisneros and Bartolomé de las Casas the 'Procurator and Universal Protector of All Indians in the Indies,'" in *Journal of Hispanic/Latino Theology* 9, no. 3 (February 2002): 60–77; and Leticia A. Guardiola-Sáenz, "Reading from Ourselves: Identity and Hermeneutics among Mexican-American Feminists," in *A Reader in Latina Feminist Theology: Religion and Justice,* ed. María Pilar Aquino, Daisy L. Machado, and Jeanette Rodríguez (Austin: University of Texas Press, 2002), 80–97. See also my own work, "Contesting an Interpretation of John 5: Moving beyond Colonial Evangelism," in *John and Postcolonialism: Travel, Space, and Power,* The Bible and Postcolonialism 7, ed. Musa W. Dube and Jeffrey L. Staley (London: Sheffield Academic Press, 2002): 76–93. From a theological perspective, see Orlando O. Espín, "Toward the Construction of an Intercultural Theology of Tradition," *Journal of Hispanic/Latino Theology* 9, no. 3 (February 2002): 22–59; and María Pilar Aquino, "Latina Feminist Theology: Central Features," in *A Reader in Latina Feminist Theology: Religion and Justice,* 133–60.

3. For those Latino/as in the field of religious studies who have addressed the issue of teaching, see Fernando F. Segovia, "Pedagogical Discourse and Practices in Contemporary Biblical Criticism," in *Teaching the Bible: The Discourses and Politics of Biblical Pedagogy,* ed. Fernando F. Segovia and Mary Ann Tolbert (Maryknoll, N.Y.: Orbis Books, 1998), 1–28; Jean-Pierre Ruiz, "Four Faces of Theology: Four Johannine Conversations," in *Teaching the Bible,* 86–101; Francisco García-Treto, "Crossing the Line: Three Scenes of Divine-Human Engagement in the Hebrew Bible," in *Teaching the Bible,* 105–36; Fernando F. Segovia, "Pedagogical Discourse and Practices in Cultural Studies," in *Teaching the Bible,* 137–67; Ralph Casas, "'Making-Face, Making-Heart': The Spiritual Foundations of an Indigenous Pedagogy," *Journal of Hispanic/Latino Theology* 9, no. 2 (November 2001): 17–47.

its structure and narrative; ideological in the sense of its political and religious expressions; and rhetorical in the sense of its didactic or polemical dimension displayed through a variety of rhetorical intentions: admonition, consolation, and exhortation.[4] Second, with regard to readers, the readers' social location and agenda are critically examined within their contexts. Third, with regard to readings, the question of who serves to benefit and who does not is also at the forefront. This threefold analysis of the text, readers, and readings marks intercultural criticism and employs a "reading-across" strategy that aims to stress a broader dialogue with the public, an intensified focus on the geopolitical dimension of liberation, and a close evaluation of all discourses as constructions.[5] As such, intercultural criticism is my point of departure to analyze and engage teaching and learning in the classroom.

CONTEXTUALIZATION

One of my interests in the field of biblical studies is the study of identity.[6] I am interested in the study of identity from the point of view of the text (identity in the ancient Jewish texts), from that of the readers of the text (identity of the readers), and a study from the point of view of how identity is used to construct interpretations. The latter two foci have consumed most of my attention in the last several years as well as undergirded my pedagogical discourse and practices. Identity, for many postmodernists, is usually discussed around the tension between essentialist and nonessentialist perspectives of identity: between the notion of identity as something given and something that is always in process.[7] As one who espouses the latter perspective, identity is understood in the classroom not as something static and singular, but as shifting and multiple. I seek to discover identity not to restrict but

---

4. See Fernando F. Segovia, "John 1:1–18 as Entrée into Johannine Reality," in *Word, Theology, and Community,* ed. John Painter, R. Alan Culpepper, and Fernando F. Segovia (St. Louis: Chalice Press, forthcoming).

5. Segovia, "Reading-Across," 80–81.

6. By identity, I follow the lead of Stuart Hall who refers to the term as "the meeting point" which attempts to bring together those social factors that speak to us and those social factors that are constructed by other subjects or discourses. See Stuart Hall, "Introduction: Who Needs 'Identity'?" in *Questions of Cultural Identity,* ed. Stuart Hall and Paul du Gay (London: Sage Publications, 1996), 1–17.

7. Kathryn Woodward, "Introduction," in *Identity and Difference,* Book 3 of *Culture, Media and Identities,* ed. Kathryn Woodward (London: Sage, 1997), 11.

to appreciate that complexity or ambiguity cannot be limited.[8] This latter debate between the binary oppositions of clarity/complexity is most
evident, for example, when some students of Mexican American ancestry identify themselves differently as Hispanics, Latino/as, Tejano/as,
and Chicano/as. This panoply points not only to the heterogeneity of
Latino/as, but also to the difficulty in trying to produce clarity.

For many who are not part of this collective group, the complexity
can be frustrating because clarity of ethnic identity is not achieved. The
issue here is that many essentialists — consciously or unconsciously —
believe that complexity only leads to fragmentation, conflict, and difference, rather than unity, community, and sameness. I, for one, believe
that ambiguity or complexity of identity can be a positive state of being. I
see it as breaking down fixed patterns of identification, universality, and
coherence, all of which lead to dominating the other and undermining
diversity. Furthermore, cultural universalists or assimilationists prefer
identity in the singular rather than the plural. Sometimes universalism
results in a politics of erasure — that is, a politics that attempts to blur
and thereby obliterate the cultural identities and histories of many of the
underrepresented in our democratic society, resulting in a failure to deal
critically with racial and ethnic issues across the nation and globe. This
is the fear of many with regard to the impact of globalization.

In the study of the Bible, this politics of erasure is also found among
early Jewish/Christian studies when Hellenism or Judaism is understood
in the singular rather than in the plural. The collective noun in the singular does help with simplicity in explaining Hellenisms and Judaisms
in the classroom, especially to students unfamiliar with the topic. It
can likewise leave students with the myopic impression that the ancient
world was monocultural, resulting in an image of homogeneous identity in the ancient world.[9] Belief in a single culture and history based
on universalism runs the danger of an oppressive universalism in today's
world. For example, in the area of ancient Christianity and Judaism,
Daniel Boyarin perspicaciously points out the dangers of universalizing
Christianity or essentializing one's identity when he challenges the traditional line of interpretation of Galatians 3:26–29. This text suggests

---

8. Ibid., 1–6; Henry A. Giroux, *Border Crossings: Cultural Workers and the Politics of Education* (New York: Routledge, 1992), 24–25.

9. Daniel Boyarin, *A Radical Jew: Paul and the Politics of Identity* (Berkeley: University of California Press, 1994), 1–12.

that differences between individuals should be set aside in favor of a new identity in Christ Jesus: "all one in Christ Jesus." For Boyarin, identity should not disappear but rather be engaged in order to understand sameness and difference in the world today.[10] If not, violence, racism, and ethnocentrism are strong possibilities.

In the classroom, students at times enter with the strong assumption that all the Jewish people in the biblical texts are the same, all the Christians are the same, and even all the Greeks are the same. Their assumptions are based on the essentialist notion of identity. Sometimes this false assumption of identity spills over in their essentialist statements about other identities. For instance, all Latino/as are the same, white women and black women are the same, Jewish people are all the same, Muslims are all the same, to name a few. Contrary to such essentialist politics, I prefer a politics that aims, although not always successfully, toward celebrating diverse identities. I am interested in highlighting cultural identities and histories, whether in the biblical text or not, and demonstrating that diverse identities do not lead to radical separateness, but to self-reflection, openness to otherness, and seeing more of the world's horizons.[11]

The argument here is that intercultural criticism is one approach among many that emphasizes a strategy of reading-across of texts, readers, and interpretations of texts. This reading-across strategy calls for a greater emphasis on a public dialogue, a focus on imperial/colonial formations in and out of texts, and an intense questioning of all interpretations and constructions — including one's own. The goal is to yield diverse readings, but diverse readings that have carefully and seriously taken into consideration the questions of who serves to benefit and who not from such readings. In other words, it is a call to explore different ways in which we might invite and celebrate diverse identities in our classrooms using nontraditional pedagogic practices to challenge empiricism, objectivity, hierarchism, and competitiveness.[12]

I would like first to begin this call with a brief discussion of my present teaching context. Recognition of the teaching context, I believe, is a

---

10. Ibid., 228–60.

11. See Howard Thurman, *Jesus and the Disinherited* (Boston: Beacon Press, 1976), for an earlier and powerful call for engaging difference.

12. I understand competitiveness to mean arguing for one final reading of a text by showing how one's own reading is right and everyone else's is wrong.

prerequisite to understanding my particular context. It allows me to expand my own horizons and appreciate the horizons of others. Second, I consider certain pedagogic strategies designed to foster diverse identities in the classroom, which by no means suggests that my strategies are universal. I do believe that teaching is contextual, and that every teaching context is very different and particular to its location.[13] Third, I provide reviews of two texts that aim to introduce the topic of diverse identities by way of analyzing their reading strategies. This analysis serves to better understand intercultural biblical criticism. Put otherwise, I would like to propose an ethical framework for teaching biblical studies in this age of diversity and globalization. It is important to move toward understanding for and respect of the Other and an appreciation of the opportunities provided by diverse identities. However, I would argue that such an approach does not mean that debate ceases with regard to issues of diverse identities; debate is essential with an intercultural approach to reading texts.

Before I proceed, the teaching context from which I speak must be disclosed. Since it is well attested now that social location shapes meaning, this essay is surely not excluded. I teach at the University of the Incarnate Word, which is a predominantly Hispanic or Latino(a) school in San Antonio, Texas. The U.S. government considers it a Hispanic-serving institution. As the name of the school implies, it is a church-related university (Roman Catholic), founded in 1881 by the Congregation of the Sisters of Charity of the Incarnate Word (C.C.V.I.), who in 1984 adopted liberation theology's preferential option for the poor. I have not only embraced the Congregation's option for the poor, I have also expanded it to include all the oppressed or marginalized. Liberation from a postcolonial perspective underlies my pedagogical discourse and practice — that is, the liberation, empowerment, and decolonization of all marginalized peoples of God through critical engagement in the classroom of texts, readers, and readings. For instance, my pedagogy aims not so much to transmit knowledge that students can readily digest and adopt, but rather to take received knowledge and critically examine it. For me, this means preparing students in areas such as liberationist, feminist, and contextual approaches to religious studies from a postcolonial

---

13. If I taught at another institution, a school with very few Latino/as in the classroom, I am sure that my pedagogy would need to be modified. Also, I am tenured, which allows me the space to experiment in the classroom with various pedagogical practices.

perspective.[14] Content is still pertinent, but understanding the content in relationship to whom it serves to benefit and whom it does not is likewise necessary.

PEDAGOGIC STRATEGIES

I firmly believe that the study of ancient texts must be made meaningful before students can critically engage in learning. Not all students come to class motivated and ready to discuss the text at hand. Not always, but most often, particularly in introductory courses, students do not know enough to know whether they might be interested.[15] For me, this means I deliberately aim to make the subject matter connect with their lives.[16] The entry point I use is the topic of identity of the student/reader. Several strategies, centered on the diversity of identity, are employed in the classroom to help make the biblical text a site where students can critically reflect upon their identity and, more important, mobilize them politically to demand recognition of their culture and voice. I am not interested in using the biblical text in a colonialist fashion of homogenizing identity, nor in the traditional liberationist sense of correlating one's identity with the marginalized in the text. Rather, I am interested in using the biblical text as a point of departure to define and redefine the students' identity in relationship to their own history and agency within their world. This, of course, means that the biblical text itself undergoes interrogation in terms of how it constructs identities and as a literary, ideological, and rhetorical product. It also entails a critical assessment of the teacher, students, and texts.

   1. Identity of the Teacher: Teaching biblical studies is a partisan engagement.[17] I begin my classes usually with an introduction of my particular identity. This is by no means an easy task. Even though I have been trained in the context of postmodernism, the ethos of the academy

---

14. For a similar understanding of a postcolonial approach to teaching see Richard King, "Disciplining Religion," in *Orientalism and Religion: Postcolonial Theory, India, and "The Mystic East"* (London: Routledge, 1999), 35–61.

15. bell hooks, *Teaching to Transgress: Education as the Practice of Freedom* (New York: Routledge, 1994), 13–34.

16. Giroux, *Border Crossings*, 14–15.

17. This does not mean that I am doctrinaire. I understand "partisan" and "doctrinaire" to mean two different things. Whereas the partisan implies openness for debate and scrutiny, doctrinaire does not. See ibid., 15.

and the university is still dominated and shaped by the apersonal, objective paradigm.[18] To disclose one's identity is surely a risky endeavor and one that I constantly struggle with in the classroom. Nevertheless, in the context from which I teach, I believe such an exercise is a first step toward approaching the topic. It consequently empowers the voice of students coming from similar backgrounds. For example, the first time I realized that my experience and voice were legitimate forms of knowledge came when I heard another culturally underrepresented professor use his experience of marginalization as a lens to read texts and culture.

The disclosure of one's cultural social location does not need to reside only with ethnic/racial "minority" professors. Most people usually assume it is fruitless for white, middle-class teachers to discuss their identity. However, "whiteness" is also a racially/ethnically constructed identity. If one works with a general understanding that ethnicity and race are social categories and not biological ones, then by failing to name whiteness, or any ethnic identity for that matter, white professors maintain their "dominance by appearing to be invisible."[19] Just like any ethnic identity group, whiteness must undergo scrutiny as a site of privilege and oppression as well as a site of efforts to challenge oppression. The same interrogation must focus on other identity factors as well. If the dominant identity positions we hold are not scrutinized with regard to our interpretive system, then we reify their attitudes and norms in the classroom.[20]

2. Identities of the Students: Another strategy that is pertinent to making the subject matter more meaningful is to find out more about one's students' identities. Students must be encouraged to cross, remap, and challenge each other's readings of texts. Yet their experiences must be affirmed and critically interrogated. A pedagogical exercise that I learned some years ago in relationship to gender identity involves critically reflecting on one's power in society. I have modified the exercise a bit

---

18. Ingrid Rosa Kitzberger, ed., *The Personal Voice in Biblical Interpretation* (London: Routledge, 1999), 1–11.

19. Giroux, *Border Crossings,* 17.

20. For instance, I can remember many — not all — of my Anglo teachers (and some ethnic minority professors) couching their lived experiences around the myth that social mobility is open to those ethnic minorities who lift themselves up. In other words, what was being espoused was that upward mobility is an individual rather than a structural matter, and any barriers that one experienced were not due to racism or sexism within the structure but rather resulted from one's "bad" or "lazy" attitude. Sadly, students can come to believe in such cruel stereotypes — as I did before deconstructing the myth.

to focus on ethnicity. For example, what are the cultural advantages and disadvantages of being a person of color/white/mixed or mestizo, man/woman, white woman/woman of color, straight/gay, etc.? What things about these groups make the student angry, scared, uncomfortable, and comfortable? What makes it difficult to talk to people of the other group about differences? Over the course of years, I have experimented with three primary assignments to encourage students to articulate their own identities. By no means are these assignments without their difficulties, nor do they always produce spectacular results. However, I have found it easier to do these exercises with students coming from "minority" groups because they tend to be more open to questions of diversity. My supposition is that because they perceive themselves as powerless, there is less to lose in being vulnerable.

a. Autobiographical paragraphs: One assignment is the autobiographical paragraph that creates a space for students to think through questions of identity. The autobiographical paragraph exercise is one that I assign at the beginning of the semester with students reading out loud (without comments from students or myself) a paragraph on how they define their identity. Sometimes I provide a guiding question, such as: How does gender, race/ethnicity, or class define your identity or identities? The autobiographical process also begins with me. Students are more apt to speak and disclose themselves if they understand from the outset that I, the professor, believe in the assignment. It also provides a forum for students to express their ideological positions later in the semester when they write or provide interpretations of the biblical texts.

b. Assigned Readings: Another exercise requires students to read a particular biblical text (e.g., Gen. 1–2, 9, 34; John 4; Gal. 3:28–29; Philemon, etc.) and then asks them to reflect how their own identity might influence their reading of the particular text. I also sometimes ask them to read a religious or theological essay from a different identity perspective from their own. This exercise allows students not only to understand the world behind the text and the story itself, but also provides an opportunity to see similarities and differences between the text's, the author's, and their own worlds.

c. Writing Assignments: A third strategy I sometimes use to draw out the question of difference are identity-writing assignments. For example, I have required students to interpret texts from a postmodern perspective (i.e., ideological perspective) in order to participate in the construction of the ancient world within a politics of identity and difference.[21] The intent of this assignment is to call into question the construction of meaning and knowledge. Finally, it helps students to break down the high and low culture distinctions by making their lived experience a valid source of meaning.

The goal behind these strategies or exercises is to help students develop a sense of who they are and a sense of social issues associated with constructing their social worlds and histories. It is also a way to train them to think in terms of intercultural criticism. In other words, the pedagogical practices aim to teach them intercultural criticism in an inductive fashion in which they begin to evaluate consciously or unconsciously the reader of texts and the readings.[22]

3. *Identity of the Text:* Texts must be understood as literary (I would add here historical as well), ideological, and rhetorical products. However, I believe that the pedagogy of biblical studies that perhaps is dominant at many universities and colleges (unwittingly I hope) keeps students from examining it from a literary, ideological, and rhetorical product. The fear, it seems, is that students will stray from viewing the text as an authoritative source of their identity. However, what can and does often happen is that students are taught how *not* to critically engage the text. For instance, historical criticism, the dominant paradigm used to teach biblical studies, functions, I believe, to silence rather than give students a voice. It does this by trying to construct the ancient identity of the other from the position of neutrality. Its referent is positivism, which is not to say that historical criticism is not valuable; in fact, it has given me much information about the ancient Other. However, historical criticism has not provided me with much wisdom on how to engage and dialogue with the ancient Other. The examination of the identities in the text from a variety of methods (including historical criticism) is crucial if the goal is liberation and decolonization.

The disclosure of one's identity, therefore, functions at the beginning of my classes to redefine the role of the professor in terms of an engaged critic — not only with students, but also with the biblical text.

---

21. This assignment is also done from a historical perspective, without the lens of identity, in order to help them compare and contrast the difference between a modernist and a postmodernist reading of the Bible.

22. Along with this, I try to help students develop a sense of the ancient social world and its histories.

Personal disclosure begins the process by creating an open, comfortable, and challenging multicultural classroom environment. Most important, personal disclosure provides students with a prism to begin examining the biblical text from the perspective of diversity. In short, to make the text meaningful, it is pertinent to acknowledge one's identity, including white identity, and it is pertinent to read-across the readers, text, and readings.

READING STRATEGIES

What follows is a review of two texts from within the discipline of biblical hermeneutics with an ideological agenda of liberation. The goal here is to better understand intercultural criticism and its application. The first text is entitled *Reading the Bible from the Margins,* by Miguel A. De La Torre.[23] This text serves as a sample of the reading-with strategy that many liberation biblical scholars adopt to argue for diversity among readings. I examine it here as representative of a different approach in order to demonstrate that not all texts with a liberation agenda necessarily fall under intercultural criticism. At the same time, I provide an examination of this text in order to highlight further characteristics of the reading-across strategy that intercultural criticism employs.

The second text is *Reading the Bible in the Global Village,* edited by Justin S. Ukpong et al. This text arose from a symposium held in Cape Town, South Africa, at the Society of Biblical Literature's International Meeting. This text collectively is representative of the reading-across strategy and focuses on the topic of the discipline of biblical studies, hermeneutics, readings of biblical texts, and the assumptions of the enterprise of Christianity. Both texts are viewed from the perspective of reading strategy and attitude or posture toward the biblical text. The point here is to demonstrate that different reading strategies aim to promote the diversity of readings in the classroom. However, as I argue briefly below, even reading strategies must undergo a critical assessment asking who stands to benefit and who does not. These questions must also be asked of assigned texts, including those that claim to promote liberation. I believe that intercultural criticism asks this question.

---

23. Miguel A. De La Torre, *Reading the Bible from the Margins* (Maryknoll, N.Y.: Orbis Books, 2002).

Reading-With Strategy — Miguel A. De La Torre (2002)

Miguel De La Torre in *Reading the Bible from the Margins* focuses on marginalized readings and on how social identity factors, such as race, class, and gender, influence the reading experience of the Bible.[24] It is also a text meant to teach all readers, but especially those who are members of the dominant society, how to read the Bible and how to "read-with" the margins. The aim is to undermine dominant and thereby oppressive readings of the Bible in order to bring forth liberation of the Bible, the dominant society itself, and the marginalized.

As a literary product, *Reading the Bible from the Margins* is divided into seven chapters, not including the introduction.[25] Each chapter focuses on a particular topic, accompanied with a particular rhetorical aim. This purpose is usually a combination of three: didactic in the sense of teaching readers *how* to read the text with the margins, polemical in the sense of defending the good news against misreadings, and hortatory in the sense that our moral responsibility as Christians is to read-with the marginalized. The ideological aim overall is the liberation of the dominant class, the Bible itself, and the marginalized. Closely implied in the notion of liberation is the concept of salvation. De La Torre states, "Reading the Bible from the margins is as crucial for the salvation of the dominant culture as it is for the liberation of the disenfranchised."[26] In other words, there is a strong correlation between liberation and salvation.

De La Torre is working with the traditional theological framework of liberation hermeneutics. It is a hermeneutics governed by the liberation principle of the preferential option not just for the poor alone — as advocated by many Latin American theologians — but for the marginalized as well. The marginalized include African Americans, Native Americans, Asian Americans, Latino/as, women, the gay community, and the

---

24. This study arises from a series of lectures by De La Torre at Hope College in a course entitled "Reading the Bible from the Margins." The objective of the course was to encourage his predominantly European American students to read the Bible as non–European Americans and to contest their traditional interpretations of the Bible which have led to racism, sexism, and classism. Despite my serious reservations with his "reading-with" approach, De La Torre's work is an honest effort to make students hear anew familiar stories in the Bible.

25. The chapters are delineated as follows: (1) Learning to Read, (2) Reading the Bible from the Center, (3) Unmasking the Biblical Justification of Racism, (4) Unmasking the Biblical Justification of Sexism, (5) Who Do You Say I Am? (6) Jesus Saves, and (7) Can't We All Just Get Along?

26. De La Torre, *Reading the Bible from the Margins*, 5.

economically disadvantaged in the United States and those living in developing countries oppressed by U.S. economic and political policies. In other words, "to read from the margins" refers to reading from the perspective of those who historically have been and still are being oppressed by the European American male community in the United States. De La Torre does acknowledge that he himself plays the role of oppressor at all times because of his dominant male gender and his middle-class privileges, but he is also one of the oppressed — and speaks principally from this position — because of his "minority" status as a Latino — one of the many underrepresented groups in the United States. He strongly believes that all readings should be done from the margins, because it is at the margins where one encounters God.

His theological justification to locate God at the margins is biblically based. God does not manifest him or herself through the readings emanating from the middle or wealthy classes or from the readings emerging from European American men, but rather with the disenfranchised, including gays and lesbians, as illustrated in many biblical stories where God has chosen to side with the poor, women, ethnically marginalized, and the sexually marginalized. Furthermore, according to De La Torre, Jesus is a member of this marginalized culture since he was born not within the geographical center (Jerusalem) of Jewish life but rather on the margins (Galilee). In addition, Jesus is a marginalized person in his society as demonstrated through his crucifixion, which excluded him from the center and placed him among the margins with other crucified or marginalized people. Thus, one must search for Christ among the margins.

Working with this liberation principle of preferential option for the margins, De La Torre proceeds to liberate the Bible from the dominant society's interpretations of various texts that have been used to oppress the margins themselves. The dominant society is not directly identified in his work, but nevertheless is suggestive of Anglo American men and those who choose an individualist and spiritual approach to reading texts. The latter is consistent with fundamentalists, who have traditionally interpreted the Bible from an objective and positivistic position.[27] Working with the principles of objectivity and positivism, the dominant societies have used a hermeneutics of superiority to exclude marginalized

---

27. Ibid., 160.

readings by the underrepresented groups mentioned above. The dominant societies' readings have also been used to justify racism, classism, and sexism. De La Torre sets out to subvert the dominant readings by a process of rereading various texts throughout the Bible through the voices at the margins. He believes that his particular reading strategy is a part of liberating the Bible from the hands of the dominant society, thus allowing the good news of the Bible to save the dominant society. His strategy is pertinent to the salvation of the dominant culture as it is for the marginalized. It is a sin to allow the dominant society to continue in its hierarchal quest to exclude the margins from participating in the practice of reading texts and from reading them from their marginalized positions.[28]

Throughout his book, De La Torre continues this strategy of inserting the voice of the marginalized. In many of the major chapters, De La Torre sets out to dismantle privileged or oppressive readings, and then proceeds to provide the voice of the marginalized through "their" perspective. Actually, he becomes the voice of the marginalized. De La Torre's reading-with strategy is one in which it is a moral necessity to read with the margins — African Americans, the poor, and women, to name a few. It is neither "speaking about the margins" that he is calling for nor a "listening to" the margins; rather, it is a reading-with the margins on a universal level that De La Torre is proposing. This reading-with strategy does not call for a careful reading suggestive of historical criticism or a reading of the story world using literary methods, but rather a materialist reading that is characterized as reading the daily struggles of life into the Bible. In other words, close attention is given to the social location of the margins alone within the story world and outside the story world, but there is no strong critique of all the readers, including the marginalized ones, nor of his own construction of reading-with strategy. The result of this materialist reading leads to liberation or salvation for the dominant and marginalized in society.

For De La Torre, this reading-with strategy also calls for converting biblical scholars to turn away from the concerns of biblical criticism and to read with the marginalized. The Bible serves as repository of God's revelation and is the panacea for reforming all oppressive institutions and readings, but only if we all read with the marginalized and apply biblical truths that are inherent in the Bible can liberation and salvation

---

28. Ibid., 148–49.

be achieved. This biblical truth is not simply based on personal belief, but the very action of siding with those at the margins. It is based on imitating Christ, who is a member of a marginal society and whose mission was to undermine oppressive and colonialist injustices in the world.

Reading-Across Strategy — Musa W. Dube (2002)

Another approach that challenges readers/students to focus on a larger dialogue with the public, on a closer examination of the geopolitical dimension of liberation, and on an intense scrutiny of discourse as construction can be found in a recent work entitled *Reading the Bible in the Global Village*.[29] This book is a product of eight scholars, either from Africa or who have a strong commitment to African biblical scholarship, who aim to respond to various issues related to reading the Bible by international voices or in relationship to globalization. Collectively, *Reading the Bible in the Global Village* is an attempt to bring together, along with their tensions, the story of Africa (of pre- and postcolonial times) and the Bible.

As a literary product, the collection is organized along the lines of the order in which the essays were delivered at the 2000 SBL International Meeting in Cape Town, South Africa.[30] The first two essays by Justin S. Upkong and Musa W. Dube both set the scene by way of unfolding an African hermeneutical approach (Upkong) and by responding to the implications of Upkong's approach (Dube). I focus on Dube's essay below. The next two aim to map African biblical scholarship by way of European discipline and the role of the Bible in Africa (Masoga). The following essay proposes a method using the sociohistorical situation of the biblical text to avoid a simplistic reading of marginalization in the ancient world of Israel and thereby addressing as well today's issues of marginalization in the world (Gottwald). The penultimate essay is a reading of Paul's notion of freedom from a postcolonial perspective (Punt), and the final offering is a brief response to all the essays (Wimbush).

---

29. Justin S. Upkong et al., *Reading The Bible in the Global Village: Cape Town*, Global Perspectives on Biblical Scholarship 3 (Atlanta: Society of Biblical Literature, 2002).

30. The table of contents in *Reading the Bible in the Global Village* is as follows: Justin S. Upkong, "Reading the Bible in a Global Village: Issues and Challenges from African Readings"; Musa W. Dube, "Villagizing, Globalizing, and Biblical Studies"; Gerald O. West, "Unpacking the Package That Is the Bible in African Biblical Scholarship"; Alpheus Masoga, "Redefining Power: Reading the Bible in Africa from the Peripheral and Central Positions"; Norman K. Gottwald, "The Role of Biblical Politics in Contextual Theologies"; Jeremy Punt, "Towards a Postcolonial Reading of Freedom"; Tinyiko S. Maluleke, "What if WE Are Mistaken about Bible and Chrisitianity in Africa?" Vincent L. Wimbush, "Response."

As an ideological product, the authors all challenge readers to examine closely their assumptions. All are guided by a heterogeneous liberation perspective, but without the positivistic ethos that a particular reading is definitive. With the possible exception of Jeremy Punt's "Towards a Post-colonial Reading of Freedom," the contributions overall do not focus on any particular biblical text. Rather, the focus tends to be on the discipline of biblical studies and "how one can know and how one can know it."[31] In other words, this collection is theoretical rather than applied. The essays are more interested in the assumptions and principles that originated in the Western world and have gained hegemonic influence. From a rhetorical product point of view, the essays are didactic in the sense that they present various reading approaches — not just a single one — from Africa and in the sense that readers would benefit by considering seriously the ethical implications of the teaching of the Western world. The essays are neither polemical in the sense that they need to save the Bible, nor do they assert that the Bible is the panacea to the ills of oppression in Africa (Maluleke). What follows is a review of two essays, both excellent examples of the reading-across strategy. I begin first with Justin S. Upkong's essay, "Reading the Bible in a Global Village: Issues and Challenges from African Readings," followed by Musa W. Dube, "Villagizing, Globalizing, and Biblical Studies."[32]

Upkong's "Reading the Bible in a Global Village" advocates a particular reading approach called inculturation hermeneutics. This is an approach that takes seriously the social-cultural context of ordinary African readers of the Bible with the goal of social-cultural transformation.[33] The assumptions of inculturation hermeneutics include: (1) a holistic approach to culture that replaces a dualistic framework of high/low, secular/religious, or expert/ordinary readers with all of these dimensions; (2) an African conceptual frame of reference, which includes the reading practice and the reading method; and (3) the functional condition of readers, which entails the social location of readers and the

---

31. Wimbush, "Response," 176.
32. Other examples by Dube of the "reading-across" strategy can be found in *Postcolonial Feminist Interpretation of the Bible* (St. Louis: Chalice Press, 2000); "*Batswakwa:* Which Traveller Are You (John 1:1–18)?" 150–63, and "To Pray the Lord's Prayer in the Global Economic Era (Matthew 6:9–13)," in *The Bible in Africa: Transactions, Trajectories, and Trends*, ed. Gerald O. West and Musa W. Dube (Boston: Brill, 2000), 611–32.
33. On the one hand, Upkong is advocating a reading-with strategy by arguing that his reading must be done with ordinary African readers. On the other hand, Upkong believes that every reading is contextual and particular rather than universal, as De La Torre's reading is claiming.

implications that these identity factors contribute to the reading practice. This results in the following principles: (1) meaning is a construction; (2) the Bible is both a sacred text and a classic; making the Bible a "living book" for critical investigation, (3) readings are contextual and particular; (4) readings must be done with a commitment to the people; and (5) the people and their context must be the subject of the readings. All this leads to a final principle, reading "with" the people, which is quite similar to the reading-with strategy outlined above. However, Upkong's inculturation hermeneutics is more than a reading-with strategy. In the remainder of his essay, he provides an intense analysis of globalization in the world and in relation to the academy. He concludes with proposing a model of globalization that encourages difference or harmonization.

Dube's response to Upkong's proposal for an inculturation hermeneutics is grounded in African experience — like that of Upkong himself. But Dube's approach is particularly informed by her experience living in the Western world, as well as Botswana, and traveling throughout the world. More so than Upkong, Dube highlights or intensifies the call for diversity and the need to read without suppressing differences. She does so by bringing the public of South Africa into her conversation with Upkong. In other words, her dialogue with the public refers to her walk through the roads of Khayelitsha, an economically disadvantaged section of Cape Town, and other spaces marked by the scars of apartheid history. She also examines closely the geopolitical dimension of liberation — that is, the implications of the phenomenon of globalization — and she provides an intense look at the discourse of inculturation hermeneutics. In what follows, I look at each of these dimensions of her work and examine them in light of Upkong's essay.

a. Dube begins her response by narrating what happened after she traveled to South Africa from Botswana. When she arrived she went directly to her hotel to prepare for her presentation to the Stellenbosch Faculty of Theology. She did not regret not having much time to visit Cape Town, since she was staying at a beautiful hotel, apparently in a very privileged part of the city (Cape Sun Intercontinental Hotel). However, on her way to the SBL meetings where she was to deliver her paper, a close friend of hers picked her up and showed her another view of Cape Town. The section that she visited was Khayelitsha, which suffered immensely from the horrific consequences of apartheid. Khayelitsha was a "Black only" section, but she also visited the "Colored only" and the "Indian only" places. She experienced much in her journey through

these places as well as other places, such as visiting Robben Island, where
Nelson Mandela and Robert Sobukwe and many others fighting against
the evil system of apartheid were imprisoned for their efforts. Dube's
point in starting her response to Upkong's essay is intended more for the
guild (Society of Biblical Literature) by challenging these mainstream
scholars to include a broader public context in their work, after leaving
the luxurious hotel. Her call for contextuality, however, is clearer than
Upkong's in that she avoids obscuring the particularity of her contextuality (Khayelitsha, for example), whereas Upkong masks the particularity
through reference to generic "ordinary readers." In fact, Dube finds such
a term, "ordinary readers," problematic, for it avoids taking on issues
of race, gender, and class among readers.[34]

b. Upkong's essay provides a very clear and close examination of
globalization, delineating the benefits and the ills of globalization, but
also calling readers to resist it. For Dube, the issue of globalization is
not simply about outlining the positive and negative traits that it produces; rather, globalization is a phenomenon, a reality, that increases the
number of people who cannot participate in the benefits of globalization
because they do not have electricity, a home, or adequate nourishment.
For instance, she surely benefits from globalization every time she uses
her computer for her work, yet she cannot send an electronic message
to her mother or read the "village" news on-line. Dube does agree with
Upkong that globalization is a continuation of colonization, but like
colonization she proposes that questions need to be asked about who is
writing the rules of globalization as well as the rules of how to read biblical texts.[35] She proceeds in the remainder of her essay to provide a close
reading of Upkong's inculturated biblical hermeneutics and focuses on
whether his approach is congruent with his call to resist globalization.

c. Dube begins her examination of Upkong's inculturation hermeneutics proposal with a major concern: that Upkong does not really provide
a mapping of inculturation hermeneutics in relationship to African biblical scholarship and history generally, nor does he address seriously the
term "ordinary readers" or their identities.[36] So Dube sets out to map
inculturation hermeneutics and address the issues surrounding the term
"ordinary readers" that is such an integral component of his approach.

---

34. Dube, "Villagizing, Globalizing, and Biblical Studies," 50.
35. Ibid., 48.
36. Ibid., 49–50.

First, Dube points out that inculturation hermeneutics emanated from political liberation movements and had been primarily associated with sub-Saharan Africa. One form of this resistance approach she calls "inculturation from above." "Inculturation from above" is a phrase that was espoused by scholars who wanted to confirm both their Christian identity and their African identity. It functioned to resist any dismissal of their latter identity as pagan. Another form of this resistance approach Dube calls "inculturation from below," which is older than the "inculturation from above" strategy and which was advocated by the African Independent Churches. "Inculturation from below" is much more radical and espoused a nonapologetic hybridity as the stance against colonization and its resultant ills. This approach "arises from, for, and with the community."[37]

Second, inculturation hermeneutics, as presented by Upkong, overlooks the voice of women, despite the history of women that engendered inculturation hermeneutics. Dube is also quick to point out that Upkong's version of inculturation hermeneutics does not take race seriously as clearly illustrated through the colorless phrase, "ordinary readers." Dube's point here is that for inculturation hermeneutics to truly resist globalization and colonization, it needs a more intense examination of gender and race and its role and implications vis-à-vis inculturation hermeneutics. Dube concludes by emphasizing that inculturation hermeneutics has a contribution to make, but she also wonders whether those outside Africa even care to know about it. She argues that the voices of Africa must be heard in order to resist globalizing forces, including certain forms of biblical hermeneutics that continue to colonize "the Other."

Comparative Analysis

When comparing both reading strategies, I position myself along the latter strategy, namely, the reading-across strategy. Both strategies aim to involve a broader spectrum of the public. For De La Torre, his focus is strongly with the marginalized in the United States: African Americans, women, Asian Americans, Latino/as, gays, and the poor. For Dube, her focus is on Africans (both men and women) and the disinherited throughout the world. The difference is that the strategy represented by Dube avoids inverting the hierarchical system with the marginalized on the top

37. Ibid., 53.

and the rest of the world on the bottom. De La Torre, with the best of intentions, works with a hermeneutics of superiority. In other words, one
either sides with the perspectives of the marginal readings or one will
not be liberated or saved. This approach for me obscures any critical
analysis of readings from the margins.

Both strategies have a focus on the geopolitical dimension. The
reading-with strategy advocated by De La Torre provides limited discussion on this dimension. The only space provided is a discussion with
regard to poverty and hunger on a global level. Dube's reading-across
strategy is much more serious in looking at the implications and the
ethics of globalization. Finally, De La Torre provides no critical evaluation or critique of his hermeneutics. Dube, on the one hand, provides a
critical evaluation of Upkong's approach of inculturation hermeneutics
and its failure to take seriously the role of gender and race. She also
examines critically her role in doing scholarship within the academy
vis-à-vis her social location in Khayelitsha.

The reading-with strategy does have merit, especially in bringing the
voices of the margins to the center, but I question if it is indeed the voice
of the others. Is not De La Torre reading for them? How can De La
Torre read as an African American, feminist, and other underrepresented
groups? Also, I find the reading-with strategy problematic in its stance as
the Bible as the ultimate authority. Like Maluleke, I question whether the
text can solve all the ills of racism, classism, and sexism today. A simple
rereading of texts does not lead to liberation, but rather to inverting
the hierarchy of privilege. Hierarchalism remains rather than being dismantled. By idealizing the world of the margins in and out of the text
we establish a modern norm of the very world that Jesus challenged.[38]
The reading-with strategy does not necessarily allow for diverse reading,
but rather it advocates for a corrective reading, one that comes from the
point of view of the margins. This is no different from fundamentalists'
positivism. De La Torre does not read it from the perspective of the
whole, but like other modernist readings, he fragments his reading in
order to recontextualize those portions of the biblical text that illustrate
oppression. De La Torre's reading-with approach does differ from other
modernist readings in that he does not disguise his role in the reading
process.

---

38. Tolbert, "A New Teaching with Authority," in *Teaching the Bible*, 177.

The reading-across strategy I find more persuasive because it challenges the assumptions of biblical studies, by reading in light of the larger geopolitical situation, not suppressing particularity but allowing it to exist and to challenge universal readings of biblical texts. It fights against positivism, objectivism, hierarchalism, and a competitiveness that aims to show defective readings.

ETHICS OF INTERPRETATION

This brief section on the question of ethics is motivated by my interest in exploring the relationship between teaching biblical studies and students' appropriation of the biblical text. A critical reflection on the ethical implications of teaching biblical studies contributes to the morals, attitudes, and values of students. Teaching is always political. Whether one teaches from an objective standpoint or subjective standpoint, ethics plays a role.[39] In particular, I am interested in how teaching biblical studies can help move us beyond judgments of identity to an appreciation of diversity — if at all possible. As such, I am very much interested in the ethical implications of teaching biblical studies in the context of everyday praxis in this age of diversity. This also includes teaching biblical studies via the Internet, especially when it deals with globalization or gender identity.

Let me suggest two ethical stances that join theory and praxis and that might be integrated into the teaching of biblical studies.

1. As I argued above, disclosure of one's identity is a very important step in teaching biblical studies. However, this step must undergo critical self-reflection and interrogation by oneself and by others. Simply disclosing one's social location without critical reflection leads nowhere. One needs comparison to understand difference. Such a practical exercise is a prerequisite for growth. It allows one to see her/his identity in terms of power (privilege/marginality), and also allows one to see more than one culture. Additionally, comparison forces us to think about whether we want to maintain our values on diversity or move forward to reforming or remapping them.

---

39. Elisabeth Schüssler Fiorenza, *Rhetoric and Ethic: The Politics of Biblical Studies* (Minneapolis: Fortress Press, 1999), 195–200; and Josina M. Makau and Ronald C. Arnett, eds., *Communication Ethics in an Age of Diversity* (Urbana: University of Illinois Press, 1997), vii–xi.

2. Another value worth considering is openness to others. Here, I am
not advocating mere tolerance, which does not allow one to enter the
world of another, nor am I advocating radical relativity, which presumes
that one can suspend judgment in critiquing another context or particular identity. What I am advocating is the notion of respecting otherness
on its own terms and in its own contexts. Openness to diversity is a
very costly investment. One has to suspend one's views and codes of
conduct and try to understand the viewpoint of others. This takes a lot
of time, energy, and thought. The long-term investment, I would argue,
is that it opens up one's circle of dialogue partners. This is not to say
that one is no longer capable of judging particular racist attitudes, patriarchal hierarchies, or certain codes of "straight behavior." Rather, it
means trying to understand the diverse identities of students and others
on their own terms as a starting point toward a world that is enriched
through (more) liberation. I hope students have become conscious of
some of these ethical values by the time they leave my classroom.

In conclusion, I envision my role as a professor of biblical studies as
crossing many borders. Given the influx of new ethnic students (students
traditionally excluded from the privilege of higher education) and new
ethnic faculty in the profession of biblical studies, the primary borderland is that of intercultural criticism. Focusing on identity factors in the
Bible or in the reader is not divisive, but rather integral to constructing
knowledge about the worlds behind the text, of the text, and before the
text. And there is only enrichment of diversity to be gained! As I mentioned above, my initial emotion when crossing this border is fear, but
as I move forward, backward, and crisscross between all sorts of other
borders, I soon realize that the only thing to fear is remaining on one
side of the border.

2

Visions of Hope

The Legacy of the Early Church
ZAIDA MALDONADO PÉREZ

INTRODUCTION

We all yearn and search for historical connectedness. The knowledge, for instance, that we are the progenitors of a long line of descendants helps us grasp this connectedness by giving our existence historical importance. While perhaps not the center of our quest for existential meaning, this historical connectedness or rootedness plays a formative role in the way we view ourselves and our place in this world.

Latino/as in the United States[1] have been engaged in a quest for historical connectedness and rootedness that belies the untruth we have been told about ourselves and our peoples since the *Conquistas*. Latino(a) theologians and scholars share this passionate, though not uncritical, quest for the historical legacies that confirm our place and honorable role in the historical process — be this in Latin America, North America, or elsewhere. Recent books about the development of Latino(a) Protestant churches, for example, are uncovering the forgotten work and role of Latino(a) missionaries, lay leaders, and pastors, many of whom fought denominational hierarchies against the racism and stereotyping that relegated their leadership to the sidelines.[2] Their history of perseverance, courage, and faithfulness in the face of unjust and often very trying circumstances is not only a source of pride but, above all, a source of hope and a challenge to continue this legacy.

Protestant Latino/as have another legacy that has not been claimed but to which we have equal rights. I refer to that legacy willed to us

---

1. From here on, all references to Latino/as mean those in the United States.
2. See, for example, David Maldonado Jr., ed., *Protestantes/Protestants: Hispanic Christianity within Mainline Traditions* (Nashville: Abingdon, 1999).

by the early church, especially that which called into question political, social, cultural, and ecclesial norms that contradicted the good news of a new order. In this new order men and women, slave and free, are each other's equals and all are *hijos* and *hijas* of the one God. By following the mainline church's tendency to focus on the ecclesial histories and theology mainly from the time of the Reformation, we too have ignored the rich history that is ours to explore.

Along with its rich theological heritage, the Reformation also bequeathed us with a leeriness toward anything that smacked of Roman Catholicism. Our emphasis on *sola scriptura* over against Roman Catholicism's emphasis on tradition for the development of faith and dogma relegated the wealth of early church thought to the theological margins, rendering silent important voices. This act of benign neglect would not be condoned by the very reformers to whom we claim allegiance and who relied heavily on early church writers for their inspiration and guidance.[3]

Early (and medieval) church writings lie waiting to be discovered like a precious pearl within its shell. Only when we open the shell can we appreciate its worth. We read early church writings, not necessarily for what they might prescribe, but for the insights they inspire concerning matters of faith and practice. We also read them for the witness of persons and faith communities that, not unlike us and our own communities, also struggled to understand God's leading for a particular time and place. We need more of us to take up and read the treasury of early church writings and claim them — the good and the ugly — as part of our legacy as Christians committed to a faith that seeks understanding based on a communal dialogue that does not preclude the voices of their ancestors. Like our early church sisters and brothers, we need to engage those writings from our own contexts and perspectives. This too is their legacy to us.

MARTYRS, VISIONS, AND THE LEGACY OF HOPE

The corpus of material on the martyrs of the early church is one example of writings that have been neglected by our Protestant communities. Protestants have relegated them to the Roman Catholic Church, which has benefited from its testimony of courage and defiance unto

---

3. Luther and Calvin were very familiar with the writings of Augustine. Calvin, for instance, espoused his teachings on divine election. John Wesley had a special affinity for the Eastern fathers, especially Macarius.

death against oppressive structures. Roman Catholicism's canonization of some of these martyrs in honor of their faithful witness, as well as the early church's practice of attributing to them special mediating powers, contributes to Protestant's neglect of this material. Thus, the Protestant church has lost the opportunity of gaining insight from this witness.

Stories of the martyrs are an account of a government's quest to disarm the church of her faith and life. The martyrs subverted this attempt by their defiance. They chose to die rather than to deny Christ. The records of their deeds were passed on from church to church, encouraging its resolve to mobilize itself to address her enemy. The "scholars" of the church appealed to the government's sense of reason, calling for justice and compassion. They tried to dispel misconceptions by explaining their faith and Christian practice. Pastors, bishops, presbyters, and their communities sought discernment as they interpreted the Gospels in light of their circumstances. Their letters and sermons reflect the pain and passion of a pastor for the flock, especially given that they themselves were being arrested, oftentimes condemned to torture or death. In their absence, the churches circulated these letters. The testimonies of these martyrs were used as instruments of instruction and a call to a recommitment and reevaluation of what was truly important.

The martyr's visions, defined here as a visual imagery believed to be "supernatural in origin and revelatory in significance,"[4] were also a part of this popular literature that made its way through the churches. These visions affirmed promises of the glory awaiting the suffering communities after death. Most important, visions became powerful conduits of a new existence characterized by a reign that was present and yet still to come.[5] As conduits of this newness, "visions helped the reader transcend present circumstances by compelling the Christian to...live out of that new interstitial domain manifested in her/his hope of what is and is yet to be."[6] But they did more than just encourage the persecuted church. Early church understanding of the authority of visions as a God-initiated act over which authorities (church and otherwise)

4. Robert W. Frank, "Visions," in *An Encyclopedia of Religion*, ed. Vergilius Ferm (New York: Philosophical Library, 1945).

5. See "Death and the 'Hour of Triumph': Subversion within the Visions of Saturus and Polycarp," in Zaida Maldonado Pérez, "The Subversive Dimensions of the Visions of the Martyrs of the Roman Empire of the Second through Early Fourth Centuries" (diss., Saint Louis University, 1999), 88–117.

6. Ibid., 101, 102.

had no control had subversive implications. Visions, for instance, revealed a nuanced view of God, the world, power and powerlessness, death and life that at times challenged what was construed as normal by the early church or Graeco-Roman society.[7] This incongruence with prevailing Gentile and/or Christian religious and sociopolitical thought and practice — or "subversive dimension" — provided a foundation and inspiration for a dynamic grassroots (or popular) theology rich in symbolic content.

This early and medieval understanding of "vision" eventually ceded to the Enlightenment bias against what was perceived to be superstitious or "unreasonable." Nevertheless, "vision" has retained its subversive dimension within our communities.[8] Latino/as continue to use the language of "vision" as something God-given or inspired: it usually refers to something other than status quo — to *algo mejor. Sentir que* (to feel that), *creer que* (to believe that), and *entender que* (to understand that) God is *mostrándonos algo mejor* (showing us something better) is to see with the *vientre* (gut, belly, womb) what our intellect and experience tells us is unreasonable because it is unattainable. These individual and communal visions — like those of the early church — provide the inspiration to move forward. They aid our communities to face challenges with hope despite the risks. They allow us to walk with resolve and to do the "unreasonable" — to *festejar*[9] even amid the *meollo*[10] of poor housing, low wages, and continued marginalization of our peoples. Why? Because we believe that these visions are God-given and therefore, God-empowered. More than intellectual knowledge, we have a "gut knowledge" that our *ay benditos* and *Ave Marías* do not fall on deaf ears — even when "things as they are" encroach on our vision of things "as they should be,"[11] forcing us to cry out, "Lord, I believe, help my unbelief."

The visions of the martyrs allowed them to exist between horizons, defying all boundaries of time and space, life and death, powers and

---

7. Ibid., 6.

8. This is also very true of our African American sisters and brothers, especially as portrayed through Rev. Dr. Martin Luther King Jr.'s "I have a dream" speeches and his life and death.

9. *Festejar* is the verb form of the noun *fiesta*.

10. *Meollo* can mean "mess," "mix," "issues," "deep and messy," etc. It is used to refer to something intricately complex and "messy."

11. "Things as they are" refers to the dominant paradigm, the norm or prevailing context (e.g., behavior, thought, attitude). Things "as they should be" refers to that new way of being, thinking, or seeing that the visions portray and that goes against the prevailing norm.

principalities. This subaltern existence was uniquely subversive.[12] Like
the visions of the martyrs, our visions also allow us to live out of present-
future horizons that compel us to work and pray for that *algo mejor* that
God has in store. We are all too well aware of the proverb that cautions,
"where there is no vision, the people perish."[13]

We can learn from the content, role, and function of the visions of the
martyrs even today. Like them, we too are in need of seers and subversive visions that will unite our energies and challenge our complicity. The
Roman Empire sought to make the followers of Christ surrender their
name and therefore also their faith. Latino/as today face other challenges.
We are often required or enticed into surrendering our Latino-ness, our
compromiso[14] (commitment), vision, and struggle for a reign where the
right to dignity and the pursuit of happiness is not tied to the color of
our skin, our "accent," or the origin of our surname; where our children are free from self-fulfilling prophecies that crush their spirits and
limit their opportunities to develop their God-given potentials; where
the lowly are lifted up and the boundaries that keep us in certain parts
of town and limit our political voices are dissolved. The few of us who
have reached certain levels of economic and professional achievement
are especially challenged not to forget our *comunidades;* to remember
that we are supported by them, that we were empowered and called to
represent those in the margins in order to challenge those in the center.
We must recall the pain from the emotional scars we suffer, the casual-
ties we endure from breaking through the glass ceiling. Wounded in the
process, we could easily be left to bleed. Instead, those who went before
us, and whom God puts along the way with the *pneuma* of God's vision,
sustain us.

We have much to glean from the role and function of visions in the
early church and how they can empower our communities. We ignore
this history to our own detriment, for our communities too find themselves struggling against institutional powers and principalities. Their
seeming indomitableness often causes us to question our faith in a God
who promises never to leave nor forsake us. What does it mean to be

---

12. For examples see Pérez, "The Subversive Dimensions of the Visions of the Martyrs of
the Roman Empire of the Second through Early Fourth Centuries."

13. Prov. 29:18 (KJV). Or, "Where there is no prophecy, the people cast off restraint" (NRSV).

14. I like the word *compromiso* in Spanish because it not only points to a "promise" we
make *con,* with another — in this case, our communities and all of God's people — but it also
suggests that enacting that commitment holds "promise" for those involved.

faithful in light of daunting circumstances? What is a faithful response? How do we know? What resources might be considered authoritative? How might these be weighed and interpreted? These were questions of our brothers and sisters of the early church. Today, they must also be our questions. We can learn from this tradition, emulating its resolve and its creative ways of encouraging and supporting each other against what was meant to divide and conquer.

The martyrs' ordeals, their visions and courageous words and deeds, the appeals by the church, and how the church interpreted all of this provide a rich source of information regarding early church beliefs on life, death, ecclesiology, God, Christ, the sacraments, judgment, salvation, and the nature of the church, to name but a few. The visions of the martyrs were used to empower, encourage, and subvert their oppressors. These visions can reflect our own struggles to overcome helplessness, hopelessness, and the surrendering of that *algo mejor.*

What follows is a historical and theological overview on the subversive dimensions of the visions of the martyrs from the Hebrew and early Christian traditions.[15] We begin with a brief look at how and why the visions of the martyrs came to be understood as belonging to and empowering not just the seer, but the whole people of God.

THE VISIONS OF THE MARTYRS
AND THE ROLE OF SUBVERSION

Visions, though directly related to the visionary's questions and situation, were nevertheless believed by the martyr and the church to address not just the martyr, but the church community as a whole.[16] Two major events in the life of the church help explain this phenomenon. One

---

15. Many of the earliest Acts of the Martyrs, or *acta martyrum,* were copies of *hypomnematismoi* (*commentaries* in Latin), or official court discourses between magistrates and martyrs (e.g., the *Acts of the Scillitan Martyrs,* the *Acts of Justin Martyr*). Many *Acts,* however, also contain *Passiones* (or *martyria*) — stories about the arrest, imprisonment, and execution of the martyr that claim to have been written by Christian eyewitnesses, contemporaries, or by the martyr her/himself. The visions of the martyrs are found in the accounts of their *passiones.* The *passiones* (as well as many of the *Acts*) was a literature especially written for the church by church people. Lay, as well as clergy, compiled and redacted the stories that would powerfully influence the life and thought of the third- and fourth-century church (and beyond). The *Acts* began circulating among the Christian communities around the mid-second century with the *Martyrdom of Polycarp,* if not earlier.

16. Augustine's use and mention of them in his sermon on Perpetua and her companions, on Crispina of Thagora, and on the Forty Martyrs provides evidence that they functioned as communal property aimed at "the consolation of the church." See Augustine, *Sermo 280* in

pertains to their historical context and the other to a theological development. This essay looks briefly at how these contexts influenced the emerging church's understanding of the martyrs' visions as prophetic, and also how this view reinforced the authority and influence of their visions.

The Visions of the Martyrs as Communal Property

For the early Christian, there was no sense of a merely private vision, no conception of private encouragement not also intended to stimulate and strengthen the whole people of God. Persecuted and martyred, the church looked to their martyrs — whose witness and visions it claimed — for strength and encouragement.[17] The martyrs' stories of faithfulness became the church's stories of victory over their oppressors: they were communal property. This was especially true of the martyr's visions.[18] The church identified the martyr as a prophetic figure. The Hebrew idea that "every prophet was believed to be a martyr...every martyr a prophet"[19] gained particular expression within Christianity in times of persecution. This analogy between the martyr-prophet is ingrained in the martyrological-hagiographical accounts of the martyrs' death.[20] Among the evidence used in these accounts to support this analogy is

Patrologia Latina, ed. J. P. Migne (Paris: Migne, 1844–64), 38:1281; Tertullian, *De anima* 55.4 in *Corpus Christianorum,* ed. J. H. Waszink (1954), 862.32.

17. This is not to say that many Christians did not "apostatize" during persecution.

18. The tradition likening the martyr to a prophet has precedence in Jewish and Christian scriptures and literature. For a discussion on Hebrew and Christian (and some Hellenistic) sources referring to the role of the prophet as martyr and the prophetic role of martyrs see H. A. Fischel, "Martyr and Prophet: A Study in Jewish Literature," *Jewish Quarterly Review* 37 (1946/47): 364–70. In the early second-century document, the *Didache* (or the *Teaching of the Twelve Apostles*), the author's exhortation regarding the "true" and "false" prophet provides several important guidelines that the martyr-prophet embodied to the fullest extent. First, the writer sets parameters by which the true "prophet" is distinguished from the false prophet. The most important of these is their "conduct," that is, a prophet practices what s/he preaches (chap. 11.8). This qualification would be directly related to and fulfilled by the martyr and prophet who gave (or was about to give) her/his life as witness to their faith. The document also exhorts its readers against prophets who would ask or accept "anything save sufficient food to carry him till the next lodging (ch. 11.6)." In accordance with this rule, the martyr-prophet did not demand anything but the privilege of self-sacrifice (in *Early Christian Fathers,* ed. Cyril C. Richardson [New York: Macmillan, 1970], 161–79). Although the document was addressed to rural Christian communities in Syria-Palestine, its popularity and authority were such that it was regarded by many as pertaining to canonical literature prior to the end of the fourth century. The issue of credulity as dependent on the prophet's life is also taken up by Roland E. Murphy's essay, "Prophets and Wise Men as Provokers of Dissent," in *The Right to Dissent,* ed. Hans Küng and Jürgen Moltmann (New York: Seabury, 1982), 61–66.

19. Fischel, "Martyr and Prophet," 1.

20. Fischel includes a list of twenty-four traits that were used to emphasize the identification of the prophet with the martyr (383–84).

the martyr's experience of visions. In his book, *The Martyrs: A Study in Social Control,* Donald W. Riddle correctly argues that martyrs were not only venerated, but that "the abilities of the apostles were ascribed to them," the charism of prophecy, especially through visions, "being the most valued of these."[21] According to Violet MacDermot, the essential characteristic of the saints was not their power to effect miracles but their ability to see visions and communicate with the divine world.[22] The experience of visions testified to the martyrs' "prophetic faculties."[23] Because visions were considered prophetic, they were deemed communal property — the common heritage of the church.

Probably the most important aspect influencing the early church's belief in the communal ownership of the martyrs' visions was their theological understanding of the "church" as "one body" with "one faith" and "one baptism" (Eph. 4:4, 5). This view is found early on in Paul's analogy of the church as the "body of Christ."[24] By the third and fourth centuries the church saw the martyr as a faithful representative of that body. As their representative, the community also claimed their visions.

In conclusion, the early church viewed the witness and visions of the martyrs as communal property. As a result, visions were shared with fellow Christians on their way to martyrdom, and most were recorded and

---

21. Donald W. Riddle, *The Martyrs: A Study in Social Control* (Chicago: University of Chicago Press, 1931), 73. Arguing for his thesis that the deeds of the martyrs were the result of socioreligious control, he adds that "the thought that the martyr obtained this special power had great effect, it would appear, in inducing candidates to undertake the experience.... It was of value in inducing the attitude of willingness to undertake martyrdom to assure a potential martyr that he would, through his experience, achieve the role of prophet." Riddle comes at the study of martyrdom from a sociological perspective which, to the detriment of the full implication(s) of the study of martyrdom, minimizes the role and function of theology in informing and shaping the religious experience. While his study throws important and necessary light to the role of religion in shaping attitudes and controlling behavior, it would be simplistic to assume that this was all that was being signified by the martyr's willingness to die. In his study regarding the work of the Holy Spirit in contexts of persecution and martyrdom in the New Testament and early church, Weinrich presents and affirms this position. In agreement with and support of Karl Holl and Marc Lod, Weinrich declares that a martyr was "an ecstatic to whom revelations were given. The martyr became a prophet by virtue of a special gift of the Spirit which enabled the martyr to view into the invisible world. In this manner the confessor and martyr became a "witness" to the resurrected Christ." See William C. Weinrich, *Spirit of Martyrdom: A Study of the Work of the Holy Spirit in Contexts of Persecution and Martyrdom in the New Testament and Early Christian Literature* (Washington, D.C.: University Press of America, 1981), xii.

22. She further argues that the visions of the martyrs "reassured" those who "unable to create such a world for themselves, might doubt its existence." *The Cult of the Seer in the Ancient Middle East: A Contribution to Current Research on Hallucinations Drawn from Coptic and Other Texts* (Berkeley: University of California Press, 1971), 94.

23. Fischel, "Martyr and Prophet," 368.

24. See 1 Cor. 10:17, 12:12–13, and 12:20.

passed on from church community to church community, and interpreted and reinterpreted throughout Christendom.

In the Hebrew Scriptures, the identification of the martyr with the prophet carried subversive implications. Is this also true for the visions of the Christian martyrs? A historical and theological overview of the Hebrew and Christian subversive tradition follows.

A Historical Overview of the Subversive Dimensions of Visions from the Hebrew Scriptures to Formative Christianity

Despite the exalted nature of their calling, prophets were not always esteemed; nor were their prophetic messages welcome. King Ahab, for example, called the prophet Elijah a "disturber of Israel" (1 Kings 18:17) and sought to kill him. Disturbing Israel seemed to be a common trend among prophets whose messages almost always challenged the political and religious powers of the times (e.g., Amos 5:9–15 speaks against social injustices and religious practices; Jeremiah protests against a false sense of security that shows itself in the blatant neglect of the needy, injustices, and pagan worship [7:1–7]; Isaiah protests against Israel's "adulteress" behavior and prophesied concerning God's judgment against Zion [1:21–31; 3:1–4:1]). This challenge took the form of "dissent" and subversion.[25] That is, their message went against the current patterns of behavior and/or thought and upset or overturned them.

By the mid-second century, early Christianity's view of the prophet had undergone some change. Not only is the martyr considered a prophet (see above), s/he is also highly esteemed and revered for her/his participation in the suffering and death of Christ through martyrdom.[26] This *imitatio Christi*, however, is not without its own subversive dimensions, as we shall see below. As with the Hebrew prophets, subversion becomes especially explicit through their prophetic message(s) (vis-à-vis their life/death).

The visions of the martyrs, when studied in relation to their context, reveal the continuation of the prophetic tradition of dissent and subversion, that is, of upsetting, undercutting, or reversing "things as they are" for things "as they should be."

One might rightly argue that visions, because of their presumed divine origin, and because neither the state nor the Christian church could either

---

25. On the subject of dissent and the prophetic message see Murphy's essay cited above.

26. This reverence later led to their veneration through relics. See Lawrence S. Cunningham, *The Meaning of Saints* (San Francisco: Harper, 1980).

preclude the experience, rule the content, or delimit the choice of its recipients, were of themselves subversive. This can be seen, for instance, in the account of Stephen's martyrdom (Acts 7:54–60). Through his death, the Pharisees could prevent him from ever preaching about Christ. However, they could not stop divine prerogative from choosing Stephen over the Pharisees as the one to whom to reveal God's glory (Acts 7:55).[27]

Furthermore, the nature of martyrdom itself as a subversive act against the state and the dominant pagan culture is acknowledged. For instance, Eusebius (c. 260–c. 340) reflects this view in his account of four women who, despite being severely tortured, would not give into the governor's demand to deny Christ and offer sacrifice. Of the governor, Eusebius says, "he was ashamed to apply continued tortures all to no end, and to be worsted [i.e., defeated] by women."[28] Origen's *Exhortation to Martyrdom* perhaps best captures the subversive role of martyrdom or *imitatio Christi*:

> God, moreover, says by the Prophet: *In an acceptable time I have heard thee, and in the day of salvation I have helped thee.* What time could be more acceptable than when, because of our piety towards God in Christ, we make our solemn entry in this world surrounded by a guard and when we are led out, more like triumphant conquerors than conquered? For martyrs in Christ *despoil* with Him *the principalities and powers* and triumph with Him, by partaking in His sufferings and the great deeds accomplished in His sufferings — among which is His triumphing over principalities and powers, which you will soon see conquered and overcome with shame. What other day could be for us such a day of salvation as the day of so glorious a departure from her below?[29]

Origen's inversion of "conqueror" and "conquered" and his reference to despoiling "the principalities and powers" is indicative of the nature

---

27. The content and significance of Stephen's vision is dealt with further in the pages that follow.

28. This subversive attitude is further reflected in his comment regarding the death of Nemesion. Eusebius states that the governor had ordered Nemesion to be burned between two bandits. The governor's probable intentions of mocking the Christians with a reenactment of Christ's death is subverted by Eusebius's comment that the governor had instead "honor[ed] him — blest indeed! — with a resemblance to Christ." *Eusebius: The Ecclesiastical History and the Martyrs of Palestine,* trans. and notes Hugh Jackson Lawlor and John E. L. Oulton (New York: Macmillan, 1927), 1:VI.41.18.

29. In *Ancient Christian Writers,* trans. John J. O'Meara (New York: Newman Press, 1954), 186.

and degree of subversion inherent in the actions of the martyr-prophet. Martyrdom is, for the believer, "the day of salvation"; death is subverted by new life, power by powerlessness, and the world (or below) by the triumph of Christ's death and resurrection in which the martyr participates.

On occasion (and as with Israel), the messages and actions of the martyr-prophets also upset the church's teachings. One such occasion is related to the church's espousal and promotion of the dominant patriarchal values shared by Jews and Gentiles toward the beginning of the second century.[30] By this time, women's social and religious roles were relegated and intricately tied to procreation and motherhood.[31] Addressing the extent of acculturation to the dominant culture, Clarissa W. Atkinson points out that writings, for example, that contained and exalted egalitarianism in gender relations (as characterized by the Jesus movement of the first century) were slowly excluded from the scriptural canon. However, she clarifies that the egalitarian view was not totally eradicated given that glimpses of this eschatological vision of equality were preserved in certain Pauline passages and other writings such as the Apocryphal Acts and the Acts of the Martyrs.[32] While the Apocryphal Acts became marginalized along with other "heterodox" texts, the Acts of the Martyrs "held a central place in doctrine and devotion."[33] Most important, Atkinson points out that:

> during the long period of persecution preceding the establishment of Christianity in the fourth century, *martyrdom* and persecution undercut the values of the dominant culture, breaking traditional [patriarchal] bonds and forging new ones. Faced with violent, immediate death, the martyrs recreated the family of discipleship

---

30. See Clarissa Atkinson, *The Oldest Vocation: Christian Motherhood in the Middle Ages* (Ithaca, N.Y.: Cornell University Press, 1991), 18–19.

31. Atkinson makes an interesting and, I think correct, interpretation of the meaning between, for example, Ignatius's work and instruction regarding the (male) leaders of the church and the further development and institution of patriarchy. She states, "at the beginning of the second century, Ignatius of Antioch instructed Christians to 'regard the bishop as the Lord himself.' Bishops soon became teachers, rulers, and 'fathers'; Ignatius told the Magnesians, whose bishop was a young man, 'to render him all respect according to the power of God the Father.' The patriarchal authority of men was easily conflated with the authority of God and restored to the 'households' of the new churches" (*The Oldest Vocation*, 17–18 and notes 26 and 27).

32. Atkinson, *The Oldest Vocation*, 19.

33. Ibid., 19.

modeled by the men and women who followed Jesus to his crucifixion. In many respects they shared the voice and vision of the
disciples as well as their experience of *communitas*.[34]

She further argues that "these Acts present very different models of family and of gender relations; they demonstrate the martyr's renunciation
of traditional concerns and a reversal of ordinary priorities."[35]

The argument for the subversive role of martyrdom itself is thus firmly
attested. However, there is much more to be said about the nature and
degree of subversion that can be discovered only through the careful
analysis of the *content* of the visions of the martyrs in comparison with
the prevailing religious and sociopolitical *contexts* of the times.[36] How
are these visions subversive; that is, how are they upsetting, undercutting,
or reversing things as they are for things as they should be? Who or what
is being subverted? How does the content and context aid our understanding of the nature and degree of subversion? The Christian Scriptures
provide us with various examples and answers to these questions. Just
before his death, the deacon Stephen experiences a vision that subverts
the prevailing socioreligious notions of life and death, of power and powerlessness. His vision of Jesus' (the "Son of Man") exalted position at
the right hand of God (Acts 7:56) challenged Hebrew understandings of
Jesus as a false prophet whose existence was terminated at the criminal's
cross. This intimate revelation of the glory awaiting him at his departure
from this life — his place of destination — also challenged dominant notions of power.[37] The accuser's power to take life is surpassed by God's

---

34. Ibid.

35. Ibid., 18–19. For example, in regards to the *Martyrdom of Perpetua and Felicitas,* she
states, "God facilitated the martyrdom of Perpetua and Felicitas despite their physiological
condition. The biological demands of motherhood, accepted in the ancient world as marks
and determinants of female incapacity, were not allowed to stand in the way of the martyrs'
witness. Motherhood was not in itself redemptive, but neither did it preclude participation in
the most sacred vocation" (21–22).

36. I am aware that visions and their interpretations, when given, may be literary creations
rather than actual transcriptions or summaries of the visions of the martyrs. This, however,
in no way hinders the possibility of studying the visions for their subversive elements vis-à-vis
their religious and/or sociopolitical contexts.

37. In his desire to distance Stephen's vision from the view that it was merely a "typical
feature of stories of martyrdom," Weinrich maintains that the vision held no benefit for Stephen
and was instead intended for the benefit of the Jewish leaders. His first argument, that the vision
held no benefit for Stephen, is simply a judgment that cannot be substantiated. That it did not
"reveal the future fate of the martyr" is a narrow explanation of the vision and overlooks the
theological connection of "the heavens" where God (and Jesus) is with the believer's ultimate
"place" of destination. As Christ died and rose to be with the "Father," so it was taught that
the Christian would also die and rise to be with the "Father." Only in this sense is the vision's

power not only to give life but *eternal* life, with Him. Most important for the developing church of the first four centuries, Stephen's experience provided a *visual* affirmation[38] to the countercultural view first articulated and modeled by Jesus that "Whoever would preserve his life will lose it, but whoever loses his life for my sake and the gospel's will preserve it" (Mark 8:35).

This subversive view of life and death would find expression in the fertile ground of the persecution and martyrdom of early Christians. The martyrs' visions offer a compelling window into the nature and extent of this and other subversive dimensions.

In one of his visions, Paul says that he was "snatched up to Paradise to hear words which cannot be uttered, words which no person may speak" (2 Cor. 12:1–4). Though very little information is given, the choice of words used to describe his experience is telling. From this description the reader is able to make at least two important observations. First, Paul's use of the word "Paradise" to describe what he saw sets up binary opposition between it and the "world," that is, between "paradise" and earthly existence. The state's use of suffering and the threat of death to create apostates assumes the primacy of earthly existence. The opposition between "paradise" and his earthly existence implies the contrary (the primacy of eternal life with God in paradise), and the stress on the unutterability of the words he heard strengthens the depth

---

prophetic thrust fully appreciated. Hence, the man that they are about to stone not only has a vision of the glory of God, but, despite their efforts at finishing with his life, their evil actions only serve to precipitate his participation in the glory just revealed to him. (It also serves, as Weinrich points out, to spread the gospel.) One cannot but ascertain that the vision *does,* then, reveal something about the martyr's fate! In his argument for the distinction between early Christian martyr-texts and the vision of Stephen, he uses "consciousness," vs. ecstasy or trance, as the line of demarcation. He states "there is no indication that Stephen was in a trance or ecstasy. He was conscious enough to relate on the spot his vision to his hearers" (42). First, one might ask what does "conscious enough" mean? Second, while one might agree with him that Stephen's vision was not just another "typical" occurrence related to martyrdom (but then we can also say the same for any other vision), his argument actually serves to place undue emphasis on "mode" rather than on *content,* the main focus. Furthermore, and in agreement with Violet MacDermot, "distinction between seeing the visions in a state of dream, ecstasy, or trance, and the exercise of the conscious imagination, was not clear to the writers of the Hellenistic or early Christian period" (54). Thus, whether a "vision" or not a vision — in Weinrich's view, we must acknowledge that the recorder understood and recorded it as such. See Weinrich, *Spirit of Martyrdom,* 38–43.

38. The author's proof that Stephen's vision can be trusted as true or real for all believers is based on his reference to the Holy Spirit in him. Thus it states that Stephen was "a man filled with faith and the Holy Spirit.... A man filled with grace and power, who worked great wonders and signs among the people." And again before his stoning, it states that Stephen was "filled with the Holy Spirit." See Acts 6:5, 8; 7:51.

of this opposition (e.g., the words are inexpressible because they refer
to things unlike any he has experienced in this world). The significance
and import of this vision and the opposition it sets up are further solidified through Paul's later statement, "For, to me, 'life' means Christ;
hence dying is so much gain" (Phil. 1:21). Once again, and within the
context of martyrdom, visions function to subvert any action aimed at
undermining Christian views of life and death, power and powerlessness.

Another example of the subversive dimension in the visions of the
martyrs is found in the book of Revelation, where the author, who had
been exiled to the island of Patmos because he "proclaimed God's word
and bore witness to Jesus," experiences an array of visions (Rev. 1:9). His
visions not only served to strengthen him during his own persecution,
they were also aimed at encouraging the faithful through visions revealing the imminent end of their suffering and the proximity of a new reign
of peace and justice. The powerful effect of these visions against impend-
ing death is heard in John of Patmos's subversive statement, "Happy is
the person who reads this prophetic message, and happy are those who
hear and heed what is written in it, for the appointed time is near!"
(Rev 1:3).[39]

As shown above, sufficient evidence exists on behalf of the role of subversion in the visions of the martyrs of formative Christianity. The term
"subversion" was defined in light of the relation between the *content* of
the vision and the *context* and referred to that which upset, undercut,
or reversed "things as they are" for things "as they should be."

It is important to remember that the visions were had within the context of martyrdom. Stories about this context became engraved in the
early church literature called the Acts of the Martyrs. These stories not
only framed the visions, they also provided the reader with clues that
helped unlock the meaning(s) of the visions. Together, the Acts of the
Martyrs and the visions they framed powerfully undermined their oppressors.[40] The stories about the martyrs and their response to those
who would rob them of their hope provide only a glimpse of the kinds

39. Reference to the "appointed time" meant not only their redemption from oppression,
but the avenging of their suffering "when Jesus will return in glory" (note 1:3 in the New
American Bible, 1970). See also Rev. 12.

40. For examples see my dissertation, "The Subversive Dimensions of the Visions of the
Martyrs of the Roman Empire of the Second through Early Fourth Centuries" and "Death and
the 'Hour of Triumph': Subversion within the Visions of Saturus and Polycarp," in *Theology:
Expanding the Borders*, ed. María Pilar Aquino and Roberto S. Goizueta (Mystic, Conn.:
Twenty-Third Publications, 1999), 121–44.

of treasures that are in store for those who read them. Latino/as can claim this historical and theological legacy by critically attending to this great corpus of witness and struggle otherwise called "the early church." As my mother says, *"familia es familia."* Latino/as are progenitors of a long line of descendants of familia that we have yet to meet!

3

Dis-covering the Silences

A Postcolonial Critique
of U.S. Religious Historiography

HJAMIL A. MARTÍNEZ-VÁZQUEZ

The production of historical writing should be in constant process of revision and critical examination so that unjust systems of power and oppression do not remain hidden. Through this process of revision, historians need to uncover and expose colonial discourses. Colonial discourses are those modes of representation created by the colonizer "to construe the colonised as a population of degenerate types on the basis of racial origin, in order to justify conquest and to establish systems of administration and instruction."[1] In *The Location of Culture* Homi Bhabha argues that these discourses locate the colonized as both being present in society and as Other, at the same time. He writes, "colonial discourse produces the colonised as a social reality which is at once an 'other' and yet entirely knowable and visible."[2] On the other hand, "colonial discourses have been successful because they make the colonisers feel important, valuable and superior to others."[3]

Colonial discourses create a colonial normative knowledge, an imaginary that people in the center of power see as the truth by silencing the voice of oppressed people. In this regard, Frantz Fanon argues that "colonialism is not satisfied merely with holding a people in its grip and emptying the native's brain of all form and content" but "by a perverted logic, it turns to the past of the oppressed people, and distorts, disfigures,

---

1. Homi Bhabha, *The Location of Culture* (London and New York: Routledge, 1994), 70.
2. Ibid., 70–71.
3. John McLeod, *Beginning Postcolonialism* (Manchester, Eng.: Manchester University Press, 2000), 38.

and destroys it."[4] So political decisions in the centers of power are made on the basis of this imaginary configured by colonial discourses. At the same time it is important to acknowledge that colonial discourses are based in the project of modernity.

MODERNITY AND THE "WEST"

Modernity is the impetus behind traditional and colonial historiography. Modernity, understood as a period in time, emerged with Columbus's voyage to the Amerindian territories and developed through the period of the Reformation, the Renaissance, the scientific revolution, and the Enlightenment.[5] But modernity should not be seen simply as an epoch or as a period in time, but as a discourse, "a highly complex yet coherent narrative containing assumptions about how it is possible to represent the state of nature as supported by a new realist historical consciousness of change over time."[6] In other words, beliefs, characteristics, cultural trends, and rules defined modernity. The period of the conquest and colonization of the Amerindian territories gave Europe, represented by Spain, a reason to locate itself in the center of a world-system — the modern/colonial system — while events like the Enlightenment and the scientific revolution helped northern Europe displace Spain as the center of the system.[7] The Reformation was also part of this process of displacement and marginalization because it locates Catholicism at the periphery of the Christian world. The discourse of modernity, then, locates Europe, which becomes the West, at the center of the modern/colonial system and

---

4. Frantz Fanon, *The Wretched of the Earth* (New York: Grove Press, 1963), 210.

5. This contradicts the common Eurocentric understanding, which situates the development of modernity, as Enrique Dussel argues, "from the Italy of the Renaissance to the Germany of the Reformation and the Enlightenment, to the France of the French Revolution" (Enrique Dussel, "Beyond Eurocentrism: The World-System and the Limits of Modernity," in *The Cultures of Globalization,* ed. Fredric Jameson and Masao Miyoshi [Durham, N.C.: Duke University Press, 1998], 4). This understanding leaves out of the development of modernity Spain and the ideology of conquest and colonialism, so that the Spanish territories in the "new world" are left out from the traditional discourse of modernity and the present postmodern discussion.

6. Alan Munslow, *The Routledge Companion to Historical Studies* (London: Routledge, 2000), 163.

7. For a better understanding of the modern/colonial system, see Walter D. Mignolo, *The Darker Side of the Renaissance: Literacy, Territoriality, and Colonization* (Ann Arbor: University of Michigan Press, 1995).

the Rest at the periphery. This is what Stuart Hall calls the idea of "the West and the Rest."[8]

Hall takes on the challenge of explaining the idea of "the West and the Rest" in order to provide the relationship between the two parts. He starts by stating "that 'the West' is a *historical,* not a geographical, construct."[9] This concept can be explained, according to Hall, in four ways: (1) the categorization of things between "Western" and "non-Western," (2) as a system of representation, (3) as a structure for comparison and establishing difference, and (4) a principle for evaluation that creates an ideology. I do not here summarize in detail Hall's argument or each of these ways, but it is important to acknowledge some of the central aspects Hall points out. As I have mentioned before, the West needed the Rest in order to form itself. Hall argues that "the West's sense of itself — its identity — was formed, not only by the internal processes that gradually moulded Western European's sense of difference from other worlds — how it came to represent itself in relation to these 'others.' "[10] Thus, the West became that which is different from the Rest, and even if difference exists within each of them, they were essentialized as a whole system of representation. For Hall it is in the period of exploration when this idea of "the West" came to be. He establishes:

> But in the Age of Exploration and Conquest, Europe began to define itself in relation to a new idea — the existence of many new "worlds," profoundly different from itself. The two processes — growing internal cohesion and the conflicts and contrasts with external worlds — reinforced each other, helping to forge that new sense of identity that we call "the West."[11]

This formed relationship between the West and the Rest was not innocent because the parts involved were presented as equals. In this regard, Hall states,

> The Europeans had outsailed, outshot and outwitted peoples who had no wish to be "explored," no need to be "discovered" and no desire to be "exploited." The Europeans stood, vis-à-vis the Others

---

8. Stuart Hall, "The West and the Rest: Discourse and Power," *Formations of Modernity,* ed. Stuart Hall and Bram Gieben (Cambridge: Polity Press, 1992).
9. Ibid., 277.
10. Ibid., 279.
11. Ibid., 289.

in positions of dominant power. This influenced what they saw and how they saw it, as well as what they did not see.[12]

Colonialism, then, becomes the instrument to enforce and maintain this unequal and unjust relationship.

The modern/colonial system creates colonial discourses based on colonial difference, which are the bases for this relationship. Through these discourses the West writes the history of the colonized by projecting its own history and agenda. Colonial discourses serve the colonizer by creating an imaginary that details the "truth" about the world, a world in which the colonized needs the colonizer because of the superiority of the latter. This kind of imaginary helps to create and maintain this apparent superiority by giving rationality and scientific knowledge the greater status within society. Since they have it and the colonized do not, then they can help the colonized through their life. In this regard the colonized sees the colonizer as her/his helper without understanding the system behind this relationship.

The West was created by the discourse of modernity, and the idea of superiority of the rational over the irrational is one of the principles of modernity, which gave birth to Western imperialism. As Enrique Dussel and other scholars have argued, "modernity is, in fact, a European phenomenon." But Dussel goes further in his argument by stating that modernity is "constituted in a dialectical relation with non-European alterity that is its ultimate content. Modernity appears when Europe affirms itself as the 'center' of a *World* History that it inaugurates; the 'periphery' that surrounds this center is consequently part of its self-definition."[13] So in this sense, modernity cannot be explained in respect to a Europe considered as an independent system, but as a Europe conceived as the center of the system.[14] The Others, the non-European alterity, those outside Europe, are part of the system and should be taken in consideration. Europe in its own modern mind located itself in the center and the Rest at the periphery, and as Walter Mignolo states, modernity "carries on its shoulders the heavy weight and responsibility

---

12. Ibid., 294.
13. Enrique Dussel, "Eurocentrism and Modernity," *The Postmodernism Debate in Latin America*, ed. John Beverley, Michael Aronna, and José Oviedo (Durham, N.C.: Duke University Press, 1995), 65.
14. Dussel, "Beyond Eurocentricism," 4.

of coloniality."[15] Thus, to be able to break away from coloniality and the colonial discourses, modern epistemology needs to be challenged.

DIS-COVERY AND POSTCOLONIAL CRITICISM

Historiography, understood as a colonial enterprise, as well as other disciplines is facing a series of challenges in this regard. The twentieth century turned out to be a century of decolonial processes, both outside and inside the academic world. Chela Sandoval states:

> The twentieth century season of reproachment shook the Western will to know in all its settling points, permitting a release of new knowledges in the science, arts, and humanities. This decolonizing period cultivated knowledge formations that defied and transgressed the traditional boundaries of academic disciplines: ethnic studies, women's studies, global studies, queer theory, poststructuralism, cultural studies, New Historicism, and the critique of colonial discourse developed as intellectual movements that similarly understood Western rationality as a limited ethnophilosophy — as a *particular* historical location marked by gender, race, class, region, and so on. Their shared aim was to generate new analytic spaces for thought, feeling, and action that would be informed by *world* historical conditions.[16]

Currently, colonial discourses and the normative history it creates — a history that determines the way people see and interpret the past — are being challenged by postcolonial discourses. People in former colonies and present ones are in the process of recovering their stories and rewriting their history. The new history exposes the colonial agenda within the one offered by the colonial discourse. These discourses break patterns of understanding and knowledge by shifting the role of the people from objects of a dominant history to subjects of their own history. While colonial discourses relegate people outside the center of power to the margins or borders of the normative knowledge, postcolonial (or decolonial) discourses challenge the normative knowledge to *dis*-cover the voices of

---

15. Walter Mignolo, *Local Histories/Global Designs: Coloniality, Subaltern Knowledges, and Border Thinking* (Princeton, N.J.: Princeton University Press, 2000), 37.
16. Chela Sandoval, *Methodology of the Oppressed* (Minneapolis: University of Minnesota Press, 2000), 8.

these marginalized people. *Dis*-covery is not the process by which someone finds for the first time a land or an idea. Rather, following María
Pilar Aquino's conception of *dis*-covery, it should be understood as a process in which the subject realizes that covering up has been part of her/his
past. Talking from the standpoint of Latin American women, Aquino
says, "the five hundred years of European presence in Latin America
have served not so much as an occasion for imagining what our history
actually was or could have been but rather as an occasion for a continuing *dis*-covery."[17] She goes on to say, "The great European invasions did
not *discover* but rather covered whole peoples, religions, and cultures
and explicitly tried to take away from natives the sources of their own
historical memory and their own power."[18] Thus, *dis*-covery becomes
a process of uncovering and re-creating one's own past and memory. It
serves the marginal, the subaltern, in the quest for an identity, a self-
identity, different from that which has been placed upon her/his by the
people who covered up the memory. It is a way of breaking away from
the colonial heritage imposed on knowledge.

This process of *dis*-covery helps in the development of a new history in
which the voices of the people who have been silenced by the dominant
historiographical discourse though method and interpretation are uncovered and exposed as part of the historical process. Arif Dirlik argues:

> For the marginalized and oppressed in particular, whose histories
> have been erased by power, it becomes all the more important
> to recapture or remake the past in their efforts to render them-
> selves visible historically, as the very struggle to become visible
> presupposes a historical identity. In the face of a "historiographic
> colonialism" that denies them their historicity, capturing the truth
> of history, of oppression and the resistance to it, is a fundamen-
> tal task.[19]

This is why it is important not only to *dis-cover* stories and memories
that challenge the colonial discourse, but also to develop new ways of
writing history so that voices currently in the borders may be brought

---

17. María Pilar Aquino, "The Collective "Dis-covery" of Our Own Power: Latina American
Feminist Theology," *Hispanic Latino Theology: Challenge and Promise,* ed. Ada María Isasi-
Díaz and Fernando F. Segovia (Minneapolis: Fortress Press, 1996), 241.
18. Ibid.
19. Arif Dirlik, *Postmodernity's Histories: The Past as Legacy and Project* (New York and
Oxford: Rowan and Littlefield, 2000), 215–16.

to the historical process. This inclusion should not be in the form of a footnote, nor should it be peripheral; instead it should be a significant part of the history and the actual process of writing that history.

The dominant historical discourses tend to focus their argument on the creation of heroes of the past and events that could help the people in the center of power acquire an identity. It is a way of using the past to read the present. David J. Weber, talking about the approach historians of the Texas revolution have used to understand and interpret this event, says:

> But it is more than a traditional big brag that has led Texans to exaggerate the events of 1836 and to make mortal men into heroes of mythological proportions. This certainly reflects a more universal tendency — the tendency to write pietistic history and to use the past as a kind of Rorschach test, seeing wistfully in the past what we wish to see about ourselves in the present. In the interest of creating a usable past, the peoples seem to engage in the making of myths and passing them off as historical fact.[20]

People in society live out the myths created by the dominant discourses in the form of traditional history. "Traditionalist historiography produces a fictive past, and that fiction becomes the knowledge manipulated to negate the 'other' culture's differences."[21] Although postcolonial discourses do not challenge the fictive character of history (representation of the past), they reexamine traditional history and its myths and challenge its interpretation and the universal character it attains. In other words, postcolonial discourses work in a certain kind of subversive way against the normative imaginary.[22] In them, the myths and the fictional pasts

---

20. David J. Weber, *Myth and the History of the Hispanic Southwest* (Albuquerque: University of New Mexico Press, 1988), 140.

21. Emma Pérez, *The Decolonial Imaginary: Writing Chicanas into History* (Bloomington: Indiana University Press, 1999), xviii.

22. Many scholars agree that the "field" of postcolonial studies traces its origins to the publication of the book *Orientalism* by Edward W. Said in 1978, without disregarding its connections to earlier works by Frantz Fanon and Albert Memmi. In the present, no one can claim that postcolonial studies are housed in a single discipline or program. While most of the work has been done in English departments and within literary criticism, postcolonial studies have challenged disciplines such as political science, law, sociology, and history, just to mention a few. For this project, I take postcolonial studies as whole, although I recognize the diversity of uses in various disciplines. Postcolonial studies have served Third World scholars to critique and examine colonial discourses and to reconstruct the history of the colonized. Fanon, Memmi, and Said are most responsible for the development of theories of colonial discourses, or colonial discourse analysis, and these are the foundation for the development of postcolonial

are dismantled and subaltern people, "those of inferior rank, whether class, caste, age, gender or any other way,"[23] find the sources and voices for the construction of "an identity uncontaminated by universalist or Eurocentric concepts and images."[24] A decolonial imaginary is formed different from the one colonialism constructed, and as Emma Pérez indicates:

> The difference between the colonial and decolonial imaginaries is that the colonial remains the inhibiting trace, accepting power relations as they are, perhaps confronting them, but not reconfiguring them.... The decolonial imaginary challenges power relations to decolonize notions of otherness to move into a liberatory terrain.[25]

U.S. RELIGIOUS HISTORIOGRAPHY AS A COLONIAL ENTERPRISE

Traditional U.S. religious historiography has to be understood and analyzed in terms of this paradigm of colonial/decolonial discourse. A critical look at the sources, the content, and the form in traditional U.S. religious historiography uncovers its silences and leads to the *dis-covery* of voices, places, and stories from the people at the borders of its discourse. At the same time this approach leads to the uncovering of unjust systems within the discourse and the imaginary it creates.

U.S. religious historiography has depended upon a canon, a standard narrative, which began its development in the nineteenth century with Robert Baird's *Religion in America,* but all this process had its climax in the writing of *A Religious History of the American People* by Sydney Ahlstrom.[26] This work became the grand narrative of U.S. religious

studies. These theories explore the ways the colonized are kept under subjugation by the modes of representation used by the colonizer and emphasize the role of language in this process of representation.

23. Anna Green and Kathleen Troup, *The House of History: A Critical Reader in Twentieth-Century History and Theory* (New York: NYU Press; 1999), 283.

24. Simon During, "Postmodernism or Post-colonialism Today," *The Post-colonial Studies Reader,* ed. Bill Ashcroft, Gareth Griffiths, and Helen Tiffin (London: Routledge, 1995), 125.

25. Pérez, *The Decolonial Imaginary,* 110.

26. Robert Baird, *Religion in America; or an Account of the Origin, Relation to the State, and Present Conditions of the Evangelical Churches in the United States with Notices of the Unevangelical Denominations* (New York: Harper & Brothers, 1856), and Sydney E. Ahlstrom, *A Religious History of the American People* (New Haven, Conn.: Yale University Press, 1972).

history, the conclusion of a tradition. As Jerald C. Brauer puts it, "This became the classical way of interpreting and writing the religious history of the United States. Sydney E. Ahlstrom has produced the definitive history in this tradition."[27] Brauer finds that the scholars in this tradition, those whom I have mentioned above, followed two assumptions: (1) it was possible, even with the diversity in denomination, "to sketch out a unified picture of the development of religion in America and to place it, in varying degrees, in dialogue with a complex social context"; (2) there was a particularity in the structure of the religious experience in the United States, "particularly European yet uniquely American — a Protestant reality," which shaped and formed the history.[28]

Sydney E. Ahlstrom completed the work of the historians in the tradition that he followed, from Baird to Gaustad.[29] Though this tradition, as I have pointed out, suffered changes through time, it is now completed with this piece. He recovered most of the main material uncovered by earlier historians, giving a new meaning to the understanding of religion in the United States by trying to focus on religion, and not merely Protestantism. In this regard, Henry Warner Bowden argued, "Ahlstrom's publication is a landmark in modern historiography, because it adequately summarizes the best work of colleagues to date and will provide the standard correlation of such material until decades of new spadework require another one."[30] He set out to write a revisionist history of

27. Jerald C. Brauer, Review of *A Religious History of the American People,* by Sydney E. Ahlstrom, *Church History* 42, no. 3 (1973): 406.

28. Ibid.

29. The long tradition he followed included Daniel Dorchester, *Christianity in the United States from the First Settlement Down to the Present Time* (New York: Phillips & Hunt, 1888); Leonard W. Bacon, *A History of American Christianity* (New York: The Christian Literature, 1897); Henry Rowe, *The History of Religion in the United States* (New York: Macmillan Company, 1924); William Warren Sweet, *The Story of Religions in America* (New York: Harper & Brothers, 1930), and *The American Churches: An Interpretation* (New York: Abingdon-Cokesbury Press, 1947); H. Richard Niebuhr, *The Kingdom of God in America* (Middletown, Conn.: Wesleyan University Press, [1937] 1988); and *The Social Sources of Denominationalism* (Cleveland: World Publishing, 1929); Jerald C. Brauer, *Protestantism in America: A Narrative History* (Philadelphia: Westminster Press, 1953); Clifton E. Olmstead, *History of Religion in the United States* (Englewood Cliffs, N.J.: Prentice-Hall, 1960); Sidney E. Mead, *The Lively Experiment: The Shaping of Christianity in America* (New York, Evanston, and London: Harper & Row, 1963); Winthrop S. Hudson, *American Protestantism* (Chicago: University of Chicago Press, 1961), and *Religion in America* (New York: Charles Scribner's Sons, 1965); Edwin Scott Gaustad, *A Religious History of America* (New York: Harper & Row, 1966); and H. Shelton Smith, Robert T. Handy, and Lefferts A. Loetscher, *American Christianity: An Historical Interpretation with Representative Documents* (New York: Charles Scribner's Sons, 1960–63).

30. Henry Warner Bowden, "Landmarks in American Religious Historiography: A Review Essay," *The Writing of American Religious History,* ed. Martin E. Marty (Munich and New York: K. G. Saur, 1992), 128.

religion in the United States, a new perspective, but as Brauer found out, that was not accomplished. Brauer affirmed,

> Though there are a number of important differences between Ahl-strom and his predecessors, such as his comprehensiveness, the far greater weight he gives to intellectual history, his attention to groups previously ignored or given inadequate treatment, the suppression of a particular chauvinism which marked Baird or Sweet, the fact remains that this is not a new interpretative per-spective on religion in America which essentially rearranges our basic understanding of that history.[31]

The amplitude of this work provided the space for several movements and religious experiences to be analyzed, but "the classic 'Protestant-Puritan' tradition remains the interpretative center of his history."[32] Although arguing for a renovation and a new paradigm in U.S. religious historiography, Ahlstrom continued to focus on the "Protestant-Puritan" tradition in order to construct his narrative to the point that it could be considered "one of the very best synthetic constructs of the develop-ment and role of that tradition in America."[33] I go a little further and argue that this became the canon of religious history in the United States and that the classical historiographical interpretation was just brought together in this work. This is why understanding the magnitude and import of Ahlstrom's argument is so important.

Sydney Ahlstrom built this narrative on the tradition that preceded him, but the inclusion of religious pluralism is what makes this work so important. As David Daniels argues, "the Ahlstrom narrative serves as an apologia for religious pluralism."[34] He saw the United States of his time as a post-Puritan era and thought of the history as a process in which different religious groups developed and helped in the developing of the nation. Of course, he was not the first to include religious pluralism, but without a doubt the massive space he dedicated to it gave him a better chance of proving the importance of it. The problem in Ahlstrom's work is that he did not see this religious pluralism as an actual new way of

---

31. Brauer, "Review," 406.
32. Ibid., 407.
33. Ibid.
34. David Daniels, "Teaching the History of U.S. Christianity in a Global Perspective," *Theological Education* 29, no. 2 (1993): 94.

interpretation, and the historiographical paradigm he set out to revise was kept unchanged. In this sense I agree with Henry Bowden's statement that this work did not provide any detailed revision, but that it merely adds new material to the already established tradition.[35]

A Religious History of the American People serves the purpose of summarizing material and introducing new material, but it does not change the basic point of view of interpretation, which remained the "Protestant-Puritan" tradition. It opened the door for new research but it did not contribute to the changing of lenses through which the historian interprets, reconstructs, and represents the past. Even his mentioning of the importance of the black experience in the study of religion in the United States to point out that he thought of it as the "basic paradigm for a renovation of American church history"[36] did not open the door for new historiographical scaffolds. The inclusion of religious pluralism and the black experience are not part of the theme of the book; they are included only inasmuch as they are related to the Puritan tradition because even in the last part of the book the relationship to Puritanism is made through the reference to a post-Puritan era. This gives Puritanism the central role in the interpretation of U.S. religious history; everything else has to be referenced to their relation to Puritanism, and this is what happened to religious pluralism and the black experience. *A Religious History of the American People* became the definitive work of a tradition and closed the canon of that tradition. Other scholars wrote (or composed) syntheses, macronarratives, not of the magnitude of Ahlstrom's but with somehow the same commitment.[37] In this sense, Mark Noll's *A History of Christianity in the United States and Canada* closes the canon of U.S. religious historiography because it is the last synthesis (macronarrative) written in the discipline.

I will go further to describe this canon as a closed standard narrative, which sees groups, experiences, and ideas outside the classical tradition

35. Bowden, "Landmarks in American Religious Historiography," 133.
36. Ahlstrom, *A Religious History of the American People,* 12.
37. Robert T. Handy, *A History of the Churches in the United States and Canada* (New York: Oxford University Press, 1977); and Mark A. Noll, *A History of Christianity in the United States and Canada* (Grand Rapids, Mich.: Eerdmans, 1992). Other works in the area are Martin Marty, *Pilgrims in Their Own Land: Five Hundred Years of Religion in America* (Boston: Little, Brown, 1984); and revised editions of previous works as Edwin Scott Gaustad, *A Religious History of America,* new revised edition (San Francisco: HarperSanFrancisco, 1990); and Winthrop S. Hudson and John Corrigan, *Religion in America: An Historical Account of the Development of American Religious Life* (Upper Saddle River, N.J.: Prentice Hall, 1999).

as outsider, as the Other. Religious pluralism has been addressed within the canon but has never become part of it, and as far as the black experience goes it has not been seen, as Ahlstrom proposed, as the basic paradigm of renovation of the discipline. This experience has become an important research topic for many scholars and a large amount of material has been uncovered and included in the standard narrative. In a sense, the inclusion of the black experience has been seen as the key aspect to complete the narrative, which does not mean that the black experience has taken a protagonistic role within it. In this sense, race has become an important issue but many times has been treated as a "somewhat separate topic to be added to the already existing topics in the story of religion in America."[38] Thus, race has not been an integrative part of the main topic and theme of the standard narrative.

The canon, the standard narrative, has been closed to the issue of race and other issues as part of its subject matter because of its dependence on the modern project, which "assumed a universal truth with core and periphery relations, giving privilege to the rationality and sensibility that undergirded its cosmology as normative."[39] This traditional way of doing U.S. religious history follows the modernist impulse as it locates the "Protestant-Puritan" tradition at the center and other issues at the periphery and tends to universalize this tradition, leaving groups outside this experience without an actual participation in the historical project. So these groups, as Others, are left without a historical voice or consciousness. The standard narrative works to maintain the privileged position of U.S. white male America at the center through its use of power in writing by leaving hidden the voices and stories of the Others. In its representation, the narrative constructs the past through the use of emplotment in which the events are seen in a progressive and continuous way from the European Reformation to an authentic U.S. Christianity to a religious plurality. Of course the main catalyst, which explains this progressive character, is the "Protestant-Puritan" tradition that serves, as Noll acknowledges, as the thread of the narrative. This thread is the lens through which everything is interpreted and defined. In this sense a connection can be made between this standard narrative

38. Roger D. Hatch, "Integrating the Issue of Race into the History of Christianity in America," in *The Writing of American Religious History,* ed. Martin E. Marty (New York: K. G. Saur, 1992), 181.
39. Daniels, "Teaching the History of U.S. Christianity in a Global Perspective," 95.

(canon) and the idea of universal history[40] or Foucault's *total* history.[41] This standard narrative, then, becomes the dominant discourse, which creates an imaginary that becomes the norm and tends to be universalized. This imaginary is a colonial imaginary since it is sustained by the modern project.

On the other hand Hayden White's argument about the use of narrative form can also be used to analyze this canon. In these works as in other historical accounts, narrative has been used to establish the presence of a coherent argument without gaps or empty spaces.[42] Narrative as a form has provided U.S. religious historians a structure to construct one grand synthesis in which every event included is connected to each other. So if an event, theme, or geographical space does not have a connection with the main argument of the narrative it is left out or included as peripheral (footnote). Hence, the voices and stories that break the continuity are seen as secondary and nonessential. This approach provides the central thread in the narrative with a superior character and the people represented through it with a central role in society because they have a historical voice and consciousness. In conclusion, the use of narrative has helped in the construction of an imaginary, which is seen as normative. It is a colonial discourse because it relegates the Other to the borders and imposes a standard narrative (a master-narrative) that has "focused disproportionately on male, northeastern, Anglo-Saxon, mainline Protestants and their beliefs, institutions, and power."[43] It has been used as the means by which voices have been silenced and memories

---

40. See Immanuel Kant, "Idea for a Universal History with Cosmopolitan Intent," trans. Carl F. Friedrich, *Basic Writing of Kant,* ed. Allen W. Wood (New York: Modern Library, 2001), and for a critical discussion on the issue of a universal history see Dale Irvin, *Christian Histories, Christian Traditioning: Rendering Accounts* (Maryknoll, N.Y.: Orbis Books, 1998); and Walter Benjamin, "Theses on the Philosophy of History," *Illuminations,* ed. Hannah Arendt, trans. Harry Zohn (New York: Schocken Books, 1985).

41. Foucault differentiates between *total* history and *general* history, the second project being the task for new historians. "The project of a *total* history is one that seeks to reconstitute the overall form of a civilization, the principle — material or spiritual — of a society, the significance common to all the phenomena of a period, the law that accounts for their cohesion — what is called metaphorically the 'face' of a period." *General* history, on the other hand, focuses on the correlation between the phenomena not to draw them together as *total* history does but to "deploy the space of a dispersion" (Michel Foucault, *The Archaeology of Knowledge and the Discourse on Language,* trans. A. M. Sheridan Smith [New York: Pantheon Books, 1972], 9–10.)

42. See Hayden White, *The Content of the Form: Narrative Discourse and Historical Representation* (Baltimore: Johns Hopkins University Press, 1987).

43. Thomas A. Tweed, "Introduction: Narrating U.S. Religious History," *Retelling U.S. Religious History,* ed. Thomas A. Tweed (Berkeley: University of California Press, 1997), 3.

hidden. Thus, traditional U.S. religious historiography works within the contours of the modern/colonial system. As Steve McKinzie declares:

> The older versions have omitted key events, neglected important constituents, and failed to consider a diversity of points of view. They have, in short, given us a narrative that is truncated and short-sighted, dominated by a Protestant elite, and riddled with prejudice.[44]

NEW WAYS, OLD WAYS

In the past decades, there have been several new approaches to the writing of U.S. religious history. It is important to first acknowledge the work of R. Laurence Moore, *Religious Outsiders and the Making of Americans,* and that of Catherine L. Albanese, *America: Religions and Religion,* which offer new perspectives on religious pluralism in the United States.[45] Without entering into a meticulous description of these books, I want to recognize the importance of their arguments in favor of a more plural narrative of U.S. religious history. Both scholars question the actual canon by promoting a more exhaustive examination of the experience of non-Protestant religious groups in the United States. Their work is crucial in the understanding of religious diversity, and the introduction of new themes and geographical settings (outside New England). Peter W. Williams's *America's Religions: Traditions and Cultures* has to be mentioned in order to complete the voices that have argued for a more religious diverse narrative.[46] But these are not the major alternatives historians have taken.

U.S. religious historians have taken the paths of micronarratives and case studies in order to continue the process of writing. Syntheses, macronarratives, are no longer being written, so the major works in the discipline are concentrated in studies of regions, themes,

---

44. Steve McKinzie, "Saints and Revisionists: Refashioning the American Religious Narrative," *Cross Currents* 48, no. 1 (1998): 103.

45. R. Laurence Moore, *Religious Outsiders and the Making of Americans* (New York: Oxford University Press, 1986); Catherine L. Albanese, *America: Religions and Religion* (Belmont, Calif.: Wadsworth, 1992).

46. Peter W. Williams, *America's Religions: Traditions and Cultures* (New York: Macmillan, 1990).

people/communities, religions and periods of time.[47] I want to recognize and examine the increased production of collections, so called "Readers." Through the evaluation and comparison of these collections a better view of the status of the discipline can be captured. In these anthologies scholars are proposing new directions and propositions, while at the same time subtly promoting the continuation of the traditional historiography. In other words while some scholars have challenged the traditional model of writing the history of U.S. religious experience, others have taken new approaches but still maintain the content.

I should start with the examination of *Retelling U.S. Religious History*, edited by Thomas A. Tweed, which shows that the grand narratives have left certain regions and communities out of the normative historical account.[48] Scholars in this book uncover the religious story of different regions of the United States. The "aim is not to reconstruct a single grand narrative, but to offer several situated stories and ask readers whether these illumine regions of the past that had remained obscured in the older surveys."[49] This work demonstrates the importance of considering geographical location as a locus of analysis. This shift not only highlights the geography of U.S. religious history, but it also recuperates the voices of people in the borders both geographical and socially. Lauren F. Winner points to the importance of this approach to the recovery of marginalized voices as she states, "the scholars in *Retelling U.S. Religious History* rightly insist on showing that 'outsiders,' to alter the metaphor, are more than just raisins in the cake."[50] This is a way of breaking away from the normative discourse by establishing the presence of other legitimate stories previously absent from the standard narrative.

The authors in this anthology find that motifs (sexuality, contact and exchange, colonialism) and locations (Canadian borders, the southwestern territory, and Pan-Pacific area) serve as important hermeneutical keys in order to bring new perspectives to the table. This "retelling," is important because the absence of a group in a discourse is more than the absence of a voice. Tweed argues:

---

47. The one exception is the revisions to Hudson's *Religion in America* by John Corrigan, who although integrating new material including that from Albanese's book has not been able to step away from the predominance of the dominant tradition.

48. Tweed, ed., *Retelling U.S. Religious History.*

49. Ibid., "Introduction," 6.

50. Lauren F. Winner, "Retold, Redirected, Rethunk: Form and Content in the Study of American Religion," *Books and Culture: A Christian Review* 4, no. 3 (1998): 21.

... the stories that fill history textbooks are important because they negotiate power and construct identity. They situate us in society and tell us who we are. Historical narratives often reflect, and shape, the social and economic order: individuals and groups excluded from narratives are excluded from more than stories. Those who do not find themselves or their experience represented in the most widely told stories engage in struggles — private and public, quiet and noisy — to make sense of themselves and locate their place among others in the wider society. Historical narratives, then, never are "just" history. There always is a great deal at stake for narrator and readers, always much to gain and lose in power and meaning.[51]

In other words, he is calling for the *dis*-covery of those stories, places, and voices that have been excluded from the grand narratives. While he acknowledges that the major surveys have dealt with the issue of diversity, the main characters and the storyline are still the same, which was Roger D. Hatch's argument on the nonrevision of the subject matter of the standard narrative. This process of *dis*-covery enables the inclusion of new stories, voices, and places not in an external way (footnote), but as part of the subject of history. In other words, the essays in *Retelling U.S. Religious History* go beyond a mere introduction of new topics and themes to actually providing new interpretative lenses and paradigms. The essays, as Steve McKinzie has acknowledged, lack cohesiveness as a whole but I believe that this proves the discontinuities within the writing of history, and that in those discontinuities, in those spaces, hidden stories are found. It is a matter of looking for them and exposing them.[52]

Although other collections of the last decade, have brought to the table new approaches and perspectives, they have not challenged the traditional and modern/colonial character of U.S. religious historiography. A first example of this kind of work is the collection *New Directions in American Religious History,* edited by Harry Stout and D. G. Hart.[53]

---

51. Tweed, "Introduction," 2.
52. A great example of how to explore and expose is present in David G. Hackett, ed., *Religion and American Culture: A Reader* (New York: Routledge, 1995).
53. See Harry Stout and D. G. Hart, ed., *New Directions in American Religious History* (New York: Oxford University Press, 1997).

The articles in this anthology were collected from a conference with the
same name in 1993. The articles were written following these guidelines:

> Given the decisive shifts in historiography from mainline to sideline
> in the past twenty years, the conference planners asked the partici-
> pants to think of the new groups they are studying and the histories
> they yield in dialectical tension with the old Protestant mainline
> histories, thus bringing the old "Church History" — Protestant
> centered and intellectually based — into dialogue with the new,
> non-mainline-centered and socially based "religious history."[54]

Although this premise conveys hope to the readers that the articles in
the book will serve as groundbreaking material, both in the content and
method, the book falls short of this objective. While a period of growth
and transition in the study of religion in the United States is acknowledged, the essays in the book do not provide new material to work with
as much as new perspectives on the same old topics and themes.

The authors in *New Directions in American History* looked at the old
stories and introduced a "new" way of rethinking and rewriting them.
Again, there is no intent of writing new stories, because as Laura F. Winner says, "Stout and Hart are more concerned with refining the stories
we have."[55] The authors want to create a change in the way religious
history in the United States is being told so they took the already existing
topics and themes (Puritanism, voluntarism, African American religion,
Catholicism, and Judaism, and others) and worked on them, trying to
find out how would they fit in the present condition of the study of religion in the United States. The new perspectives should be taken into
consideration if those topics and themes are going to be reexamined,
but besides the discussion about the use of sociology and the new social
history in the first chapter and large amount of works cited within the
different texts, the book does not offer really new paths to follow. Paul
Boyer makes an excellent critique of the fact that this book does not take
into consideration the changes in the religious life of the United States;
it does not pay attention to the religious and ethnic diversity present
in today's society. He establishes the importance of different groups in
the development of the social, political, and economic structures of the
United States. Boyer points out:

---

54. Ibid., 4–5.
55. Winner, "Retold, Redirected, Rethunk," 20.

With a few exceptions, this book addresses specific sectors of *white American Protestant* history. One would hardly guess from this volume the Hispanics (mainly Catholic, with a strong evangelical and Pentecostalist admixture) will soon overtake blacks as the nation's largest minority; that Islam is poised to supplant Judaism as America's second largest religion after Christianity; that Pentecostalism has been the most vital and dynamic force in the twentieth-century American religious life; that Quakers, Unitarians, and Episcopalians, while relatively few in number, have played outsized roles in American social, intellectual, political (and military) history; that America has spawned new religions that today enroll many millions worldwide, including Mormonism, Christian Science, Jehovah's Witness, and Seventh-Day Adventist; that televangelist Billy Graham was this century's most influential American Christian leader worldwide; or that heterodox religious innovators, from the Fox sisters and William Miller to the latest New Age guru or Bible-prophecy popularizer, have profoundly shaped the American religious scene.[56]

It is a matter of reviewing the book to be able to see that this initiative failed to grasp most of the dimensions that can shift the nature and direction in religious history in the United States.

This critique applies in the same way to other collections in the area of U.S. religious history.[57] These collections have been used to preserve the status quo and the normative character of the dominant discourse. The only difference with the surveys is that now macronarrative has been replaced by micronarrative as the form of discourse. Stories are still silenced and covered, and the historical voice of the people in the borders is still excluded from the discourse. In this regard, Harry Stout and R. M. Taylor state that "historians do not need to pursue ever-new topics so much as they need to relate their work to broader, theoretical concerns."[58] Contrary to Stout and Taylor, I argue that historians

---

56. Paul Boyer, "Testimony Time: Historians Reflect on Current Issues in American Religious History," *Evangelical Studies Bulletin* 15, no. 3 (1998): 4.

57. Other examples are Jon Butler and Harry S. Stout, eds. *Religion in American History: A Reader* (New York: Oxford University Press, 1998); Henry Warner Bowden and P. C. Kemeny, eds., *American Church History: A Reader* (Nashville: Abingdon Press, 1998).

58. Harry S. Stout and R. M. Taylor, "Studies of Religion in American Society: The State of the Art," *New Directions in American Religious History,* ed. H. Stout and D. G. Hart (New York: Oxford University Press, 1997), 36.

should not treat the theoretical concerns and the new stories and topics separately, because both need to be revisited.

U.S. religious historiography has benefited from the developments of these collections, for the introduction of new material or for the reevaluation of the old. The different projects available serve as proof of the many ventures in which scholars in the field are engaged while at the same time serve as proof that the standard narrative is still the basic paradigm for most of these ventures, with the few exceptions mentioned above. The micronarratives in many cases are not serving the purpose of revising the dominant discourse, but on the other hand serve as projects of legitimation of the standard narrative and the modern project. Revisions like these have continued to support the modern project and have not challenged it. The micronarratives have not produced any alternative knowledge to modernity, but instead have become part of the colonial project. Even when they set out to include more participants they have not explored the discontinuities. Mark Noll includes people who have been left out of the standard narrative, but at the same time argues, "It may still not be entirely clear how to integrate such groups fully into the written story of Christianity in America, which until recently has been dominated by leaders of elite groups who did leave extensive published records."[59] And after analyzing the "new" micronarratives and the projects they represent, the problem clearly resides in the lack of critique of the scaffold that sustains the standard narrative, that being the modern project.

The inclusion of a critique of the modern project would actually expand and redefine the understanding of pluralism in U.S. religious historiography. Although some of these texts help unmask the dominant discourse (canon) as exclusive by leaving in the borders other religious expressions beyond the mainline Protestant world, David Daniels declares, "a serious critique of the modern project and its constriction of alternative narrative is necessary before a new direction in historiographical narrative is actually possible."[60] He argues that the last revisions of the standard narrative dealt with the making of religious pluralism, but still supported the modern project. So Daniels goes on to propose,

---

59. Ibid.
60. Daniels, "Teaching the History of U.S. Christianity in a Global Perspective," 99.

To revise this thesis and move toward a globalized interpretation, the making of religious pluralism needs to shift from procedural discourse which distinguishes pluralities, majorities, and minorities, to ecological discourse of post-modern musings. For example, the making of religious pluralism might be re-defined in terms of heterogeneity instead of homogeneity.[61]

But while scholarship in religious pluralism in the United States can be expanded with proposals like Daniels's, scholarship in the area of racial/ethnic pluralism in religion has not had the same impact and the revisions in this area are scarce. Postmodern musings are needed within this area as well.

A BLACK/WHITE PARADIGM

One reason for the lack of emphasis on racial/ethnic pluralism is the scholars' assumption of a black/white paradigm that leaves out of the analysis and interpretation people in the middle of this spectrum. "Historically, race in the United States has been perceived as a black-white issue."[62] Most of the work in the field has opened up to the study of African American (Black) religion, although Roger D. Hatch's article provides the condition of that inclusion. In this regard, the "revised" traditional U.S. religious historiography has created and solidified a paradigm to deal with the issues of race and ethnicity. The issue of race is only dealt with as a binary opposition between black and white. Every topic or issue is studied, interpreted, and analyzed based on the relationship between these two groups. In this paradigm the white still has the control over the voice of the black, and still dominates the discourse, but the inclusion of a black voice, although peripheral, has given the white a sense of accomplishment since it appears as if the standard narrative has been revised and opened to diversity. But as a matter of fact the standard narrative is still closed not only to the black voice, but also mostly to the voices outside (or in the middle) of the black/white paradigm.

61. Ibid., 97.
62. Teresa Chávez-Sauceda, "Race, Religion, and la Raza: An Exploration of the Racialization of Latinos in the United States and the Role of the Protestant Church," in *Protestantes/Protestants: Hispanic Christianity within Mainline Traditions*, ed. David Maldonado Jr. (Nashville: Abingdon Press, 1999), 178.

On the other hand, the issue of ethnicity has been dealt with only as much is it pertains to the situation of European immigrants. "In short, a great deal of the writings and discussions on the topic of American religion has been consciously or unconsciously ideological, serving to enhance, justify, and render sacred the history of European immigrants in this land."[63] Ethnicity, in this sense, is seen only through the male WASP lens, so although the mention of U.S. Native Americans, U.S. Latino/as, and U.S. Asian Americans is available in some of the literature, the issue of ethnicity enters the discussion only if it relates to the condition of the European immigrants and their relationship with each other.

U.S. religious historiography has revised its standard narrative in order to keep the dominant discourse dominated by the male WASP perspective, which translates in control over what Harry S. Stout called "the American Way of Life."[64] The construction of a black/white paradigm in order to interpret the racial/ethnic relation within the religious experience in the United States is just proof of these internal revisions. Before this paradigm, the three-party system opened the canon to two non-Protestant groups, Catholicism and Judaism, in order to give the impression that the Protestant-Puritan perspective no longer dominated the standard narrative.[65] It is clear that the Protestant-Puritan perspective defined those two groups and selected the spaces they were going to share. These groups have voice inasmuch as they contribute to that "American Way of Life," dissenting voices are considered exceptions and make the texts as footnotes. The same happens with the inclusion of the black perspective. This racial/ethnic paradigm sustains the standard narrative by including African Americans as addenda to the male WASP–dominated discourse. African Americans' voices have been retrieved and many of their stories have been uncovered, but other Others have been relegated to the borders and their voices are kept silenced and covered. This black/white paradigm has created two valid poles, so the groups that do not fit in either of the poles are boxed into one of the poles or just left out.

---

63. Charles H. Long, "A New Look at American Religion," in *The Writing of American Religious History*, ed. Martin E. Marty, 87.

64. Stout, "Ethnicity."

65. Will Herberg, *Protestant-Catholic-Jew: An Essay in American Religious Sociology* (Garden City, N.Y.: Anchor Books, 1955).

A NEW PERSPECTIVE FROM THE BORDERLANDS

The standard narrative in U.S. religious historiography is a colonial discourse in the sense that it silences voices and covers memories of whole groups. The apparent revisions and openness exhibited by this canon have not challenged the subject matter or the paradigms of interpretations used. This canon positions the Others at the borders not only of a text, as footnotes, but at the borderlands of society, and their inclusion in the narrative has been for the sole purpose of reinforcing their own identity and their control over those Others. The construction of the standard narrative followed the path of traditional modern historical discourse through which the past can be seen as it really happened as narrative proved to be the form of discourse. In this standard (or master) narrative, the Protestant-Puritan tradition was the central aspect through which everything was interpreted, so the superiority of this tradition, which is part of the construction of the West in the Americas, was established through this dominant discourse. This discourse was given a universal character, so every other particularity has to be explained through it to acquire any kind of validity. The canon of U.S. religious history, as a traditional historical discourse, can be characterized for the impetus of continuity, and supported the ideas of progress and the superiority of the West over those in the periphery, the Others (Rest). This is the way a colonial imaginary was created, leaving the Others outside.

In order to accomplish and perpetuate this control, this dominant discourse gave way to revisions, which came for the most part from the inside, of the same discourse. These projects of revisions, as I have argued, varied but none opened up the field to voices from the outside to talk back to the center. The voices involved in the processes came from the inside opening up space for voices of the outside to come in but not on their own terms. The dominant voice, which is the U.S. white male American, controlled the definitions, terms, and subject matter of the discourse. Of course, during this time many proposals from the outside have appeared, and people from border groups keep writing their own stories and keep talking back to the center — not from within the dominant discourse but from the borderlands. The canon has to be deconstructed in order to be reconstructed, leaving aside the models that divide into parties the population, the homogenization of plurality, and the racial/ethnic and gender paradigms that support the marginalization of peoples and the perpetuation of the standard narrative. The openness to voices from the outside has to come without any kind of control or hidden agenda. As Charles H. Long argues:

> It is no longer possible for us to add the "invisible ones" as addenda to a European dominated historical method for such a procedure fails to take into account the relationships of the omitted ones to the Europeans throughout American religious history. Nor it is possible for us, simply in imitation of the historical method we are criticizing, to begin the project of writing history in which the ideological values of blacks and Amerindians dominate. This procedure has no merit for it could not make sense of that problem of invisibility which allowed us to raise the issue of our discussion. The issue raised here is a subtle one and questions must be asked concerning the very nature of historical method.[66]

This is exactly what I am looking for. I am not arguing that the Protestant-Puritan tradition or that white male U.S. America should be left out of a revised discourse. I feel that the deconstruction of the canon should bring the reconstruction of a new scaffold. The deconstruction of the modern project embedded in the standard narrative would bring down the colonial imaginary promoted by it in which the northeast Puritan experience serves as the catalyst for the rest of the religious history in the United States.

The deconstruction of the black/white paradigm is the key to bringing down the dominant scaffolds together with the inclusion of the issues of class and gender. The issue of gender has been introduced in many of the anthologies and other literature, but it has focused for the most part on the women of the dominant groups with the inclusion of some African American women.[67] So in this sense I am arguing that the black/white paradigm has also guided the work dealing with the issue of gender. The issue of class is not present in the literature and many times is relegated to an addendum of the issue of race/ethnicity/gender. This issue cuts through religious groups and denominations because the voices that are heard within the dominant discourse are usually coming from a higher class, in the economic sense obviously. The voices and experiences of those in the lower classes, no matter their positioning within the spectrum of society, are mostly relegated to the borders, and do not take part in the

66. Long, "A New Look at American Religion," 87.
67. See Rosemary Radford Ruether and Rosemary Skinner, eds., *Women and Religion in America: A Documentary History*, 3 vols. (New York: Harper & Row, 1981–85).

discourse. This is why it can be argued that the winners, those in power, control the standard narrative. A way to bring justice to these groups is to include a paradigm, which follows feminism on the border or Third World feminism. Through these approaches the issues of class, gender, and race/ethnicity are not seen as individual topics but as integrative issues in order to *dis*-cover the voices of the subaltern and attain their liberation. It is a way of creating ties between different subaltern groups (people of color in the United States, for example) and resisting the oppressive character of the dominant discourse, a white male upper-class discourse, and change the geopolitics of theories and knowledge.[68]

The racial/ethnic perspective with the integrative inclusion of the issue of class and gender opens the discourse to new voices, places, stories, and relationships and breaks through all the established models available.[69] U.S. Latino/as are one of those groups left out of the U.S. religious historical discourses because of the imposition of the black/white paradigm. They are in the middle of the spectrum, so their voices are lost in a vacuum. Their geographical spaces are forgotten; their stories are erased and destroyed. The colonial imaginary leaves U.S. Latino/as without a historical voice, at the borders of the historical discourse. Regarding this issue, Daisy Machado says, "If an entire population group has no historical voice, and if that group seems to have occupied no significant historical space, then it is very easy to relegate that group to the margins of a national and religious epic."[70] U.S. Latino/as, then, have become invisible people, subaltern people. They have been left out of the master narrative; their voices and stories are silenced and covered.

As I argued before, the modern project, embedded in the standard narrative, constructed an image of these people and their stories that benefited the dominant groups. In the canon, the land the Other occupied is seen as empty and open for destruction, conquest, and colonization. Their memory is stolen and destroyed. It is said that nothing good can

---

68. See Sonia Saldívar-Hull, *Feminism on the Border: Chicana Gender Politics and Literature* (Berkeley and Los Angeles: University of California Press, 2000).

69. An example of these models is the two-party system proposed by Martin E. Marty in his *Righteous Empire: The Protestant Experience in America* (New York: Dial Press, 1970). This model argues that Protestantism can be explained through the binary opposition of liberal/mainline and fundamentalist/evangelical. For a better understanding and critique of this see Douglas Jacobsen and William Vance Trollinger Jr., eds., *Re-forming the Center: American Protestantism, 1900 to the Present* (Grand Rapids, Mich.: Eerdmans, 1998).

70. Daisy Machado, "The Writing of Religious History in the United States: A Critical Assessment," in *Hispanic Christianity within Mainline Protestant Traditions: A Bibliography*, ed. Paul Barton and David Maldonado Jr. (Decatur, Ga.: AETH, 1998), 83.

come out of these people because of their characteristics of savagery and barbarity. These images are constructed and imposed on the Other in order to maintain and increase the power of the dominant group, and the present racial/ethnic paradigm does not provide a critique of these misrepresentations and silences.

The history of the Southwest serves as one of the best examples to understand these constructions and silences. Traditional U.S. religious historiography sees the Southwest and its history through the lens of progress, and westward movement. Notions like the vacancy of the land, the conquest of the wilderness, and the superiority of the Euro-American race were supported by the ideology of manifest destiny embedded in the missionary activities of the first two centuries of Protestant growth in the United States. "To the extent that the Protestant heritage has been characteristic of the religious ethos of the United States in its first two centuries of growth, it might be said that Manifest Destiny expressed the ideological rationale of the Protestant empire."[71] Manifest destiny established a culture of supremacy and a racial domination; it created a myth of a frontier, wilderness, and a virgin land. "America" is based on this myth, a sentiment of chosen people. Manifest destiny and the myth it creates are still embedded in the writing of U.S. religious history. Although Turner's frontier thesis has been challenged and confronted, the sentiment behind it is still rooted on the beliefs of superiority and domination.[72] The Southwest is not part of the imaginary as a space of encounter and exchange or subjectivity, but as an empty space available for conquest, progress, and missionary activity. It has been the frontier, which needed to be conquered and tamed. The history of U.S. Latino(a) Protestantism in the Southwest breaks up the pattern of domination established by a Protestant-Puritan northeastern tradition.

The Southwest should be seen as the borderlands, as a place where colonization happened. The borderlands are a place with a history of miscegenation and racism. This is the space where invisible people

---

71. Edwin Sylvest, "Hispanic American Protestantism in the United States," in *Fronteras: A History of the Latin American Church in the USA since 1513*, ed. Moises Sandoval (San Antonio: Mexican American Cultural Center, 1983), 283.

72. Frederick J. Turner proposed his thesis in a paper entitled, "The Significance of the Frontier in American History," which was first presented in July 12, 1893, at the American Historical Association meeting in Chicago and was later an address to the State Historical Society of Wisconsin on December 14, 1893. It is printed in the *Annual Report of the American Historical Association for the Year 1893* and later reprinted by Irvington Publishers as part of *The Irvington Reprint Series*, History Reprint H-214.

live. The borderlands have been defined in many ways. Herbert Eugene Bolton talked about the borderlands as "the meeting place and
fusing place of two streams of European civilization, one coming from
the south, the other from the north."[73] Gloria Anzaldúa goes beyond a
geographical definition to talk about the borderlands as a place where
violence, ambivalence, and death reside.[74] So as Daisy Machado argues:

> The Borderlands are a geographical reality that one can find on a
> map, but they are also a lot more than that. The U.S. Borderlands
> are *that* place where Latinas and Latinos live, struggle, love, fight,
> and strive to define who they are in the midst of a society that
> has for centuries kept them an invisible mass, a footnote in the
> homogenizing historical process of an entire nation. In this broader
> sense the Borderlands have no geographical boundaries and are
> both a symbol and a reality, not just for Mexican Americans but
> also for the millions of other Latinas and Latinos who currently
> make up the new diaspora.[75]

The colonial imaginary created by traditional U.S. religious historiography has objectified this space and the people that live there. Scholars
in the field have not considered the history of this space as part of
the imaginary. The main reason for this silence is the continuation and
perpetuation of the black/white paradigm.

In order to construct a decolonial imaginary the borderlands have to
become a discursive space from which history is written. In this space,
historians can locate themselves on the side of the oppressed and write
history from that space, acknowledge not merely the marginalization,
but celebrate the resistance. The borderlands give a new meaning to
history; for example, the Puritan story then becomes regional and not
universal or normative. The Puritans become key characters in the history of U.S. religion, but not the only ones. Looking at the borderlands
as a paradigm exposes colonial, xenophobic, and racist attitudes, roots
of the ideology of manifest destiny. From this place, history is not seen

---

73. Herbert E. Bolton, "Defensive Spanish Expansion and the Significance of the Borderlands," *The Idea of the Spanish Borderlands*, ed. David J. Weber (New York: Garland, 1991),
36.
74. See Gloria Anzaldúa, *Borderlands/La Frontera: The New Mestiza* (San Francisco: Aunt
Lute Books, 1987).
75. Daisy L. Machado, "Kingdom Building in the Borderlands: The Church and Manifest
Destiny," in *Hispanic/Latino Theology: Challenge and Promise*, ed. Ada María Isasi-Díaz and
Fernando F. Segovia (Minneapolis: Fortress Press, 1996), 63.

as the narrativization of events but as the means by which "those voices that have become barely audible whispers" are heard: "the voices of those who were conquered and because of their defeat have in many ways been silenced and made invisible."[76] The borderlands become a discursive location where the histories can be *dis*-covered without the influence of the normative discourse. Colonization, racism, marginalization, oppression, and paternalism are revealed in this space from the side of the suffering. In other words, the histories are not told to benefit the peoples in the center of power, but to liberate the peoples outside of it. The voices that have been silenced by the dominant historical discourse for so long are now *dis*-covered.

The borderlands as a discursive location become the space where concepts, paradigms, and hermeneutical keys are deconstructed and reconstructed. This space is where history is seen through the eyes of the peoples excluded from the historical narratives — peoples outside the dominant discourse. The historian, if s/he wants to write a more inclusive history, has the responsibility of locating her or himself in this border space in order to write a new discourse that reveals the voices of the people left outside the normative discourse. As Emma Pérez reminds us, "as historians, our project is to decolonize the writing of history to create a decolonial imaginary of the future."[77] In other words, to be able to engage in a decolonizing project, history has to be done from outside the center of power. Daisy Machado recognizes the importance of this place in the writing of Latino(a) religious history, as she states:

> But if one is to uncover the Latino church, both its past and present, one must recognize that research for this endeavor cannot begin in the center of the established scholarly world. Nor can it begin in the center of denominational structures. Instead, the religious history of Latinos [and Latinas] in the United States is researched and written in the margins of both academic and denominational worlds. It is in this other place, this place "outside the gate," where the Latino church can be found and where her history has been made, continues to be made, and is currently being lived and told.[78]

---

76. Daisy L. Machado, "A Borderlands Perspective," *Hidden Stories: Unveiling the History of the Latino Church,* ed. Daniel Rodríguez-Díaz and David Cortés-Fuentes (Decatur, Ga.: AETH, 1994), 49.

77. Pérez, *The Decolonial Imaginary,* 79.

78. Machado, "The Writing of Religious History," 84.

CONCLUDING REMARKS

U.S. religious historians need to locate themselves in this space in order to unveil the unjust systems of power and oppression that have been hidden in the traditional discourse. The present racial/ethnic paradigm has to be replaced to open the spectrum for all people of color. The present paradigm has avoided the questions of race in the borderlands by focusing primarily on the issues of black/white. Because brown people do not fit in the race paradigm or the ethnic paradigm, ethnorace can function as an alternative, especially for Latino/as, because it "would remind us that there are at least two concepts, rather than one, that are vitally necessary to the understanding of Latina/o identity in the United States: ethnicity and race."[79] The colonial imaginary would be decolonized because ethnicity would include immigrants from all over, not only Europe, and race would include brown people, not only black and white. This will lead to the recognition of the Spanish Southwest as a place of encounters, with history and subjectivity, and most important to the acknowledgment of manifest destiny as the ideological framework of the missionary activity as well as the historical discourse. It will open the discussion about the condition of the people in this colonial space beyond the relationship between blacks and whites. It will *dis*-cover the wars, the occupation of the land, and the paternalistic approach by the missionary activity, and it will remind the colonizer that history should be seen through different lenses in order to construct a more inclusive representation of the past, in which silences and coloniality are exposed.

U.S. religious historiography has not been open to the development of this kind of critique, less to the emergence of this kind of scholar. This field has been developed as a colonial enterprise by covering and reducing the importance of the histories of particular groups and communities. The colonial discourse has ignored the borderlands, yet it is a space of significance. In this space marginal voices are heard and a decolonial imaginary is constructed. The field has to construct a critique of its discourse and the myths and ideologies that sustain it, modernity and manifest destiny. Conversation with other fields serves as a key to this project, bringing new voices and perspectives to the table. But while this happens, scholars in the borderlands continue their work of decolonizing

---

79. Linda Martín Alcoff, "Is Latina/o Identity a Racial Identity?" *Hispanic/Latinos in the United States: Ethnicity, Race, and Rights*, ed. Jorge J. E. Gracia and Pablo De Greiff (New York and London: Routledge, 2000), 42.

the imaginary by *dis*-covering the hidden stories, and more importantly
by deconstructing the scaffold upon which the imaginary is built.

U.S. Latino(a) religious historians should be working toward an unmasking of the colonial discourse by recovering *la memoria rota*.[80] Their
work is seen as regional, particular, and somehow irrelevant for the field,
but they still continue to challenge the normative character of the traditional discourse uncovering the voices of the borderlands. In this process
the traditional history (the Puritan story) is exposed as particular and regional. This discourse does not seek its own validation by the center, but
the validity and historical voice of those people in the borderlands. In
this sense, they are engaged in the process of *dis*-covery, but a critique
of the modern/colonial character of the dominant discourse is still lacking. The project of *dis*-covering subaltern pasts is committed to expose
oppression and exploitation and in that same way helps to uncover the
limits of traditional history. In other words, scholars involved in the
project of *dis*-covery are following a postmodern approach by focusing
their work not on the study of what really happened, but on "the recovery of forgotten, hidden, invisible, considered unimportant, changed and
eradicated histories."[81] These scholars are organic intellectuals located
in the space where resistance to colonization resides, the borderlands.

This discursive location provides U.S. Latino(a) scholars and others a
space where a new epistemology is born. Walter Mignolo acknowledges
that to be able to step away from the modern/colonial project, a new
epistemology has to be produced, or better yet an already existing epistemology needs to be recovered.[82] This epistemology thinks from and about
the borders, so it is a border epistemology, a subaltern knowledge. This
new epistemology not only deals with the particular, but also critiques the
totalizing projects that still exist, as the standard narrative in U.S. religious
history. U.S. Latino(a) scholars have to strive to decolonize the dominant
discourses, using the already existing voices from the borderlands, their
stories and memory. In this sense the process of *dis*-covery leads to a process of liberation. While uncovering voices is vital, scholars cannot forget
to critique directly the structures and discourses to obtain liberation.

---

80. *La memoria rota* means the broken memory. The term is used by Arcadio Díaz-Quiñones
to describe the loss of identity (and the past) produced by colonialism. See Arcadio Díaz-
Quiñones, *La memoria rota: Ensayos sobre cultura y política* (San Juan: Ediciones Huracán,
1996).

81. Keith Jenkins, *On "What Is History?": From Carr and Elton to Rorty and White* (New
York and London: Routledge, 1995), 38.

82. Mignolo, *Local Histories*.

4

En-Gendered Territory

*U.S. Missionaries' Discourse in Puerto Rico
(1898–1920)*

MAYRA RIVERA RIVERA

"Puerto Rico — Paradise island since 1898." With this phrase a T-shirt at a Puerto Rican hotel sells a revised creation story for the island. Creation by subordination. What kind of creation was that? Who created? By what means? What was created? In whose image? These questions underlie my present reading of U.S. missionaries' discourse in Puerto Rico immediately following its occupation in 1898.[1] While this is an inquiry into theological ideas and symbols, it is no less an exploration into forces with very concrete social and political effects.

Methodologically, the colonial context in which mission took place warrants the use of postcolonial criticism as a reading lens. Surprisingly, the words of a missionary furnish an added link between this fragment of the Puerto Rican history and the postcolonial theoretical framework. Inaugurated by Edward Said's groundbreaking critique of the Western invention of the category of the "Orient,"[2] postcolonial theory becomes explicitly, if fortuitously, summoned to the Puerto Rican scene in a call for the U.S. missionaries to expand their knowledge of the *mind of the people* to be evangelized. "The Latin mind," the missionary explains, "is essentially Oriental."[3]

---

1. The idea of this rereading is indebted to the work of Samuel Silva-Gotay, *Protestantismo y política en Puerto Rico, 1898–1930: Hacia una historia del protestantismo evangélico en Puerto Rico* (San Juan: Editorial de la Universidad de Puerto Rico, 1997). It has also benefited from the comments of Luis Rivera Pagán.

2. Edward Said, *Orientalism* (New York: Vintage Books, 1994).

3. Robert McLean and Grace Petrie Williams, *Old Spain in New America* (New York: Association Press, 1913), 134.

My use of postcolonial theory is especially influenced by the work
of Homi Bhabha, in which the psychoanalytic contributions of Jacques
Lacan are brought to bear on the travails of colonial subjectivity.[4] For
Lacan, the formation of the ego is characterized by processes of identification. The ego, he argues, emerges from a person's internalization of
external images that it misrecognizes as the self. In contrast to the experienced lack of unity of the self, the image(s) of identification present
themselves as totalities, which the subject assumes at the cost of self-
alienation. Bhabha argues that, like the processes of ego formation
described by Lacan, the identities on which the legitimization of colonial authority rests involve constant misrecognitions of an image for the
self. "The question of identification," Bhabha contends, "is never the
affirmation of a pre-given identity, never a self-fulfilling prophesy — it
is always the production of an image of identity and the transformation
of the subject in assuming that image."[5] But the image of identity thus
assumed is tethered by the image of the Other, and thus its boundaries
are dependent upon, and hence threatened by, the Other. As it denies its
dependence on the Other, colonial identity is fraught with anxiety and
condemned to an obsessive reassertion of its fragile boundary lines. Re-
sorting to the repetition of multiple and incongruent images of self/Other,
colonial discourse attempts to mask the perceived fractures in the organizing principles of colonial rule, but unwittingly inscribes its profound
uncertainty at the heart of its self-legitimating pronouncements.

The methodological contributions of postcolonial criticism are complemented and frequently displaced by recent feminist scholarship on the
role of gender ideologies in the symbolic systems of dominant modern
thinking. In a philosophical tradition that constructed matter and flesh as
inferior realms to be controlled by reason, the subordination of women
is inscribed in the metaphoric representations of body and the land as

---

4. Homi Bhabha, *The Location of Culture* (New York: Routledge, 1994). The use of Lacan's work is potentially problematic if it entails the universalization of psychoanalytic theories
deriving from the study of a dominant Western subject. As a tool for the analysis of discourses
developed by Western colonizers, however, it seems promising. Lacan's phallocentrism has also
been subject to heated debates among feminist scholars. Bhabha's rereading of Lacan, however, seems to open a possibility for reframing the masculinist mode of subject formation that
limits Lacan's work along more complex understandings of the impact of social authority in
individual subjectivity. For details on the debates and the possible opportunities for critical feminist uses of Lacan see Elizabeth Grosz, *Jacques Lacan: A Feminist Introduction* (New York:
Routledge, 1990).

5. Bhabha, *The Location of Culture*, 45.

feminine images and as images of femininity. The stereotypical characterizations of women — as creatures inclined toward materiality rather
than spirituality, capriciously driven by emotion more than by reason,
passive receptors instead of active producers, naturally depleted of energy, dependent, and infantile — complemented and were complemented
by ideas about the nature and body, which were depicted as Other to the
male-associated principles of rational order, progress, and culture. The
denied dependence of maleness on its Other, of culture on nature, and of
reason on the body became a source of anxiety. Maleness was imagined
to be threatened by matter and flesh, land and mother.

These gendered representations have theological correlates. The hierarchical dyads — male/female, spirituality/materiality, reason/passion —
were imagined to reflect a cosmological one: God, the creator of rational order ruling over his [sic] Other — primal matter, represented as
dark chaos, that resists and threatens the created order. Chaos and darkness — and the faces associated with them — would then be construed
as threats to creation.[6] The complex web of metaphoric representations
and metonymic substitutions generated at the intersections of imperial,
theological, and gender imaginaries interweave the representations of
otherness within limited and fixed forms of knowledge characteristic of
the colonial stereotype.[7]

In the beginning — that summer of 1898 when the American troops
entered Puerto Rico — the island was not absolute nothingness. It was
not an empty land nor was colonial rule an origin(al) situation. The very
name of the island already bore the marks of the greed of conquest.
Puerto Rico (*Rich Port*), the Spanish colonizers had named it, thus replacing the formerly also-Spanish naming after San Juan. But this did

---

6. Catherine Keller's scrutiny of the sources and effects — theological and social — of the
theological elimination of the chaos of Gen. 1 and other ancient traditions through the doctrine
of ex-nihilo undergirds my interpretation of the use of chaos metaphors in colonial discourses.
The darkness of chaos, she explains, became an intolerable trace of otherness for an emerging
"Christian imaginary of mastery." Chaos as a complexity inscribed in the beginning of creation — and of theology as well as of every discourse of origin and purity — was the subject of
systematic theological and secular erasure, a/nihilation. See Catherine Keller, *The Face of the
Deep: A Theology of Becoming* (London: Routledge, 2002).

7. My use of the term "imaginary" follows Walter Mignolo's definition: "the imaginary of
the modern/colonial world is its self-description, the ways in which it described itself through
the discourse of the state, intellectuals and scholars." *Local Histories/ Global Designs: Coloniality, Subaltern Knowledges, and Border Thinking* (Princeton, N.J.: Princeton University Press,
2000), 23. For a discussion on the interrelatedness of gender, class, and race on colonial representations see Anne McClintock, *Imperial Leather: Race, Gender and Sexuality in the Colonial
Contest* (New York: Routledge, 1995).

not restrain the new colonial power from attempting to erase the past
through yet another ritual naming — naming after the colonizing father
who declared it had just been born.[8] "A nation was born in a day, in an
hour."[9] It was named *Porto Rico*.[10]

   This naming was followed by a rush of knowledge about the island and its inhabitants. These early objectifying gazes were imprinted
in the pages of a number of illustrated books produced to disseminate knowledge about the conquered islands: Cuba, Puerto Rico, and
the Philippines. The titles are revealing: *Our Islands and Their People*
(1899), *Neely's Panorama of Our New Possessions* (1898), and *Our
New Possessions* (1898). The repeated possessive "Our" discloses the
appropriating zeal of the knowledge enterprise.

   The Protestant churches were also eager to grasp the Puerto Rican
soil. Even before the United States had declared the war on Spain in
1898, the missionary societies were preparing to enter the new territories.[11] The object of conquest was also made an object of mission. As
Protestant denominations divided the island's body among themselves
for missionary work, they also marked it "Our." The knowledge ac-
cumulated by the churches was disseminated through the publication
of missionaries' memoirs and guidelines for missionary work, the titles
of which are revealing too: *Our Foreign Missionary Enterprise: United
Brethren Mission Study Course; Old Spain in New America; The Waiting
Isles; New Day Ascending; Kingdom Building in Puerto Rico: A Story of
Fifty Years of Christian Service; It Came to Pass*.[12] These works, along

   8. Luce Irigaray has persuasively argued that the ritual of naming after the father signals
a social disavowal of the origin in the maternal body and the appropriation of that role by
the male figure. (See Luce Irigaray, *Speculum of the Other Woman* [Ithaca, N.Y.: Cornell University Press, 1985], 18–24.) In the case of the colonial scene, this translates into the correlate
disavowal of the history of the conquered lands entailed in the myth of the empty lands and
the appropriation of it by the colonizer. See McClintock, *Imperial Leather*, 28–30.
   9. McLean and Williams, *Old Spain in New America*, 105.
   10. The name "Porto Rico," the official name given by General Miles on his arrival to the
island, was never used by the natives, who continued to use Puerto Rico.
   11. The U.S. Protestant churches' newsletters published a number of articles sanctioning the
invasion. Northern Baptist, Presbyterian, Congregational, and Methodist Episcopal Churches
were initially participating. Other denominations joined the missionary work at later dates. See
Silva-Gotay, *Protestantismo y política en Puerto Rico, 1898–1930*, 111–19.
   12. J. S. Mills, W. R. Funk, and S. S. Hough, *Our Foreign Missionary Enterprise: United
Brethren Mission Study Course* (Dayton, Ohio: United Brethren Publishing House, 1908);
McLean and Williams, *Old Spain in New America*, issued by Council of Women for Home Missions; Charles S. Detweiler, *The Waiting Isles* (Philadelphia: Judson Press, 1930), issued by the
Northern Baptist Convention; Fred L. Brownlee, Secretary of the American Missionary Association, *New Day Ascending* (Boston: Pilgrim Press, 1946); C. Manly Morton, *Kingdom Building
in Puerto Rico: A Story of Fifty Years of Christian Service* (Indianapolis: United Christian

with the Superintendent's Annual Reports for the Methodist Episcopal Church and their official newsletter, *El Defensor Cristiano,* constitute the textual base of this essay.[13]

IMAGINARY IDENTITIES
AND INCONGRUENT DIFFERENCES

Can one divide human reality, as indeed human reality seems to be genuinely divided, into clearly different cultures, histories, traditions, societies, even races and survive the consequences humanly?
— Edward Said

The inhabitants of the world can be divided in two classes: those who have the Bible and those who do not have it.
— *El Defensor Cristiano,* 1904

The U.S. colonial regime "deliberately placed" Puerto Rico at the churches' "doorsteps."[14] There, the military occupation was invested with a rank of divine history. It was rendered as the fulfillment of Isaiah's prophecy or as the equivalent to the extension of the Roman Empire in the times of the apostle Paul. The invasion "prepared the way for evangelization."[15] Still, the relationship between occupation and mission was also explained by the inverse logic. That is, not only was the invasion necessary in order for evangelization to occur, but mission was also considered a necessary and integral part of the project of colonization: an "occupation of Porto Rico by Christian forces."[16] After all, "Was not the protestant religion part of the new order? Were not the ruling classes of America Protestant? Ought not the Porto Ricans to embrace the religion of their liberators as well as other elements of their civilization?"[17]

A shared language of conquest and a correlative claim of divine sanction made the *religion of the liberators* and the *other elements of their civilization* almost indistinguishable from each other. Colonization and

---

Missionary Society, 1949); Edward A. Odell, *It Came to Pass* (New York: Board of National Missions, Presbyterian Church, 1952).

13. *The Christian Defendant.* All translations from this newsletter are mine.

14. Morton, *Kingdom Building in Puerto Rico,* 112.

15. Mills, *Our Foreign Missionary Enterprise,* 176; Detweiler, *The Waiting Isles,* 16.

16. Detweiler, *The Waiting Isles,* 22.

17. Ibid., 25.

mission were construed both as signs of election and as acts of compliance with the supreme duty entrusted to the conquering *race*. This
bivalent and self-legitimating conception was systematically articulated
by Rev. Dr. Josiah Strong, General Secretary of Missions of the Congregational Church in the United States. In his 1886 treatise, *Our Country:
Its Possible Future and Its Present Crisis,* he developed, based on preva-
lent scientific principles and statistical data, the postulate of the U.S.
superiority as a manifestation of the nation's providential destiny to
rule mankind [*sic*].[18] This commanding position, he argued, gave the
U.S. Christians the "opportunity and obligation" to hasten or retard the
coming of Christ's kingdom.[19]

Thus for the U.S. missionaries, mission was their "God-given duty"
to work "for the enlightenment and evangelization of millions of Puerto
Ricans."[20] It was theirs because "God [had laid] upon the American
nation the *imperious duty,* as well as conferred to it, the exceeding honor
and privilege of carrying the gospel of the kingdom to all parts of the
earth."[21] *Imperious* as imperial, mission belonged to those who identified
with (or mirrored) a discrete image that I will henceforth call *American.*

Numerous sketches of the *American* were drawn in the missionary
texts. According to Strong, for instance, the *American* was a new creation, the "new Anglo-Saxon race of the New World" "a more powerful
type of man than has hitherto existed" (220). Characterized by his [*sic*]
"money-making power," "genius for colonizing," "unequaled energy,"
"indomitable perseverance," and "personal independence," the *American* excelled "all others in pushing his way into new countries" (221).
The *American* was being prepared for the maximum test in the Dar-
winian imaginary, "the final competition of the races," a contest of
"vitality and of civilization," the most probable outcome of which was
the "extinction of lower races" (22f).

This typical characterization placed the *American* firmly on the masculine side of its contemporaneous imaginary. As a masculine species, the
American was the perfect candidate to rule over "lower races," that is,

---

18. Josiah Strong, *Our Country: Its Possible Future and Its Present Crisis* (New York: Baker
and Taylor, 1891). A second edition was published in 1891. By 1891 the book had sold over
130,000 copies and by 1916 more than 176,000. Multiples articles and even whole chapters
had been published in missionaries' newsletters.

19. Ibid., 227.

20. See 1902 and 1909 Yearbook of the *Superintendent's Annual Report and Official
Minutes of the Porto Rico Mission of the Methodist Episcopal Church.*

21. *Year Book 1909.*

over less manly ones. Senator Albert Beveridge made this assumption explicit. In agreement with Strong, the senator argued that compliance with God's plan for the United States required fostering "the disappearance of debased civilizations and decaying races before the higher civilization of the nobler and *more virile types of men.*"[22] The imagined contest of the races was then a test of virility conceived to mirror nothing less than the cosmological contest to impose order over chaos by the power of domination. Theodore Roosevelt, undoubtedly a main character in this story, argued that the virile *American* had to retain control over Puerto Rico; failing to do so "would be followed by utter *chaos* in the wretched islands themselves. Some *stronger* and *manlier* power would have to step in."[23]

Strong, manly, and white. Darkness of skin — symbolically linked to the darkness of chaos — was not to taint the image of the *American.* Hence General James Wilson disallowed black soldiers from the occupation army during the Spanish-American war. The occupation was to include, in Wilson's words, only the "best American whites"[24] — an action then reemphasized by the churches' abjection of black missionaries from the mission occupation forces.[25]

The image of the *American* produced a myriad of discursive "equivalences, samenesses, identities": *American* and Protestant, Christian and Protestant, Progress and Protestantism, Civilization and *American* values, Freedom and Protestantism, and many more.[26] Exemplary of these

---

22. Kevin A. Santiago-Valles, *"Subject People" and Colonial Discourses: Economic Transformation and Social Disorder in Puerto Rico, 1898–1947* (Albany: State University of New York Press, 1994), 63. Likewise, Roosevelt states, "Of course there have been many instances of brutality, cupidity and stupidity by the conquerors, but by and large, the subject nations have benefited. To begin with, in all logic, the conquering nation has been more civilized, *certainly more virile*" (Theodore Roosevelt cited in ibid., 1, emphasis added).

23. Ibid., 74.

24. Nélida Agosto Cintrón, *Religión y cambio social en Puerto Rico (1898–1940)* (Puerto Rico: Ediciones Huracán, 1996), 59.

25. Ibid.

26. Bhabha, *The Location of Culture,* 77. These identities are a recurrent feature in the missionaries' writings. The following are typical examples: "The men of importance in *this nation* were, are, and will continue to be *Protestants*" (*Defensor Cristiano,* October 1, 1903). "An anti-clerical government . . . advances in the road of *culture, industry and progress*" (*Defensor Cristiano,* November 1, 1903). "Do you think that anyone would be satisfied in being ignorant and especially of *Protestantism* when one see this marching with the most *advanced nations* in front of *progress,* while Catholicism remains in the back?" (*Defensor Cristiano,* October 1, 1903). "Hispanic-American republics have not progressed because they have been subject to Papacy" (*Defensor Cristiano,* November 1, 1903). "It is absurd the idea, pursued by some in Puerto Rico, to amalgamate freedom with Roman Catholicism" (*Defensor Cristiano,* January 1, 1905).

doublings is *Year Book*'s statement, "Under the protecting folds of the flag we move forward on all lines of activity with that *unrestricted liberty* which is the glory of *our American Christian Protestant civilization.*"[27]

This affirmation, however, also points to the fault lines concealed under the cloak of colonial discourse. The mission field revealed the split of the assumed equivalences at play in their evangelical message. Theirs was a Christianizing mission to a Christian people, an advocacy of democracy to unrepresented colonized subjects, an implementation of religious freedom through the legal restriction of Catholic practices, a separation of Church and State in which Protestant values were construed as the appropriate representation of the State.[28] The *unrestricted liberty*, undeniable trait of the *American Christian Protestant civilization*, was disjointed at the mission field.

And "the strategic splitting of the colonial discourse... is contained by addressing the other as despot."[29] If the missionaries were to occupy this space of total identification with the image of the *American*, an "absolute, undivided, boundless, homogenized despot" had to be found.[30] The *American* had to stand facing a stereotypical and antithetical Other. To the traits of this Other image of the colonial imaginary I now turn.

WHO IS THE OTHER?

The modern colonizing imagination conceives of its dependencies as a territory, never as a people.   —Sir Herman Merivale, 1839[31]

A bright young girl was sent from Porto Rico to New York to be educated. Shortly after getting fairly settled in school she wrote, "Do you know what they call me here? *Our New Possession.*"
                                                  —*Old Spain in New America,* 1916

---

27. *Year Book* 1904, 16; emphasis added.

28. The *Defensor Cristiano* gave its open support to a law project to prohibit processions, which were an important part of the Catholic tradition in the island (January 15, 1905). The *Methodist Newsletter* also asked for a law project to prohibit "external religious cult" and the ringing of the (Catholic) churches' bells (June 15, 1905).

29. Bhabha, *The Location of Culture,* 98.

30. Ibid. In colonial discourse, however, the need for an absolute Other is undermined by the colonialist demand for the colonized to mimic the colonizer. Numerous examples of the ambivalence arising from this problem of colonial authority (developed prominently by Homi Bhabha) are found in the missionaries' texts. My reading is limited to the fantasies of full identity there attested.

31. Cited in ibid., 97.

The Other of the *American* was not only the *Porto Rican*,[32] but also the newly acquired land — a distinction frequently collapsed under the tropes of colonial discourse.[33] Ultimately, the goal of the colonial project was to possess the land, to define *Porto Rico* as a U.S. territory. But to turn a living place into a territory required a forceful denial of the Puerto Ricans' claims to a Puerto Rican land and the disavowal of their ties to a motherland, to past histories, to previous beginnings. Only thus could the *American* stand as the sole creator of a new thing created out of nothing but dust. This denial — sustained by patriarchal fantasies of pure male origination — would soon be haunted by the shadow images of the repressed motherland. The missionaries' depictions of the island wavered between provocative portraits of a paradisiacal land and tenebrous sketches of a dangerous landscape. Attraction and fear were frequently combined in ambiguous expressions, such as the *Year Book*'s praising exclamation, "The very heavens seem to catch the witchery of the Island's spell."[34] Noticeably confounding land and woman, the missionary found himself trapped in the typical ambivalence toward the female body — mother *and* witch, virgin *and* seducer.

The imagined threat of being caught in the land's spell was clearly expressed in recurring allusions to the effect of climate. Drawing from scientific theories that proposed a direct link between the evolution of races (or lack thereof) and climate, colonial discourse gave the tropical weather a phantasmagoric mystique envisioned as a force haunting even the missionaries. The newly "discovered" land was reviled as more dangerous to health than any other Latin American country, "enervating and weakening...to those engaged in mental work," causing the "depletion of nervous energy," having a "relaxing effect" like that of "worldly social influences, and the secular spirit" of inducing "moral laxity."[35]

---

32. As with the term "American," I use "Porto Rican" to denote exclusively an image constructed and deployed within the discourses explored in this reading.

33. Efrén Rivera Ramos argues that the legal identity of the Puerto Rican was defined by construing the question as one of the "legal characterization of a locality" and then imposing them as a characterization of the people, and further rendering both people and territory as property, legitimately subjects to the principles of private property (*The Legal Construction of Identity: The Judicial and Social Legacy of American Colonialism in Puerto Rico* [Washington, D.C.: American Psychological Association, 2001]).

34. *Year Book* 1908. See also McLean and Williams, *Old Spain in New America,* 107f; Morton, *Kingdom Building in Puerto Rico,* 1f; Odell, *It Came to Pass,* 39f; *Year Book* 1905, 20f; 1906, 24f; 1909, 10f.

35. Detweiler, *The Waiting Isles,* 33; *Defensor Cristiano,* September 1, 1905; *Year Book* 1904; *Year Book* 1903, 16; George Milton Fowles, *Down in Porto Rico* (New York: Eaton & Mains, 1910), 98.

As a figure of masculinity, however, the *American* was called to protect himself from these feminized influences. Thus, to ward off the threat of being engulfed by the island's climate, the familiar codes of gender hierarchy were reinscribed recurring to the current myth of the virgin land. Discursively erasing as much as four hundred years of history the *Year Book* fantasized: "Porto Rico rests upon the bosom of the tropic seas as beautiful, majestic and fruitful in all its natural gifts as when Columbus first discovered it; *waiting only* the assistance of law, sound government aided by intelligent industry, enterprise and moral transformation."[36] *Porto Rico* appears as a beautiful female who invites (and incites) the manly colonizer and waits — docile and available, to be entered, inseminated, and owned. A waiting isle in need of the *American* — indeed a comforting mirage of patriarchal (and colonial) order![37]

The figure of a passive land had its correlate in the image of a passive *Porto Rican.* Facing the *American,* colonial discourse placed an image of otherness delineated in reference to land of origin, race, and culture to produce a contrasting picture that was fundamentally fixed and externally determined. The multiple and contradictory characterizations of the *Porto Rican* were homogenized under several organizing categories. For example, after providing an extensive list of differences between the *Porto Rican* and the *American,* a Baptist missionary concludes that they are all "manifestations of a more *fundamental difference* between the Porto Rican and the North American.... These islanders, *like the rest of their race, are.*"[38] The so-called race fixed the *Porto Rican* within multiple typologies: "the Spanish," "the Latin mind," "the Catholic," "the Spanish-speaking peoples" — all of them masking any specificity. Even the "Oriental" was casually invoked. The missionary's choice for the fundamental difference is this: they are "*fundamentally emotional* while

---

36. *Year Book* 1906, 25.

37. The importance of the image of the passive island is evidenced in its use as the title for a Baptist Church's mission's book for the Caribbean: Detweiler, *The Waiting Isles.*

38. Arthur James, *Thirty Years in Puerto Rico: A Record of the Progress since American Occupation* (New York: Educational Work Board of Home Missions, 1927), 20, emphasis added. According to James, the *Porto Rican is* "an embodiment of hospitality and courtesy ... seldom found among the Anglo-Saxons" (14); "possesses a fine idealism, but he seems to lack the ability to put his ideas into reality" (16); shows "appreciation of the abstract" (17); *is* a "follower rather than leader" (18); *is* "kind and generous" (18); *is* "lacking what the Anglo-Saxon considers the first element of a good sport" (29); and *is* "notoriously individualistic" (23). For a similar representation of the Puerto Rican see George Milton Fowles, *Down in Porto Rico* (New York: Eaton & Mains, 1910), 46.

the continental is unemotional."[39] The feminization implied in the em-
phatic distinction signals once again the intricate relationship between
the demarcations of race and gender differences.

To demarcate the *Porto Rican* according to race introduced a pecu-
liar challenge in the ordering structures of U.S. colonial and missionary's
discourse. Although the term "race" was used rather loosely to differ-
entiate groups based on a wide range of attributes, skin color retained a
privileged place as a marker of race in the colonial tropes.[40] In contrast
with the idea of the homogeneous white *American,* the colonized was
neither homogeneously white nor black. Precisely this indecipherability
represented a problem in the eyes of an impressive number of missionaries. Robert McLean, for example, states, "The Spaniards did not draw
the color line very closely, consequently the population was decidedly
mixed both as to color and to blood. *This mixture was bound to cause
many complications.*"[41] The complications were certainly multiple. A
race without a particular color or a people without a race? Unresolved.
For if the link between race and color is fractured, how can the *white*
define her/himself? If the people did not belong to a particular race, how
can they be fixed in the colonial order?[42]

The undecidability of a race placed in between the assumed black/
white ontological divide was soon disavowed through the repetition of
stereotypical representations. The black/white dichotomy was used as a

---

39. James, *Thirty Years in Puerto Rico,* 20.

40. In his Romanes Lecture at Oxford in 1910, for example, Theodore Roosevelt defined the
"white race" as "the group of peoples living in Europe, who undoubtedly have a certain kinship
of blood, who profess the Christian religion, and trace back their culture to Greece and Rome"
(Howard K. Beale, *Theodore Roosevelt and the Rise of America to World Power* [Baltimore:
Johns Hopkins Press, 1956], 27). Another recurrent theme on the characterizations of *races*
was language, which was particularly forceful in the missionaries' discourse of Americanization
and in the resistance against it. An appropriate elucidation of its complex characteristics is an
important aspect of the analysis of the missionary discourses which cannot be included under
the scope of the present article.

41. McLean and Williams, *Old Spain in New America,* 106, emphasis added. See also: James,
Thirty Years in Puerto Rico, 21; Fowles, *Down in Porto Rico,* 20f; Mills, Funk, and Hough,
Our Foreign Missionary Enterprise, 176; Brownlee, *New Day Ascending,* 73; Detweiler, *The
Waiting Isles,* 6.

42. Following McClintock's analysis of sexual surveillance in colonial contexts, it can be
argued that the constant search for the "color line" as a boundary between races indicates
the colonial anxiety about the integrity of the *American* as a race in the face of the threat of
miscegenation. This fear typically triggers a sense of urgency to control women's sexuality as
the site of potential racial contamination. The centrality that the missionaries gave to church's
implementation and control of marriage attest to this. Through this anxiety, concerns regarding
race become the driving force for the surveillance of sexual practices. The categories of gender
and race interwove again.

sign that the reader was supposed to understand — "common knowledge" in colonial discourse.[43] A missionary describes a new convert as
"a Negro, a very handsome man, *large* and *powerful*."[44] Meanwhile another missionary describes a group of listeners as "all white," and — in
precise stereotypical correspondence — he adds, "Many of them wore
shoes and stockings, their hair was combed, and their dresses cleaned
and ironed stiff as boards."[45] All white? White skins or white masks?

The flaunted shoes and dresses, along with other signs of civility,
would be summoned to cover up the lack of the color line. With the
warrants of scientific objectivity, photography became the ideal tool for
producing a unified image of otherness out of competing signifiers of
color, class, gender, culture — to name just a few.[46] The 1906 *Year Book*
furnishes a typical example.

Under the heading: "Two pictures in contrast: Let them teach the
lesson of our need," the *Year Book* drew the line. The text that frames
the pictures claimed to be interested in the "civilizing and progressive
influences" of the "true gospel." But the images clearly racialized the
implied effects. The first photograph is labeled: "They need the Gospel:
A group of Porto Rican children that know nothing of the Bible or the
true Christ. Truly." It displays a group of dark-skinned children.[47] The
primitive status with which Western dominant thought associated their
skin color is reinforced by the picture's setting; most of the children are
half naked and standing against a background of wild vegetation.

The second photograph — described as: "A Sunday School Parade: A
Group of Porto Rican Children that Together with Parents and Teachers
have come under the Christianizing, civilizing and progressive influences
of protestant Christianity" — stages a model of the civilized white (or
its mimic). People are wearing impeccable white suits and long dresses,
walking down the streets of the capital city. Besides the relegation of
darkness to past stages of progress and to lower attainments in redemption, these pictures disclose other associations as well. For instance, the
absence of adults in the first picture reinforces the typical infantilization

---

43. Bhabha, *The Location of Culture*, 78.
44. Odell, *It Came to Pass*, 18.
45. Detweiler, *The Waiting Isles*, 35.
46. The missionaries carried cameras when traveling, and many pictures of the natives appeared, for example, in every issue of the Methodist Episcopal Church Year Book. See *Year
Book* 1906, 31.
47. In fact, the same picture is used in *Down in Puerto Rico*, in that case labeled simply as
"Group of Colored Children," while the second picture is identified as "Public School Parade."

of the natives. Furthermore, because of their poor clothing, the gender difference between the children seems to blur. In contrast, the second group reflects the expected family composition, including men, women, and children, and their clothing clearly adheres to the accepted codes of gender distinctiveness. In one and the same image, the *Porto Rican* is represented as black, poor, infantile, and inadequately gendered; all features tightly intertwined as one indivisible difference. Meanwhile, the *American* Protestant way is proposed as a redemptive force capable of saving the *Porto Rican,* even from blackness. Almost, but not quite.

In terms of culture and religion, the *Porto Rican* was depicted as a passive receptor of Spain's culture, a subject overdetermined by a stereotypical image of *Spain.* For a definition of the Puerto Rican culture the missionary turned to Spain. Evidently, this *Spain* was an image fixed in the past, a country of the Middle Ages. *Old Spain in New America,* the revealing title of a mission's textbook, conveys this "static vision of 'synchronic essentialism,' " which marked the constructions of the *Porto Rican.*[48]

Deemed as a *product of Spanish activity,* the Puerto Ricans' agency in the creation or development of their own culture and religiosity was disavowed.[49] It is not surprising, then, that the missionaries' discourse lacked a distinction between the institutional Roman Catholic Church and popular religion. The syncretistic practices of Puerto Rican religiosity, which incorporated aspects of Spiritism, religions of the natives, and African religions, were sometimes accepted and other times severely criticized by the institutional Catholic Church. The missionaries' attacks against them were, however, directed against Spain or the Catholic Church. This does not mean that the syncretistic practices were unacknowledged. On the contrary, this hybridity was used to justify the

---

48. Said, *Orientalism,* 240. Walter Mignolo has argued for a distinction between two modern/colonial phases: the first extending from the sixteenth century to the eighteenth century in which Spain and Portugal figured as the centers of Europe. Judaism, Islam, and the Amerindian religions were the *Others* to be extirpated. In the second phase, marked by the Enlightenment and the Industrial revolution, Britain, France, and eventually the United States claimed their place at the center of the "Western" world. The *Others* were then increasingly marked by racial rhetoric. The missionaries' texts examined also show a redrawing of the borders of Christianity to allow the Catholic to become *Other.*

49. For example, the Mexicans (labeled the "Spanish population in the United States") were described as "the *product of Spanish activity* in exploration and colonization in the sixteenth century, and the character and condition of the people must be interpreted in the light of the character, teachings, and conditions *of that age*" (Detweiler, *The Waiting Isles,* 24, emphasis added). The same was assumed to be the case of the Puerto Ricans. See also ibid., 21.

evangelization of Christian countries, arguing that the Catholic missionaries had "committed the fatal error of adapting Christian worship to
the beliefs and practices of pagan tribes. Instead of Christianizing pagan-
ism, they allowed their Christianity to become paganized."[50] Unlike the
American — the accusation implied — the *Spanish* colonizer/evangelizer
failed to protect Christianity from the pagan Other.

The absolute boundary between the Christian and the pagan Other
could not be compromised; the "rules of recognition" had to be redrawn,
this time leaving the Catholic outside. Hence, churches' newsletters devoted more space to the contrast between the *Catholic* and the *Protestant*
than to any other subject. Every two weeks the essential differences
would be "anxiously repeated," "as if [the ignorance, superstition, materialism, backwardness, and idolatry of the *Catholic*] that needs no proof,
can never really, in discourse, be proved."[51] The final verdict was, "Ro-
manism is the enemy of Protestantism, because the latter teaches the
principles of the Gospel, the doctrines of Christ."[52] Thus, Catholicism
was excluded from true Christianity and included in the broad category
of the *Bible-lacking people*.

Like the race line, the boundary between the *Bible-lacking people*
(Catholics included) and the Protestants was supported with signs
of power and progress. The indicators of economic progress produced by the U.S. colonial government were lifted as evidence of the
U.S./Protestant superiority against the backdrop of the Spain/Catholic
backwardness.[53] *Bible-lacking people*, it was claimed, were marked
by "ignorance, poverty, degradation, oppression, unrest," their countries "lacking inventions, popular education and the modern advances";
while the people who had the Bible — that is, the Protestants — were

---

50. McLean and Williams, *Old Spain in New America*, xiii. "From the evangelical point of
view the principal reason that Roman Catholicism falls short of ministering to the spiritual
needs of the Porto Rican is because of the superstitious practices it sanctions in the name of
religion" (James, *Thirty Years in Puerto Rico*, 30).
51. Bhabha, *The Location of Culture*, 66.
52. *Defensor Cristiano*, November 1, 1903.
53. The following are just a few examples of this association, "Nothing gives our work
in Roman Catholic countries such influence as well located and attractive looking church
buildings" (*Year Book* 1905, 23). "Around this Santurce church there is a compact colony of
Presbyterians and it is interesting to see their growth in cleanliness, the increasing comfort and
beauty of their homes" (Odell, *It Came to Pass*, 23). "An anti-clerical government... advances
in the road of culture, industry and progress" (*Defensor Cristiano*, November 1, 1903). "Do
you think that anyone would be satisfied in being ignorant and especially of Protestantism when
one sees this marching with the most advanced nations in front of progress, while Catholicism
remains in the back?" (*Defensor Cristiano*, October 1, 1903).

characterized by "education, intelligence and the prosperity of their country."[54]

The guarded frontier between the Catholic Other and the Protestant was another site of anxiety. Identified as it was with the project of progress of the emerging industrial era, Protestantism struggled to create itself in ways that were congruent to the values of that time. It has been argued that modern representations of the Eastern traditions — *Bible-lacking people* — intended to subordinate or exclude aspects of the Christian traditions by projecting them into Other religious traditions.[55] Similarly, in the appropriation of *Christian* to denote exclusively the Protestant tradition and the constant depiction of Catholicism as external (rather than spiritual), emotional, material, irrational, unpractical, and uncivilized, U.S. Protestant discourse tried to purge itself from those elements of the Christian tradition that were perceived as being in tension with post-Enlightenment modernity's narratives of rational power and progress. These rejected elements were, predictably, feminized.

Through a rather disjointed combination of imagined identities and incongruent differences, missionary texts attempted to protect the boundaries of a self-image that was dependent upon its Other — *Porto Rican, Spanish, Catholic, Latin,* etc. This discursive protection of this intrinsically split identity demanded a continuous repetition of differences and images to mask the lack of equivalence between the missionary and the *American,* between the evangelized and the *Porto Rican,* between mission and redemption, and ultimately between God and its images.

BETWEEN GOD AND THE OTHER

Difficult is the task to effect the evangelization of centuries oppressed people. Here a false religion has done its worst. These *dark places of the earth* were full of habitations of cruelty....Puerto Rico shall yet be redeemed.   — *Year Book* 1905

---

54. *Defensor Cristiano,* December 1, 1904. The statement further argues that, "Prisons, shelters for the poor, refuge homes, and orphanages where the sons of the dunk, degraded, and abandoned hide, all these institutions are generally full of people do not know about divine revelation, but were, on the contrary, raised in darkness." Correspondingly, McLean and Williams assert, "The religious faith of a nation largely determines its progress and destiny" (xiii).

55. See Richard King, *Orientalism and Religion: Postcolonial Theory, India, and "the Mystical East"* (New York: Routledge, 1999).

The people are being *disarmed* of their suspicions, freed from many superstitions, broadened in their views of life, *infused* with lofty ideals and frequently 'tis now ours to see them *melted* and utterly *subdued* by the love of Christ.   — *Year Book* 1908

Wherever God is there is imperialism.
                                                         — *El Defensor Cristiano,* 1909

Mission was conceived through ideas of redemption as new creation. Creation from nothing — *ex-nihilo?* Certainly the colonial imaginary attempted to erase the Puerto Rican history as nothing. Only thus could occupation be construed as an absolute origin. In this schema, the *Porto Rican* was imagined as a passive receptacle, little more than inert stuff in which climate, race, and culture stamped their forms. But the missionary faced another reality — that of an evangelized who resisted the missionary attempts to re-form it. The supposed *nothing* of a Puerto Rican past was then construed as the image of chaos — "rebellious wickedness worthy of annihilation — and therefore already as nothing at all, invisible in the outer darkness of its exclusion."[56] Thus, U.S. colonial enterprise wavered between the disavowal of the Puerto Rican history and agency, and its recognition displaced in discourse as the return of the monstrous chaos that had to be controlled — order had to be imposed over the lower (and dark) forces that constantly threatened it. "God had made us master organizers of the world to establish system where chaos reigns...," announced a U.S. senator. "He had made us adept in government that we may administer government among savages and senile peoples."[57]

The land was a preferred site for the battles to impose control over chaos, and an ideal monument to the victories attained through the

---

56. Keller, *The Face of the Deep.* The discursive rendering as *nothing* as a precondition for concrete annihilation is evident also in Daisy Machado's words regarding the genocide of Native Americans: "The creation of a 'chosen' nation to be possessed by a chosen people necessitated a virgin land. God needed a 'clean slate,' the value and importance of the people already there had to be eliminated.... When thousands of Native Americans died on this terrible journey [Trail of Tears]... the fact that they had been categorized as lacking in worth, as destined to eventual extermination, transformed their deaths into further proof of their unworthiness to possess the land" ("La Otra América — The Other America," in *A Dream Unfinished: Theological Reflections on America from the Margins,* ed. Eleazar S. Fernández and Fernando F. Segovia [Maryknoll, N.Y.: Orbis Books, 2001], 225).

57. Senator Albert Beveridge before fully assembled Senate, 1900. Cited in Santiago-Valles, *"Subject People" and Colonial Discourses,* 26.

imposition of technological order. In his 1916 book, written in the context of the "national pride in the physical achievement of a completed Panama Canal," Robert McLean begins by lifting up the North American West as proof of the *redemptive* work already achieved by the United States.

> The early maps of the United States showed west of the Missouri River a vast stretch of country extending to and beyond the Rockies marked "The Great American Desert." The steady *progress of civilization has redeemed that desert* and it is now the great granary of the North American continent. The utilization of the streams, the opening of the fountains held in reserve by the bountiful Creator, and the planting of forests to conserve the rainfall, have made the "desert" the happy dwelling place of throngs of prosperous people.[58]

The West redeemed by the god of progress — dwelling place of the prosperous — was also envisioned as Isaiah's new earth and evoked in Edward Odell's celebratory account of the accomplishments in Puerto Rico:

> Puerto Rico today...is not the Puerto Rico of fifty years ago. ...Harbors have transformed the shoreline, large waterways and power plants have *altered* and *harnessed* the rivers, highways have *penetrated* the mountains, extensive airfields have *leveled* the landscape in the environs of large cities; factories, industrial plants, and factory-made houses have transformed suburban pastures into cities.... It's not the same old place.[59]

The triumphant tone of these passages fails to conceal the violence implied in the gendered fantasies of domination — to *harness, penetrate,* and possess — that linked the *redemption* of Puerto Rico to the conquest of the West. The desiring gazes at the Puerto Rican land were soon followed by the greed for possession — "its hills and mountains can be cultivated *to the very limits of productiveness,*" the "*barren* places will

---

58. McLean and Williams, *Old Spain in New America,* v, 3, emphasis added. Observe the continuity with Strong's description of "Western supremacy" (Strong, *Our Country,* 31).

59. McLean and Williams, *Old Spain in New America,* 51; Odell, *It Came to Pass,* 47; emphasis added.

become the most productive."[60] With technological weapons the *American* could indeed create a new land flowing with milk and honey under the power of the spirit. The spirit of progress, that is. "May the *spirit of true progress* carry on the work and *preserve our identity* in the great world of Christian thought and action so that at last we may give to the future the rich legacy of a redeemed land."[61]

The creation of the new (subject) land also entailed the creation of a new (subject) people. The *Porto Rican* was expected to passively receive new form — to satisfy the colonial "desire for a reformed, recognizable Other."[62] In this *New Creation* a creator replaced the Creator. In fact, a previous creator had been sent — a Spanish colonizer/evangelizer had also "possessed *splendid material* [the Latin *race*] upon which to build a strong and progressive civilization."[63] But the Spanish creator had allowed himself [*sic*] to become contaminated in blood and in religion. It had not *preserved its identity*. A new, manlier creator was needed.

Despite the apparent de-formation caused by the old culture and religion, and the supposed natural inferiority of their race, the Puerto Rican was assumed to be at least partly re-formable. The missionaries' work could create a "loftier race than the Latin world hath ever known," "sturdy, and energetic."[64] A new race, created in whose image?

> Porto Rico is ours.... Let Porto Rico become the best and truest reflection of ourselves.... Never before in American history was such an opportunity and such a material given from which could be carved character and Christ's likeness.[65]

Not surprisingly, in this new creation story the human being is created in the image of the *American* missionary. *Porto Rico* and the *Porto Rican* become only material — dark matter of tropical earth, dark (or deceivingly fair) skin of the native people — out of which a new image would be carved. This "passive and malleable" mass could be created and molded, and the "American spirit inspired in [it]."[66] In a remarkable

---

60. Morton, *Kingdom Building in Puerto Rico,* 108; emphasis added.
61. *Year Book* 1905, 30; emphasis added.
62. Bhabha, *The Location of Culture,* 86.
63. McLean and Williams, *Old Spain in New America,* 19.
64. *Year Book* 1910, 15; McLean and Williams, *Old Spain in New America,* 109.
65. *Year Book* 1909, 18.
66. "If the schools are Americanized and the *American spirit is inspired in* the professors and the students..., sympathy, points of view and the attitudes to life and to the government will become essentially American. The great mass of Puerto Ricans is still *passive* and *malleable*.

sleight of hand the *Christ likeness* of the missionaries' imaginary is given a concrete form, the *truest reflection* of the *American*.

The trinity of male power is now complete: the white male creator, the *American* Christ, and the Spirit of Progress; the whole divine trinity completely removed, wholly Other, to the land and to the native peoples.

CONCLUSION

Why are we here again? Why rehearse once more the words of an unfortunate past instead of dismissing them as a crude sample of colonial non-sense? "For the critique must attempt to fully realize, and take responsibility for, the unspoken, unrepresented past that haunts the historical present."[67] The purpose of this critique, however, is not to offer yet another description of "the Puerto Rican" or to pretend to purify our theological heritage from the touch of the *American* Other — such projects would only mimic the colonial enterprise, even if done with the purpose of reversing its hierarchies.

The aim of this critical engagement is rather to uncover and challenge the fundamental logic that supports relations of subordination in its multiple manifestations: as hierarchies of gender, race, culture, religion, nature, etc. — to open spaces for theological frameworks that can truly promote liberation for all. How does God create? Does creation entail the annihilation of the *old* on behalf of the *new,* of darkness on behalf of lightness? Are absolute control and order signs of God's creativity? How does the Spirit relate to matter, to nature? How do we envision God's image, in what color, in what gender? Proposing alternative answers to these questions lies ahead in the development of Latina and Latino theologies that realize *the unspoken, unrepresented past that haunt the historical present* in their striving to forge new visions of a redeeming future.

Their ideals are in our hands to *create and mold them.*" "Report on Public Schools of Puerto Rico, by the President of the Board of Education," Víctor Clark, in the report of the Brigadier General Geo. W. Davis, 1899. Cited in Silva-Gotay, *Protestantismo y política en Puerto Rico, 1898–1930,* 283. The re-formation in terms of which new creation was understood adhered to the entailed putting "the conscience of the American people into the islands of the sea."

67. Bhabha, *The Location of Culture,* 12.

PART II

Culture, Political Theory, and Theological Hermeneutics

Oye, ¿Y Ahora Qué? / Say, Now What?

Prospective Lines of Development for U.S. Hispanic/Latino(a) Theology

BENJAMÍN VALENTÍN

I am about to do a new thing; now it springs forth, do you not perceive it?
 —Isaiah 43:19

To create is not so much to make something new as to shift. Not to shift from a lesser place to a higher or better one, but to shift, intransitively. It is a working out of an old problem and a formulation of a new question.
 —Trinh T. Minha

Although it may seem to be a novel elaboration to many in the mainstream of U.S. theology, and perhaps even to some of its exponents, U.S. Hispanic/Latino(a) theology has existed as an academic discipline of inquiry for almost thirty years. Emerging in the mid-1970s, with Virgilio Elizondo's early theological writings on U.S. Latino(a) life, it has gone on to achieve a mature level of articulation, to develop its own conceptual motifs, and even to establish its own distinctive identity as an inimitable liberationist theological expression that provides insight into the confounding reality of life in the United States and of the varieties of religious experience found within it.[1] U.S. Hispanic/Latino(a) theology has heralded such influential theological innovations as the turn to

---

1. The focus of this essay is on the theologies of Latinos and Latinas living in the United States. Hence, I will not be considering here the distinction of Puerto Rican theology in Puerto Rico, although the island is a territory of the United States by reason of its commonwealth (i.e., colonial) status. It is important to note, however, first that there in fact exists a distinctive theology which is articulated from a Puerto Rican context, and second that dialogue and the exchange of ideas does exist between Puerto Rican theologians and Latino(a) theologians and religious scholars in the United States. To be sure, I believe that more dialogue and exchange needs to occur between these two theological analogues. For more on Puerto Rican theology

cultural memory as a theological source; the theorization of the concept of *mestizaje* — cultural hybridity — and popular religion; the elaboration of a distinctive women's theology of liberation; the advancement of historical Jesus study through the presentation of his mestizo and border sociocultural identity as a Galilean Jew; the valuation of aesthetic representations of Latino(a) life; the development of an ecclesiology that emanates from the context of the *barrio* (the inner city); a reading of the Bible from the eyes of Hispanics/Latino/as; the promotion of postcolonial studies within biblical hermeneutics; the development of a distinctive Christian ethics based on Latino(a) notions of *dignidad;* and many other innovative developments.[2] All of these developments demonstrate, as

consult the following sources: (1) by Luis N. Rivera Pagán, *Senderos teológicos: El pensamiento evangélico Puertorriqueño* (Río Piedras, Puerto Rico: Editorial La Reforma, 1989), and *Los sueños del ciervo: Perspectivas teológicas desde el Caribe* (San Juan, Puerto Rico: Ediciones CLAI, 1995); (2) *Un ministerio transformador: El Seminario Evangélico de Puerto Rico,* ed. Lester McGrath-Andino (San Juan, Puerto Rico: Seminario Evangélico de Puerto Rico, 1998); and (3) Yamina Apolinaris and Sandra Mangual-Rodríguez, "Theologizing from a Puerto Rican Context," in *Hispanic/Latino Theology: Challenge and Promise,* ed. Ada María Isasi-Díaz and Fernando Segovia (Minneapolis: Fortress Press, 1996), 218–39.
     2. For examples of these themes, see especially the following authors and works: (1) on the use of cultural memory in theology, Jeanette Rodríguez-Holguin, "Sangre Llama a Sangre: Cultural Memory as a Source," in *Hispanic/Latino Theology: Challenge and Promise,* 117–33; (2) on the theorizing of *mestizaje,* Virgilio Elizondo, *Galilean Journey: The Mexican-American Promise* (Maryknoll, N.Y.: Orbis Books, 1983), and *The Future Is Mestizo: Life Where Cultures Meet* (Bloomington, Ind.: Meyer-Stone Books, 1988); and Andrés G. Guerrero, *A Chicano Theology* (Maryknoll, N.Y.: Orbis Books, 1987); (3) on the theorizing of Latino(a) popular religion, Orlando Espín, *The Faith of the People: Theological Reflections on Popular Catholicism* (Maryknoll, N.Y.: Orbis Books, 1997); Alex García-Rivera, *St. Martin de Porres: The "Little Stories" and the Semiotics of Culture* (Maryknoll, N.Y.: Orbis Books, 1995); Virgilio Elizondo, "Popular Religion as the Core of Cultural Identity in the Mexican American Experience," in *An Enduring Flame: Studies on Latino/a Popular Religiosity,* ed. Anthony Stevens-Arroyo and Ana María Díaz-Stevens (New York: PARAL, 1994), 113–32; and Jeanette Rodríguez-Holguin, *Our Lady of Guadalupe: Faith and Empowerment among Mexican-American Women* (Austin: University of Texas Press, 1994); (4) on the elaboration of a *mujerista* theology, Ada María Isasi-Díaz, *En la lucha/In the Struggle: A Hispanic Women's Liberation Theology* (Minneapolis: Fortress Press, 1993), and *Mujerista Theology: A Theology for the Twenty-first Century* (Maryknoll, N.Y.: Orbis Books, 1996); (5) on the historical Jesus as mestizo, Virgilio Elizondo, *Galilean Journey;* (6) on the valuation of aesthetics, Roberto Goizueta Jr., *Caminemos con Jesús: Toward a Hispanic/Latino Theology of Accompaniment* (Maryknoll, N.Y.: Orbis Books, 1995), esp. 77–100; Alex García-Rivera, *The Community of the Beautiful: A Theological Aesthetics* (Collegeville, Minn.: Liturgical Press, 1999); (7) on an urban/barrio ecclesiology, Harold J. Recinos, *Hear the Cry: A Latino Pastor Challenges the Church* (Louisville: Westminster/John Knox Press, 1989), "The Barrio as the Locus of a New Church," in *Hispanic/Latino Theology,* 183–94, and *Who Comes in the Name of the Lord? Jesus at the Margins* (Nashville: Abingdon Press, 1997); (8) on the reading of the Bible through Hispanic eyes, Justo L. González, *Santa Biblia: The Bible through Hispanic Eyes* (Nashville: Abingdon Press, 1996); (9) on the use of postcolonial studies within biblical hermeneutics, Fernando F. Segovia, "Two Places and No Place on Which to Stand," 26–40, and "In the World but Not of It: Exile as Locus for a Theology of the Diaspora," in *Hispanic/Latino Theology,* 195–217; and (10) on

Fernando Segovia notes, that not only has U.S. Hispanic/Latino(a) theology burgeoned: it has also "gone on to develop deep foundations and
to mature and flourish as well."[3]

The nearness of its thirtieth anniversary provides us with a unique
opportunity both to celebrate the realization and to reflect on the future
of U.S. Hispanic/Latino(a) theology.[4] In this essay I hope to contribute
to the development of Latino(a) theologies in the United States, first, by
casting light upon three distinctive traits of this theological analogue,
and, second, by calling attention to ways in which these distinguishing
marks can be further cultivated so as to ensure the continued maturation
and public pertinence of our theological voice. I suggest that much of the
uniqueness of U.S. Hispanic/Latino(a) theology derives from the centrality that it gives to the category of culture; to matters of self- and collective
identity; and to the importance of a dialogical and collaborative spirit in

---

Christian ethics from a Hispanic/Latino(a) perspective, Ismael García, *Dignidad: Ethics through
Hispanic Eyes* (Nashville: Abingdon Press, 1997).

3. Segovia, *Hispanic/Latino Theology: Challenge and Promise*, 42.

4. Elsewhere I have offered a historical tracing of U.S. Hispanic/Latino(a) theology. I will
just briefly note here that the initial stage of U.S. Hispanic/Latino(a) theological articulation
begins in 1975 and extends until 1990. During this stage, the contributions of five theologians — Virgilio Elizondo, Orlando Costas, Justo González, Ada María Isasi-Díaz, and Yolanda
Tarango — loom especially important. I suggest that the move toward a more self-conscious,
intentioned, distinctive, and thorough Latino(a) theological perspective begins with the 1975
publication of Virgilio Elizondo's *Christianity and Culture: An Introduction to Pastoral Theology and Ministry for the Bicultural Community* (Huntington, Ind.: Our Sunday Visitor, Inc.,
1975). The work of religious scholars and theologians like Anthony Stevens-Arroyo, Allan
Figueroa Deck, and Andrés Guerrero also proved instrumental in the development of U.S.
Hispanic/Latino(a) theology during this period. In the 1990s U.S. Hispanic/Latino(a) theological production burgeoned, owing to the emergence of what could be called a second wave
in the articulation of Latino(a) theological thought with the works of authors such as María
Pilar Aquino, Arturo Bañuelas, Orlando Espín, Ismael García, Alex García-Rivera, Roberto
Goizueta Jr., Roberto Pazmino, Daisy Machado, Harold Recinos, Jeanette Rodríguez-Holguín,
Fernando Segovia, and Eldin Villafañe, among others. Owing in some form or another to the
work and/or mentorship of this first and second generation of Latino(a) theologians, we are,
I believe, beginning to witness a third stage/wave in the articulation of Latino(a) theological
thought, and more generally in the theoretical interpretation of the varieties of Latino(a) re-
ligious experience, with the writings of thinkers such as those who have contributed to this
volume. Among these we can count, for instance, Edwin Aponte, Rudy Busto, Samuel Cruz,
Miguel De La Torre, Teresa Delgado, Miguel Díaz, Gastón Espinoza, Michelle González, Leticia
Guardiola-Sáenz, Francisco Lozada Jr., Zaida Maldonado Pérez, Loida Martell-Otero, Hjamil
Martínez, Lara Medina, Manuel Mejido, Luis Pedraja, Nancy Pineda-Madrid, Mayra Rivera,
Chris Tirres, and myself, Benjamín Valentín. The works of some of these authors have begun to
promote a critical expansion of the horizons of Latino(a) theology. For more on the history and
development of U.S. Hispanic/Latino(a) theology see my essay "Strangers No More: An Intro-
duction to, and Interpretation of, U.S. Hispanic/Latino(a) Theology," in *The Ties That Bind:
African American and Hispanic American/Latino/a Theologies in Dialogue*, ed. Anthony B.
Pinn and Benjamín Valentín (New York: Continuum International Publishing Group, 2001),
38–53.

theological work. I will propose that Latino(a) theologians are now in a position to advance these worthy emphases by furthering the incorporation of Hispanic/Latino(a) cultural production into their theologies; by problematizing and/or complexifying their emphasis upon a discourse of identity; and by expanding their notion of *teología en conjunto* (i.e., collaborative or joint theology) to include and promote the necessity and desirability of transcultural/trans-Latino(a) dialogue and coalition-building across lines of difference. My guiding aim in this essay is this: to invite my fellow Latino(a) theologians to ennoble and advance U.S. Hispanic/Latino(a) theology by taking into consideration the prospective lines of development that I propose in the following pages.

FROM CULTURAL APPROBATION TO CULTURAL INCORPORATION AND RECONSIDERATION

In the last three decades there has come about a radical change in the theoretical foundations of the so-called humanities. Since the early 1980s the intellectual basis for humanist study has been transformed by the advancement of work on culture. Frustrated by some of the limits of a generalist social history approach, and by some of the constraints of a solely materialist notion of the social, intellectuals have increasingly turned toward culture to study the cultural contexts in which individuals and groups act. More and more, they have focused on "the symbolic order" of human activity, directing their thinking to the analysis of symbols, rituals, discourse, and cultural practices rather than to the study of social structures and social relations. This recent interest in the concept and theorization of culture has swept over a wide range of academic disciplines, including the field of theological study.

Even before discourse on culture was to become popular in U.S. theological scholarship during the late 1990s, however, Latino(a) theologians had already been inaugurating a turn to culture in their theologies. Latino(a) theology, I believe, has been at the fore of the movement within U.S. liberation and/or progressive theologies to add the category of "culture" to the liberationist paradigm in Christian theological discourse: to the reflexive spheres of race, class, and gender it has added culture. From its beginning, U.S. Hispanic/Latino(a) theology has placed emphasis on the concept of culture. The very first text written from a fully intentional and uniquely Hispanic/Latino(a) theological perspective, published by Virgilio Elizondo in 1975, was appropriately titled

Christianity and Culture. This book offered not only a full-length theological study and expression of the consciousness that emanates from the culture and religiosity of the Mexican American people, but also called attention to the possibility and desirability of a Christian theological interpretation that emanates from the space of the self, of identity, and begins with a contextualized cultural reading of the Hispanic experience. This stress on the concept and realm of culture was to receive continued expression in the subsequent work of Virgilio Elizondo and of other Latino(a) theologians.

The emphasis on culture is perceptible within Hispanic/Latino(a) theological works in the recurring use of, and significance attributed to, the concepts of *mestizaje* (i.e., Latino[a] cultural hybridity), *popular religion*, and most generally in the continuous and detailed attention devoted to the description of the so-called "Latino(a) cultural reality." In whatever manner the term *mestizaje* is employed, and no matter what secondary meaning may be attributed to the study of popular religion, the main thrust behind the use of these concepts and emphases is a concern with the proper remembrance, defense, and celebration of Latino(a) cultures. In this sense, the terms *mestizaje* and popular religion are employed as explanatory categories that synchronously depict the cultural hybridity that characterizes Latino(a) identity, help point to what is different and new about that identity in the United States, and provide fertile space for new formations and celebrations of Latino(a) cultural identity to take hold. In sum, U.S. Hispanic/Latino(a) theology's affinity to the concepts of *mestizaje* and popular religion demonstrates a fundamental privileging of matters of Latino(a) culture: the area of interest and struggle for Latino(a) theology is principally, then, the realm of culture (i.e., symbolic culture).

Hispanic/Latino(a) theology in the United States is manifestly a culturally contextualized theology of liberation not only by virtue of the fact that as a human construct it is always necessarily a product of culture but because, as Latina theologians Ada María Isasi-Díaz and Yolanda Tarango rightly note, it purposely gives witness to our Latino(a) struggle to "maintain the values of our culture as an intrinsic element of our self-identity and of our struggle"[5] for liberation in the United States. The reasoning behind the privileging of the category of culture in

---

5. Ada María Isasi-Díaz and Yolanda Tarango, *Hispanic Women: Prophetic Voice in the Church* (Minneapolis: Fortress Press, 1992), xii.

Latino(a) theology is easily grasped when we examine the general history of Latino/as in this nation. To put it simply, from the very beginning we Latino/as have had to struggle consistently and zealously to keep alive our distinctive historical and cultural experiences in the United States, all while also claiming our membership as legitimate citizens and active agents in this nation. In light of the cultural devaluation, hurtful negative stereotypes, ethnic prejudice, and social marginalization with which Latino/as have often had to contend, U.S. Hispanic/Latino(a) theologians have come to the conclusion that there may be sources of oppression other than economic — for example, racial and cultural — affecting the sufferings of Latino/as in our society. Appropriately, they have turned to the realm of culture in order to unearth, define, and uplift a certain set of beliefs and practices connected to U.S. Latino(a) peoples; to promote cultural affirmation among Latino/as; and in the hopes of finding there a potentially uncolonized space and agent for subversive consciousness that both offers glimpses of the creative defense of Latino(a) cultures and a basis from which to foster positive self- and group identity. In short, Hispanic/Latino(a) theologians have devoted a great part of their reflective energies to questions of culture in the hopes of both resisting the assimilatory pressures and prejudices that exist in U.S. life and promoting cultural affirmation among Latino/as.

The emergence of culture as a recurrent theme or reflexive category in Hispanic/Latino(a) theology is something to be appreciated, celebrated, and preserved. Given the historical realities and dynamics of cultural subjugation, ethnic prejudice, and hurtful negative stereotypes with which Latino/as have often had to contend, and the continued existence of strategies of cultural oppression in our so-called postcolonial era within the United States, this turn to culture is an important and necessary strategy. It concurrently provides a conceptual basis to examine neglected elements of Latino(a) cultures and histories; to highlight Latino(a) creativity and distinctiveness; to celebrate, defend, and win recognition for Latino(a) identities; to foster positive self-identity and collective cultural identity among Latino/as; and perhaps even more than that to universally "protest the disguised particularisms — the masculinism, the white-Anglo ethnocentrism, the heterosexism — lurking behind what parades as universal."[6] By placing emphasis upon the

---

6. I borrow this line from Nancy Fraser, *Justice Interruptus: Critical Reflections on the "Postsocialist" Condition* (New York: Routledge, 1997), 5.

realm of culture in their theologies, U.S. Hispanic/Latino(a) theologians have at once managed to make cultural study a theological and political project.

Although deeply appreciative of this turn toward culture in U.S. Hispanic/Latino(a) theology, I am convinced that we Latino(a) theologians are now in a favorable position within the evolution of our distinctive theological discourse to advance our mode of cultural theorizing. One of the ways in which we can make progress in our theological treatment of culture is by advancing from the stage of cultural approbation — wherein we simply affirm the importance of the category of culture — to that of actual cultural incorporation. That is to say, we can push forward our cultural emphasis by moving from a mere honoring of the concept of culture to the utilizing of Latino(a) cultural production in our theologies. Although they have placed much emphasis upon the category of culture, it is puzzling that our Hispanic/Latino(a) theologies still have not made much use of the cultural artifacts — the literature, music, art, drama, and film, for instance — generated by Latino/as in the United States. As I see it, the basic purpose or intention of understanding culture is to more fully engage in it. Yet, apart from engaging with certain forms of Latino(a) religious expression and creativity, Hispanic/Latino(a) theology has thus far rarely immersed itself in the broader cultural productivity of U.S. Latino/as.[7]

Further engagement with the matter of Latino(a) cultural creativity could greatly enrich our theologies. To begin, we must recognize that the possibility for a theology that is grounded in Latino(a) history, in the specificity of Latino(a) experience, exists in just such a cultural immersion. Sustained engagement with U.S. Latino(a) literature, music, art, film, drama, comedy, and other such cultural expressions and practices could serve to proffer an existential historicity, a contextuality, a corporeality, and a palpable "Latinidad" to our theologies. I dare say that without such an artifactual, cultural encounter and incorporation, our theologies run the risk of being "Latino(a)" just in name — in short,

---

7. Some authors have recently begun to use Latino(a) literature as a theological source. Among these we can name Nancy Pineda, Teresa Delgado, Michelle González, and, from a Puerto Rican/Latin American context, Luis Rivera-Pagán. But this sort of work has only recently begun to surface. While it gives witness to the sort of theological incorporation of Hispanic/Latino(a) cultural creativity that I am calling for, I suggest that more such work needs to be done. Moreover, I suggest that further use of other Latino(a) cultural artifacts such as music, art, film, and drama can and should be made.

they run the risk of suffering from an ahistoricity marked by an inability to make wider connections with Latino(a) forms of life, expressions, practices, and sensibilities.

Moreover, besides extending the possibility of a grounding specificity, further engagement with the matter of Latino(a) cultural production could aid our development of distinctive U.S. Hispanic/Latino(a) "constructive theologies."[8] By delving into the culture-producing practices of Latino/as, we could avail ourselves of viable images, metaphors, and other creative representations that could in turn facilitate our theological attempts to reinterpret and reconstruct the religious symbols or doctrines of faith as we seek to make these more responsive to new occasions and duties. Many are the tasks and/or potential undertakings of a theologian. Among these we can include the attempt to interpret the meaning of religious experience, and the effort to evaluate both the symbolic construction of human experience and the manifestations of ultimate concern brought into being in a specific culture or milieu. In this way, the theologian could operate as a religious hermeneut and/or as a cultural critic. I would suggest, however, that the distinctive or ultimate responsibility of a theologian is to interpret, reinterpret, reconstruct, and thus to extend the orientating meaning of the symbols and/or doctrines of a religious tradition. In the symbolic universe of Christian thought, this task could include the interpretation, reinterpretation, and reconstruction of symbols, concepts, or propositions such as creation, human being, Christ, the church, and especially "God."

---

8. What I have in mind when I employ the term "constructive theology" is a mode of revisionist-historicist-contextualist theology that roots itself in a religious tradition, its categories/doctrines, concepts, narratives, and images, but is willing to challenge, expand, and revise that tradition in light both of the critical questions raised by the modern and, now, postmodern world as well as the insights and/or cultural resources of a given context or culturally defined social group. And it does so because it wishes to interpret, reconstruct, and appropriate a religious tradition in such a way that it can contribute anew to our human quest for meaning in the lived moment and also respond to new occasions and duties in a transformative manner. The constructivist or revisionist theologian begins admittedly with a specific tradition of faith but both acknowledges the open-textured and dynamic quality of that tradition and seeks to make manifest its meaning in nonexclusive ways that are responsive to the needs and challenges of the time at hand, willing, as the occasion mandates, to reconstruct that tradition by weaving together its insights with both the best analyses of the current time and the creative agency made available to him or her within his/her culturally defined group's history. For some examples and insightful explications of constructive theology see Gordon D. Kaufman, *An Essay on Theological Method* (Atlanta: Scholars Press, 1979), esp. 21–41, and *In Face of Mystery: A Constructive Theology* (Cambridge, Mass.: Harvard University Press, 1993); and Sallie McFague, *Models of God: Theology for a Nuclear Age* (Philadelphia: Fortress Press, 1987), esp. 21–57.

Although some of this sort of theological work can be found within it, the archives of U.S. Hispanic/Latino(a) theology are not exactly replete with this kind of systematic and reconstructive pursuit. The term "God," the idea of God, of transcendence, or of the "sacred" has particularly received scant treatment in our theologies thus far. In a sense, to put it in Spanish phraseology, we can say *que se nos ha quedado Dios* — that we have forgotten about "God," the notion of God and the meanings, both beneficial/proper or unhealthy/improper, often attached to it. This inadvertency is peculiarly puzzling since it is "the meaning or status of the *theos* that is supposedly the object of theological analysis and interpretation."[9] I suggest that our efforts to reinterpret and reconstruct the symbols of the Christian faith in ways that are at once conversant with, alive to, challenging, and ultimately orientating for our people and many others could be aided by an examination of the vast imagination and spirituality found within the cultural artifacts produced by U.S. Latino/as. That is to say, through the agency of the immense wealth found in Latino(a) literature, art, music, film, and drama we may be better able to generate fresh notions of God, earthy portrayals of creation, timely renderings of human particularity, responsible and provocative theodicies, and liberating presentations of Christ. To put it simply and directly, the possibility of a distinctive Latino(a) systematic theology rests in large part upon our willingness to connect our theologies to the wider cultural creativity of U.S. Latino/as.

Finally, I suggest that another way in which we can make progress in our treatment of Latino(a) culture is by modifying the notion of "culture" with which we work. Indeed, it behooves us to keep in mind that "culture" is a theoretical category, a concept, a construct. The temptation is often to treat the term as if it were a self-evident given, as an incontrovertible aspect of life that can be abstracted out from the complex reality of human existence. Thus, culture is often taken to stand for a certain, concrete, and bounded set of beliefs, conventions, or characteristics assumed to "belong" to a society or some subsocietal group of people. This is the usage of "culture" that has thus far prevailed in U.S. Hispanic/Latino(a) theological discourse, the end-product often being unvarying, too tidy, and uncritical representations of Latino(a) cultural activity.

---

9. I borrow this line from Gordon Kaufman, *An Essay on Theological Method*, ix.

Although at times propitious, this static notion of culture can serve to hinder our attempts to look upon, explain, and esteem the disparateness, changeableness, and even disjointedness of human cultures. There are, however, other ways of thinking about "culture" that can counterbalance a notion of culture as "self-enclosed, static, completely coherent, and impervious to challenge."[10] We can, for instance, view culture as the sphere devoted specifically to the production, circulation, and use of meanings; as creativity or agency; or simply as practice. Each one of these alternative conceptions serves to countervail a portrayal of culture as logical, coherent, uniform, bound, and static, treating it instead as a sphere of signification and practice shot through with at times willful and at other times indeliberate action, power relations, struggle, contradiction, transverseness, and change.[11] These latter usages of culture, I would suggest, could open up new vistas in our theologies, allowing both for a higher-grade portraiture of the variety and complexity of Latino(a) agency and also a more critical handling of it.

"WHAT A TANGLED WEB WE WEAVE WHEN WE PRACTICE TO DEPICT IDENTITY"

The category of culture is but one of the subject matters that has drawn much attention in U.S. Hispanic/Latino(a) theology. The topic of identity has also commanded high regard in that theology. I dare say that much of the uniqueness of U.S. Latino(a) theology derives from the centrality that it gives to matters of self and collective identity. To be sure, the emphasis given to the concept of culture by Latino(a) theologians is closely connected to their concern with identity. Culture is, after all, a recurrent theme in Hispanic/Latino(a) theology, both as a basis to counteract the ethnic prejudice or cultural subjugation with which Latino/as have often had to contend and as a way of fostering self-affirming identities. As this last aspiration manifests, then, Latino(a) theologians have given the category of culture a central place in their search for and reconstruction of a denied positive identity. Although inexorably linked, these

---

10. I borrow these choice words from Victoria Bonnell and Lynn Hunt, *Beyond the Cultural Turn*, ed. Victoria E. Bonnell and Lynn Hunt (Berkeley: University of California Press, 1999), 12.

11. For more on the subject of differing conceptualizations of culture, and their serviceability and limitations, see William H. Sewell Jr., "The Concept(s) of Culture," in *Beyond the Cultural Turn*, 35–61.

two themes (i.e., culture and identity) can be analytically differentiated so that they can be seen as two distinct — yet related — core topics in Latino(a) theology.

From its beginning, U.S. Hispanic/Latino(a) theology has focused on matters of identity. This stress on identity arises from a legitimate concern with the survival of Hispanic/Latino(a) people as a people in the United States. Latino/as have, after all, shared the historical experiences of conquest, colonization, and political infringement; a general sense of the depreciation of their cultures; and common encounters with overt ethnic and racial prejudice as well as persistent assimilationist assumptions that threaten their identities. Hispanic U.S. history was marked very early on with the violent conquest of Mexicans and their lands. And even after professing and demonstrating our love for and allegiance to this country, we Latino/as — regardless of our nationalities — continue to endure questions regarding our legitimacy not only as citizens but also as persons. Latino/as have at times been deemed inadequate, as people that don't belong, and inherently as a problem people. On top of this, the assimilationist dogma that frequently creeps into our national discourse has often held that Latino/as must erase their past in order to become "authentic" U.S. Americans. This process of cultural subjugation and identity suppression has materialized in different forms throughout U.S. history. It came into view in the English-only initiatives that recently sought to undercut the advancement of bilingualism in U.S. public life, and in the inflammatory politics of immigration control that led to the passage of Proposition 187 in California. At other times the obstacles to cultural knowledge, positive self-identity, and collective identity take on more covert and personal configurations. Yet, whether overtly or covertly, of public or more personal impact, the dynamics of the depreciation of culture and the preoccupations with a viable self-identity that arise as a result continue to influence Latino(a) life.[12] Consequently, Hispanic/Latino(a) theologians have become convinced that the defense, maintenance, and rendering of a salutary sense of self and collective identity must be made part of a liberating theological discourse.

The theme of identity has extended over much of the efforts of U.S. Hispanic/Latino(a) theology, impressing upon its theological and political imagination. Theologically, it is perceptible in the recurring use of,

---

12. My statements in this section draw on my prior work, *Mapping Public Theology: Beyond Culture, Identity, and Difference* (Harrisburg, Pa.: Trinity Press International, 2002).

and significance attributed to, the concepts of *mestizaje* and popular religion; when comparing the historical Jesus' mestizo identity to present-day Latino(a) self-subjectivity; when theologizing Latino(a) agency; or when musing over the surreptitious activity and potentiality embedded within forms of Latino(a) religious expression. Politically, the motif of identity is expressed through a political imaginary that seeks to defend and advance Latino(a) identities, end cultural domination, and win recognition for Latino/as. In these ways and others, Latino(a) theology demonstrates a commitment to a discursive paradigm of identity recognition and to a politics of identity program.

As I see it, any discursive project that is genuinely concerned with the remedy of injustice must make room in its agenda for the consideration of issues related to the defense of group identity and the requirements of recognition. These concerns and struggles have everything to do with justice and must continue to be part of any comprehensive emancipatory project and, therefore, of Latino(a) theology. Nevertheless, I believe that Latino(a) theology has tended to focus predominantly on discussions of identity, symbolic culture, and subjectivity, and has, therefore, given too little attention to the critical scrutiny of the multifaceted matrices that impinge upon the realization of a broader emancipatory political project and energy.

The predilection toward and the emphasis on matters of identity and cultural or symbolic injustice in our theologies have unintentionally served to engender certain debilitating oversights. Our enchantment with a general discursive paradigm of culture and identity recognition has, for instance, served to displace other pertinent issues and axes of social stratification from the reflection chart. In a sense, our strong focus on matters of identity and symbolic culture, whether for the defense or celebration of cultural diversity and difference, has unintentionally served to disguise other serious economic and political disparities that exist in our society. Not surprisingly, Hispanic/Latino(a) theology has lagged behind in its scrutiny of issues related to socioeconomic injustice and the development of an adequately comprehensive social theory that connects the study of signification to institutions and social structures. Yet, if we truly mean for our discourses to be germane to the fruition of a comprehensive project invested with emancipatory commitments, we need to pay adequate attention to the broader material structures in society that generate disadvantage at various levels of social life. Our liberatory theological discourses must adequately address not merely how cultural identities may be defended and constructed differently, but also how they are produced and sustained within a deeply hierarchical and exploitative society wherein culture is only one among many other axes of stratification. To put it plainly, we should bear in mind that the axes of identity and culture are always in fact embedded in a larger web of shifting social, political, and economic relations that must be equally kept in mind when theorizing on matters of identity, culture, and difference. Hence, these matters must be understood in relation to broader societal constituents, stratifications, and crises that transcend the space of the self and the local, and yet, nevertheless, influence everyday personal and local realities.

In this vein, Hispanic/Latino(a) theologians must bear in mind that U.S. Latino/as suffer injustices that are traceable not only to the denigration of their culture and identities, but also to socioeconomic exploitation and inequity. It is vital, therefore, that we extend sustained and mature attention to socioeconomic injustice, which is rooted in the political-economic structure of society. Thus, in the same way that we offer detailed attention to social patterns of representation, interpretation, and communication such as cultural domination, nonrecognition, and disrespect, we must be willing to closely analyze matters of socioeconomic injustice such as exploitation, economic marginalization, and deprivation.[13] If our theological discourses are ultimately to be useful in the promotion of a reinvigorated social justice movement that aids impoverished and marginalized Latino/as, as well as disadvantaged persons from other ethnic communities in our society, they will have to search for ways of reconnecting a cultural and identity politics of recognition to a social politics of redistribution. To put it boldly and simply, our God-talk, theological anthropology, Christ-talk, church-talk, and religious practice should be connected to this kind of broader, more comprehensive emancipatory project — one that links redistribution and recognition claims for justice — if it is to be truly liberating.[14]

---

13. For more on these concerns of recognition and distribution, and the analytical distinction that can be made between socioeconomic injustice and cultural or symbolic injustice, see Nancy Fraser, *Justice Interruptus*, 11–39.

14. For more on these intimations, see my book *Mapping Public Theology*, esp. chaps. 2 and 3.

DOING *TEOLOGÍA EN CONJUNTO* ACROSS LINES OF DIFFERENCE

U.S. Hispanic/Latino(a) theology is also highly characterized by a collaborative spirit, a motivating impulse that has even been given name in Latino(a) theology and received prominence as a theme in itself: *teología en conjunto* (i.e., collaborative or joint theology). This sensibility materializes in the form of two distinct yet interrelated emphases. First, Latino(a) theologians stress that theology should be done in dialogue with one's community of faith. The ultimate hope in such an exchange is that the theologian is influenced by the specificity of his or her community and that in turn the community is enriched in some way by the theologian's participation. As Luis Pedraja puts it, Latino(a) theologians generally believe that "doing theology as dialogue avoids the Enlightenment's model of doing theology as an abstract observer."[15] In short, these theologians strive to become "organic intellectuals" who work in and on behalf of the religious communities they may be a part of. The second emphasis that materializes within this overall collaborative sensibility is that of doing theology in cooperation with other Latino(a) theologians as a communal exercise.

This overall collaborative and dialogical spirit is exemplified in a number of ways. One of the earliest examples of this communal and collaborative approach was Ada María Isasi-Díaz and Yolanda Tarango's 1988 book, *Hispanic Women: Prophetic Voice in the Church*. In this book Latina theology was described as a "communal process," and the method employed to give body to this notion was the use of ethnographic accounts, which elucidated the experiences of lay Hispanic Catholic women, as central components of the authors' life-based theological interpretations.[16] Another example of the emphasis on collaborative and communal engagement can be found in Justo González's call for, and description of, Hispanic theology as a *Fuenteovejuna theology:* a communal reflective enterprise that envisions all as one.[17] This overall spirit

---

15. Luis Pedraja, "Guideposts along the Journey: Mapping North American Hispanic Theology," in *Protestantes/Protestants: Hispanic Christianity within Mainline Traditions,* ed. David Maldonado Jr. (Nashville: Abingdon Press, 1999), 136.

16. See Ada María Isasi-Díaz and Yolanda Tarango, *Hispanic Women: Prophetic Voice in the Church* (San Francisco: Harper & Row, 1988), esp. ix–xvii and 12–59.

17. See Justo González, *Mañana: Christian Theology from a Hispanic Perspective* (Nashville: Abingdon Press, 1990), esp. 28–30.

can also be seen at work in Roberto Goizueta's descriptions of a theology of *accompaniment*,[18] as well as in the many convocations organized by Latino(a) theologians to discuss their work together and in the proclivity toward the production of theological anthologies that allow for inner collaboration.

The emphasis on collaboration and dialogue, the doing of *teología en conjunto*/theology in cooperation, should and must be sustained within U.S. Hispanic/Latino(a) theology. I suggest, however, that the meaning and purpose of this motif should be expanded by Latino(a) theologians so as to allow for the development and promotion of socially binding discourses that can connect the sociopolitical and cultural struggles of our Hispanic/Latino(a) communities both to the similar struggles of other marginalized social groups and to the progressive sensibilities of other constituencies in the United States. The specific form in which Latino(a) theologians have elaborated the idea of *teología en conjunto* has been limited thus far to "intradialogue" and "intracollaboration" among Latino(a) theologians and has, therefore, not yet made sufficient allowances for dialogue and collaboration with other discursive communities of struggle and progressive spirit. Aimed primarily at valorizing cultural specificity and the reclamation of positive self and group identity among Latino/as, our discourses have not reflected enough on the possible harmonizing of diverse interests in society and the importance of pluralistic alliances of struggle. Yet, the task of alliance-building and the need for coalitional energies is particularly pressing today, because of the increase of social antagonism, the fracturing of social movements, the deterioration of a spirit of solidarity, and the increasing chasm between the haves and have-nots in our society.

I am not naive as to the enormous challenges that come with the task of building alliances and coalitions. Indeed, at present we even lack the integrative and holistic visions that can abet progressive coalitions, and we also have to contend with diverse interests and the reality of fragmented constituencies in our society. But, as Susan Friedman correctly notes, "we cannot afford to give up the utopian dream of coalition and connection."[19] This utopic vision is especially pertinent for those historically subordinated persons and groups in society that by themselves

---

18. See Goizueta, *Caminemos con Jesús.*
19. Susan Friedman, *Mappings: Feminism and the Cultural Geographies of Encounter* (Princeton, N.J.: Princeton University Press, 1998), 66.

lack the power to single-handedly transform present institutional structures. Social change, especially in the United States today, requires the building and nourishment of wider communal bonds among different communities of struggle. Hence, the prospect for progressive institutional transformation in our society ultimately hinges on our abilities to facilitate and sustain holistic social arrangements that can engender broad-based political coalitions across racial, ethnic, gender, class, and religious lines of difference.

For the task of alliance-building and affiliation, we need discourses that highlight those spaces of shared experience and need in society, and which bring attention to the basic and full humanity that connects us all. We are in need of discourses that move "beyond theorizing difference to theorizing the spaces in between difference" and seek resolutely to facilitate "a solidarity of difference."[20] The demands for justice in our times call for discourses that can move beyond the theorization of difference to the theorization of the interstitial sites of interaction, interconnection, and exchange that may exist between our different spaces of identity and struggle. Such a discursive move does not demand that we ignore questions of particular identity, community, and difference within our theologies. It does require, however, that we highlight in them the things that persons and groups may have in common — their common or shared problems, aspirations, hopes, and humanity, as well as the possibilities that may exist for interaction — at least as much as we examine the space of specific cultural and ethnic identity and difference.

As individuals and particular ethnic communities living in the United States we all certainly have differences, and we must account for these in order to keep at bay harmful notions of homogenization that undermine particular self-defining narratives. However, we must also acknowledge that often our distinct ethnic and cultural groups can share, and indeed have shared, some parallel and even common stories, struggles, hopes, visions, and journeys. In order to allow for social change through emancipatory alliance and/or coalition building we must acknowledge and highlight these continuities and common interests in our Hispanic/

---

20. I borrow the first line in this sentence from Susan Friedman, *Mappings*, 68, and the second from Antonia Darder, "The Politics of Biculturalism: Culture and Difference in the Formation of *Warriors for Gringostroika* and *The New Mestizas*," in *Culture and Difference: Critical Perspectives on the Bicultural Experience in the United States*, ed. Antonia Darder (Westport, Conn.: Bergin & Garvey, 1995), 15.

Latino(a) theological discourses at least as much as we examine the space of specific identity, cultural difference, and local community.

As I see it, a theology that aspires to transformative social relevance, as Latino(a) theology does, should seek to provide the religious or spiritual basis for the integration of the struggle for equality and justice into broader spheres of everyday life, and should also aspire to disseminate its discourse to ever-widening arenas of discussion and association in the broader realm of civil society. The task of both Latino(a) liberation and of broader social liberation requires, perhaps especially in our trying and fractious times, the articulation of a broad and integrative vision that can attract the attention of a large and diverse audience, as well as bring together different liberationists and progressives to work toward meaningful social change and, thus, toward the improvement of the quality of our lives together. Correspondingly, beyond its current exemplification of "intradialogue" and "intracollaboration" among Latino(a) theologians and religious scholars only, the notion of *teología en conjunto*/collaborative theology should stand for this sort of broader, trans-Latino(a) and cross-cultural, discursive enterprise.

In order to be faithful to, and in order to meet the demands of, such a comprehensive emancipatory discursive enterprise, I suggest that Latino(a) theology should engage in more serious efforts of social theorizing even as it continues to reexamine and develop modes of cultural theories and critiques. Along these lines, it should seek to acknowledge, deeply analyze, and oppose all of the many and cross-cutting inequities that afflict not only Latino/as but many other suffering persons and groups in our society as well. Latino(a) theology should also be willing to traverse the boundaries of group knowledge and interest in order to envision and articulate a social ontology that can more tangibly enable relationships across local personal and group difference and particularity.[21] Finally, I suggest that it should be more willing to entertain the potentiality both of relational theologies and of dialogical exchange with theologians and religious scholars of other culturally and ethnically defined groups.[22] From these kinds of cross-cultural dialogues may arise

---

21. For more on these intimations, see *Mapping Public Theology*, esp. chaps. 2 and 3.

22. This is precisely the sort of vision and undertaking that Anthony Pinn and I have sought to initiate and encourage between Latino(a) and African American theologians in *The Ties That Bind*. More of this sort of dialogical collaboration should occur, not only between theologians and religious scholars of these two communities but also between and among those of other social groups.

new forms of comparative theologies and a further appreciation for the varieties of religious experience found in our societies and even local neighborhoods. Furthermore, perhaps by way of this more integrative, holistic, comprehensive, harmonizing, and cross-cultural mode of doing *teología en conjunto* we might be better able to create solidarities of difference that could bring more significant collective power to bear on society as a whole for the betterment of the quality of our lives together. Perhaps in this way we might also be better able to "experience God moving within, *between,* and among us."[23]

CONCLUSION

U.S. Hispanic/Latino(a) theology has certainly come a long way in its now almost three decades of existence, establishing its own distinctive identity and presenting a wide range of topics. Three characteristics that have especially marked this discursive theological analogue are (1) an interest in culture, (2) a concern with matters of self- and group identity, and (3) a desire for collaborative and communal exchange/accountability in the doing of theology. I suggest that these are emphases worthy of continuance and furtherance in Latino(a) theology. Furthermore, I propose that Latino(a) theologians can achieve this motif attunement (1) by furthering the incorporation of Hispanic/Latino(a) cultural production into their theologies, and by shifting from a conception of culture as a concrete and bounded set of beliefs and characteristics to one that views it more fluidly as practice and agency; (2) by problematizing and complexifying their emphasis upon a discourse and politics of identity; and (3) by expanding their notion of *teología en conjunto* to include the desirability of transcultural/trans-Latino(a) dialogue and coalition building across lines of difference. As I see it, we Latino(a) theologians should concern ourselves with the constant refurbishing of our distinctive theological inflections and with the attempt to make our discursive practices more accountable to the needs and particularities of our communities. I posit that we are more likely to succeed in this effort if we attend to these considerations in our theologies.

---

23. I borrow this phrasing from Carter Heyward, *Our Passion for Justice: Images of Power, Sexuality, and Liberation* (New York: Pilgrim Press, 1984), 11; emphasis added.

6

Unearthing the Latino(a) Imagination

Literature and Theology,
Some Methodological Gestures

MICHELLE A. GONZÁLEZ

To propose literature as a theological resource is not new to theology. From the writings of Dante to the poetry of Gerard Manley Hopkins, literature has been an aesthetic voice within theology. Theologians have used literature as a resource to tap into and reveal the theological imagination of humanity. Often, this is done in an ad hoc manner that does not explicitly challenge the implications of aesthetics for theology. A theological methodology that places literature in explicit conversation with theology, however, is often characterized by the ambiguity and tension of its interdisciplinary task. George Salyer, in his introduction to *Literature and Theology at Century's End,* is well aware of the uncertainty of the field.[1] Noting that those who engage this conversation are often challenged to justify the validity of their work, Salyer emphasizes the strain on those who pursue studies and writings on literature and theology. Tensions aside, one cannot ignore the vitality and growing interest in this area of Christian thought.

There are two main ways for the theologian to approach the relationship between literature and theology. One manner, which is perhaps the most popular, is to view literature as a theological resource. In other words, literature becomes a source for theology, gleaned on to understand the culture, context, history, and religious expressions of a given community. Fumitaka Matsuoka, for example, uses literature to "reveal complex, tantalizing, and intriguing glimpses into the cultural, religious, and ethical symbols and values they name as the forces bringing Asian

---

1. Gregory Salyer, "Introduction," in *Literature and Theology at Century's End,* ed. Gregory Salyer and Robert Detweiler (Atlanta: Scholars Press, 1995), 1.

119

North American communities together."[2] A second manner is to understand literature *as* theology. Literature not only becomes a theological source, but is also treated as a theological text. This approach is more complex, for contained within it is a challenge to preconceptions of what constitutes authentic theology. In this essay, I explore the relationship between literature and theology, emphasizing literature as theological text, with special attention to the implications of theological aesthetics for Latino(a) theology. While there have been some writings within Latino(a) theology examining literature as a theological resource, there has not been, I argue, a sustained reflection on literature *as* theology.

I begin with a brief overview of the relationship between literature and theology in Latino(a) theology. Because a theology that takes literature seriously as a form of theological writing must be grounded in a theological aesthetics, my second section explores Latino(a) contributions in theological aesthetics. Because of the prominence of his work both in theological aesthetics and an understanding of literature as theology, Swiss-born theologian Hans Urs von Balthasar's methodology is offered as a framework for exploring literature as theology. In my concluding section I examine the methodological implications of this study, as well as future directions for scholarship.

LITERATURE AND THEOLOGY:
LATINO(A) VOICES

One of the most important movements in twentieth-century theology was the birth and growth of liberation and contextual theologies, especially in the Third World and amid U.S. minorities. These theologies, which have exploded into the theological arena, challenge Eurocentric, patriarchal, dehistoricized assumptions about theological construction. They highlight the importance of social location and a preferential option for the oppressed and marginalized. A key methodological insight of these theologies is placing the nonperson at the center of theological reflection. Who is the nonperson? As described by Gustavo Gutiérrez,

---

2. Fumitaka Matsuoka, "Reformation of Identities and Values within Asian North American Communities," in *A Dream Unfinished: Theological Reflections on America from the Margins,* ed. Eleazar S. Fernández and Fernando F. Segovia (Maryknoll, N.Y.: Orbis Books, 2001), 119.

> To be sure, when we say 'nonperson' or 'nonhuman being,' we are not using these terms in an ontological sense. We do not mean that the interlocutor of liberation is actually a nonentity. We are using this term to denote those human beings who are considered less than human by society, because that society is based on privileges arrogated by a minority.[3]

To place the nonperson at the center of theological reflection transforms the very nature of theological discourse. "The questions asked by the 'nonperson,' the 'nonhuman,'... have to do with the economic, the social, and the political, and yet this does not make for a nontheological discussion, as some seem to think. That would indeed be a facile solution. It is a matter of a different theology."[4] Taking seriously the nonperson transforms the questions and sources theology explores.

In addition to examining the sociopolitical and historical contexts of oppressed peoples, liberation theologies also explore their marginalized voices. In other words, a central feature of liberation theologies is recovering lost voices within historical Christianity, as well as placing current voices at front and center. Latina feminist theologian María Pilar Aquino, for example, offers a clear hermeneutics of suspicion and retrieval that highlights both the historical marginalization of Latino/as and methodological gestures for recovering their voices. This methodological principle is seen in the essay, "The Collective 'Dis-covery' of Our Own Power," where the "un-covery" and consequent "recovery" of the suppressed traditions of Latina Americans is the emphasis. In this piece, the paradigm of oppression is found in the Spanish conquest of the Americas.

> The great European invasions did not *discover* but rather *covered* whole peoples, religions, and cultures and explicitly tried to take away from the natives the sources of their own historical memory and their own power.... We seek to *un-cover* the truth and bring to light our collective will to choose a different path.[5]

---

3. Gustavo Gutiérrez, *The Power of the Poor in History* (Maryknoll, N.Y.: Orbis Books, 1993), 91–92.

4. Ibid., 212.

5. María Pilar Aquino, "The Collective "Dis-covery" of Our Own Power: Latina American Feminist Theology," *Hispanic Latino Theology: Challenge and Promise*, ed. Ada María Isasi-Díaz and Fernando F. Segovia (Minneapolis: Fortress Press, 1996), 241–42.

This is a subversive principle, challenging traditional interpretations of the conquest. A feature of this recovery, found in the writings of various liberation theologians, is its emphasis on the aesthetic as an avenue for exploring such historical voices. Perhaps the greatest example of this is found in the work of James H. Cone on the spirituals.[6]

In a recent article on theology and literature in Latin America, Luis N. Rivera-Pagán highlighted the significance of literature as an avenue for tapping into the Latin American consciousness and imagination. "The Latin American existential drama, in all its manifold complexities, has expressed itself fundamentally, and in a magnificent way, in our literature, especially our novels, not in philosophical treatises."[7] Rivera-Pagán argues for the use of literature as a vehicle for unearthing the intellectual heritage of Latin American peoples. This would transform the stereotype that in Latin America there is no critical intellectual history. Rivera-Pagán cites the work of Ernesto Sabato, who recounts, "Not long ago, a German critic asked me why we Latin Americans have great novelists but no great philosophers. Because we are barbarians, I told him, because we were saved, fortunately, from the great rationalist schism.... If you want our *Weltanschuung*, I told him, look to our novels, not to our pure thought."[8]

While I agree with both Sabato and Rivera-Pagán's assessments of literature as revelatory of the Latin American imagination, I hesitate to reduce that imagination to purely literary production. The philosophical plays and literature of twentieth-century authors Jean-Paul Sartre and Albert Camus are clear examples that contest this reduction. In a specifically Latin American context, I wish to cite two contemporary examples. The first is seen in the influence of the literature of José María Arguedas on the theology of Gustavo Gutiérrez. As Brett Greider has demonstrated, Gutiérrez holds Arguedas's literature to be a significant resource in elaborating a theology that emerged from the context and culture of the people. Literature is a medium that allows one to examine the theological vision from a fresh perspective.[9] A second instance is the

---

6. James H. Cone, *The Spirituals and the Blues: An Interpretation* (Maryknoll, N.Y.: Orbis Books, 2000).
7. Luis N. Rivera-Pagán, "Theology and Literature in Latin America," *Journal of Hispanic/Latino Theology* 7, no. 4 (May 2000): 19.
8. Ernesto Sabato, *The Angel of Darkness,* trans. Andrew Hurley (New York: Ballantine Books, 1991), 194, cited in Rivera-Pagán, "Theology and Literature," 19.
9. Brett Greider, "Crossing Deep Rivers: The Liberation Theology of Gustavo Gutiérrez in the Light of the Narrative Poetics of José María Arguedas" (Ph.D. diss., Graduate Theological Union, Berkeley, Calif., 1988).

recent anthology entitled *Filosofía, teología, literatura: Aportes cubanos en los últimos 50 años.*[10] Editor Raúl Fornet-Betancourt brought together philosophers, theologians, and literary scholars in order to approach their fields in an interdisciplinary perspective. This book is an illustration of the growing number of collaborations in the fields of literature, theology, and philosophy in the Latin American context.

Within Latino(a) theology, no single author has offered a substantial treatment of literature and theology. There have been, however, various articles that have brought forth the significance of this topic, which only continues to grow within Latino(a) theology. Three articles are of special note: Ana María Díaz-Stevens, "In the Image and Likeness of God: Literature as Theological Reflection"; Shane Martin and Ernesto Colín, "The Novels of Graciela Limón: Narrative, Theology and the Search for Mestiza/o Identity"; and Teresa Delgado, "Prophesy Freedom: Puerto Rican Women's Literature as a Source for Latina Feminist Theology."[11] A brief study of these three essays demonstrates the manner in which Latino(a) theologians have appropriated literature as a theological resource.

Sociologist Ana María Díaz-Stevens begins her study by noting, "Like other art forms, storytelling serves to express and to shape our longings and inner emotions because it speaks about the spirit and to the spirit. However, art also transcends the personal worldview to reflect the values upon which a society is either maintained or transformed."[12] Storytelling has value in its reflection of society and culture. The purpose of her study is twofold: "On the one hand, the mode in which the written production constructs a vision of ourselves, the divine, and our relationship to others and to the Creator; on the other hand, the

---

10. Raúl Fornet-Betancourt, ed., *Filosofía, teología, literatura: Aportes cubanos en los últimos 50 años,* Concordia Reihe Monographien 25 (Aachen: Wissenschaftsverlag Mainz, 1999).

11. Ana María Díaz-Stevens, "In the Image and Likeness of God: Literature as Theological Reflection," in *Hispanic/Latino Theology: Challenge and Promise,* ed. Ada María Isasi-Díaz and Fernando F. Segovia (Minneapolis: Fortress Press, 1996), 86–103; Shane Martin and Ernesto Colín, "The Novels of Graciela Limón: Narrative, Theology and the Search for Mestiza/o Identity," *Journal of Hispanic/Latino Theology* 7, no. 1 (August 1999): 6–26; Teresa Delgado, "Prophesy Freedom: Puerto Rican Women's Literature as a Source for Latina Feminist Theology," in *Religion and Justice: A Reader in Latina Feminist Theology,* ed. María Pilar Aquino, Daisy L. Machado, and Jeanette Rodríguez (Austin: University of Texas Press, 2002), 23–52.

12. Díaz-Stevens, "In the Image and Likeness of God," 86.

language used to convey this vision and how such language approxi-
mates a theological source."[13] Latino(a) literature, Díaz-Stevens notes,
is saturated with Christian images and themes. In addition, she continues, religious references abound in the Spanish vernacular.[14] Authors
that are of special importance for Díaz-Stevens's study include Miguel
de Cervantes and Gabriel García Márquez, whom she sees as exemplary
of the tendency in Latin American literature to create a Christ-like main
character.[15] The importance of these authors is found in their sociocultural import and the theological themes they raise. Unbound by the
constraints of formal theological discourse, Díaz-Stevens contends, these
authors employ an artistic form to explore those questions that burn
deeply in the human quest for meaning.

While Díaz-Stevens offers an important literary and sociological analysis in this essay, the theme of "literature as theology," which her title
claims, is not treated sufficiently. The reader is given indicators of how
one could examine Latino(a) literature in order to explore religious and
cultural themes. Díaz-Stevens offers an invaluable contribution in terms
of her analysis of the above-mentioned authors and their significance
for the exploration of Latino(a) culture, identity, and spirituality. However, the deeper methodological questions that plague this type of study
are left unanswered. In other words, what would it mean for Latino(a)
theologians to take literature seriously as theology? Is there a difference
between using literature *for* theology versus literature *as* theology? Last,
is all literature theological? If not, what are the criteria for claiming a
literary piece as theological?

In the essay coauthored by Martin and Colín the authors examine
one writer, Graciela Limón. Though not trained theologians, Martin
and Colín explore the importance of four of Limón's novels in light of
Latino(a) theology. They begin with a significant and challenging insight
for contemporary theologians:

> Increasingly, theologians ponder the actual capacity theology holds
> to impact the life of the average person. Some theologians wonder if
> complex theological areas of inquiry such as exegetical studies, ec-
> clesiology, christology, and missiology are more accessible through

---

13. Ibid., 87.
14. Some examples she cites are *si Dios quiere* (God willing) and *con el favor de Dios* (by
the grace of God), ibid., 92.
15. Ibid. She also examines the writings of Miguel de Unamuno, Antonio Machado, and
René Marqués.

genres such as anthropology, film, music or literature rather than through traditional theological scholarship. To be sure, the issues and events that drive theological inquiry are also found in artistic works, for these subjects permeate everyday life and make for dynamic material. In other words, it is human nature to grapple with the divine, whether one is a university theologian, artist or blue collar worker, thus the process of exploration appears in literary works about the lives of common people as much as in the pages of theological journals.[16]

As Martin and Colín indicate, the impact of theological texts on the concrete realities of peoples is a pressing concern. One manner to combat the isolation of theology, Martin and Colín hold, is the use of literature within theology. This would not be alien to the theological task, they contend, for they see literature and theology (among other disciplines) as sharing a common path.

For Martin and Colín theology and literature share the ability to express the divine presence in people's daily lives.[17] Regarding the novels of Limón, they contend, "Limón engages the dialogue between theology and literature, lays the groundwork for an articulation of Chicano theology through literature, and arrives at a *theology from within.*"[18] The accessibility of her novels (in contrast to academic theology) further supports the importance of her contribution. After briefly articulating an overview of four of Limón's novels, Martin and Colín move to examine the theological themes found therein.[19] These include *la lucha* (the struggle), *lo cotidiano* (daily life), and *mestizaje.* Unlike Díaz-Stevens, Martin and Colín explicitly connect these themes to the writings of Latino(a) theology, specifically the work of Latina theologians. In addition to these above-mentioned themes, Limón creates female characters who are empowered and contest oppressive stereotypes surrounding women. This leads Martin and Colín to claim, "In effect, Graciela Limón's novels and characters embody the objectives of *mujerista* theology as they point to a theology from within. Graciela Limón is an artist-*mujerista* theologian. She, like Latina feminist theologians, is

---

16. Martin and Colín, "The Novels of Graciela Limón," 6–7.
17. Ibid., 7.
18. Ibid.
19. The novels are *In Search of Bernabé* (1993), *The Memories of Ana Calderón* (1994), *Song of the Hummingbird* (1996), and *The Day of the Moon* (1999). All four novels are published by Arte Público Press (Houston).

clearly an ally of the *mujer*."[20] The presence of mestizo characters in Limón's novels, who struggle with questions of identity and hybridity, resonate with the privileged locus of *mestizaje* in Latino(a) theology. This hermeneutic is also applied to biblical stories, which Limón reinterprets through mestiza eyes.

Martin and Colín offer an exciting avenue for Latino(a) theologians to pursue through a dialogue of literature and theology. Their thoughtful analysis of Limón's novels is a model for preliminary explorations in this field. Their essay represents a dialogue in the truest sense, where Chicana literature and Latino(a) theology are placed in conversation with each other. This interchange leads them to claim of Limón, "Her works are notable for the way they make theology accessible and bring complex theological concerns to life."[21] The translation of theological concerns into accessible, contemporary language is a central feature of the theological task. It is not, however, the sole task of theology. Behind these translations is the knowledge of the history of the complexity of theology and the diversity of its expressions. In this sense, the conversation Martin and Colín pose must be grounded in the broader discipline of theology. Within Martin and Colín's analysis, Latino(a) theology sets the framework for the conversation. The authors explore how Limón's novels affirm the claims of Latino(a) theologians and translate them into more accessible language. In this model, however, literature is not given an authentic voice that stands on its own. Literature's theological truth claims are subject to academic theology. Limón's theological vision, after all, is not informed by a comprehensive background in theology. As I will later argue, only an understanding of literature and theology grounded in theological aesthetics will resolve some of these tensions.

The writings of Latina authors continue as the subject matter in the essay by Teresa Delgado, where she explores the contributions of four Puerto Rican women to Latino(a) theology: Nicholasa Mohr, Judith Ortiz Cofer, Esmeralda Santiago, and Rosario Ferré. Delgado's article is grounded in the thesis that, "I believe these Puerto Rican women writers are prophets for the Puerto Rican people, specifically, and for Latino/as in general. As such, their stories provide us with a *critical source* for the development of Latina feminist theology, in particular, and

---

20. Martin and Colín, "The Novels of Graciela Limón," 17.
21. Ibid., 25.

for U.S. Latino(a) theology in general."[22] These authors, Delgado contends, present an understanding of what it means to be human through the use of narrative and story. Through the imagination, literature offers a vision of the future that is transformative of the status quo. Delgado's article is grounded on five presuppositions regarding the relationship between theology and literature. First, Puerto Rican literature embodies a tradition of subversion and freedom. Second, literature reveals something to us surrounding the contradictions of our humanity. Third, the response to these contradictions offers a vision for a transformed future. Fourth, theology must embody liberative action. Last, an authentic Puerto Rican theology must emerge from the connections between culture and ritual.[23] Delgado's selection of these four authors is based on the understanding and challenge they pose to contemporary Puerto Rican culture and religiosity.

By naming these four authors as prophets, Delgado holds that their writings contain the message of God. The center of this message is love and justice. Though she does not examine Christian theology and Scripture in a substantial manner, Delgado bases her interpretation of Mohr, Ortiz Cofer, Santiago, and Ferré on this understanding, which is perhaps the greatest weakness of this text. The insights explored in her analysis of these four authors are not established on a strong theological foundation. In her concluding comments she writes, "We must create a new vision of our future in feminist terms."[24] While I do not disagree with Delgado's claim, for a Latino(a) theology this vision must be grounded in a theological vision as the foundation of this feminist hermeneutic. Only an understanding of literature and theology framed by theological aesthetics can address some of the tensions raised in the three articles explored in this section.

THEOLOGICAL AESTHETICS

Theological aesthetics is a growing area in contemporary theology. Though not necessarily a theological "school" or "field" per se, those authors working on theological aesthetics constitute a conversation or particular theological style grounded in their concern for Beauty. Theological aesthetics holds that in the encounter with Beauty there is an

22. Delgado, "Prophesy Freedom," 24.
23. Ibid., 26–28.
24. Ibid., 48.

experience of the Divine.[25] An emphasis on the aesthetic is based on the belief that within the realm of symbol, imagination, emotion, and art one finds a privileged expression of the encounter with the Divine and its articulation.[26] Theological aesthetics serves as a "corrective" to the highly textual approach of theology, which often does not incorporate the fullness of humanity's encounter with God. The emphasis on the metaphorical and poetic, however, does not come at the expense of the metaphysical. Instead, theological aesthetics argues that Beauty is a transcendental attribute of God; as such, Beauty is an aspect of God's revelation. Theological reflection on Beauty must therefore incorporate aesthetic expressions of the human encounter with Beauty's revelation. Of special attention is the relationship between aesthetics and ethics. Often, a hasty interpretation of aesthetics leads to an understanding of its focus as downplaying or obscuring the significance of ethics and social justice.[27] However, an emphasis on Beauty does not have to be at the expense of the Good, and can in fact inform one's commitment to social justice.[28]

In the area of Latino(a) theology, the works of Alejandro García-Rivera and Roberto S. Goizueta are central. As defined by García-Rivera, "Theological aesthetics recognizes in the experience of the truly beautiful a religious dimension."[29] In other words, theological aesthetics contends that Beauty is a result of divine initiative. Beauty not only is; the human receives it. "Theological aesthetics attempts to make clear once again

---

25. As defined by Richard Viladesau, "What is meant by 'theological aesthetics' in its wide sense is the practice of theology, conceived in terms of any of these three objects, in relation to any of the three objects... God, religion, and theology in relation to sensible knowledge (sensation, imagination, feeling), the beautiful, the arts." *Theological Aesthetics: God in Imagination, Beauty, and Art* (New York: Oxford University Press, 1999), 11.

26. Margaret Miles argues that the textual history of Christianity must be recognized for its elitism as it is written by culturally privileged, male, and upper-class authors. Margaret R. Miles, *Image as Insight: Visual Understanding in Western Christianity and Secular Culture* (Boston: Beacon Press, 1985), 9. In the area of Latino(a) theology, Orlando Espín argues that study of Latino(a) popular Catholicism is an avenue for retrieving the theology of the masses excluded from the canons of textual theological history. Orlando O. Espín, *The Faith of the People: Theological Reflections on Popular Catholicism* (Maryknoll, N.Y.: Orbis Books, 1997).

27. See Manuel J. Mejido, "A Critique of the 'Aesthetic Turn' in U.S. Hispanic Theology: A Dialogue with Roberto Goizueta and the Positing of a New Paradigm," *Journal of Hispanic Latino Theology* 8, no. 3 (February 2001): 18–48.

28. This goes contrary to the claim by Manuel J. Mejido, who sees the "aesthetic turn" in Latino(a) theology as alienating theology from the everyday struggles of Latino(a) communities. Mejido, "A Critique of the 'Aesthetic Turn' in U.S. Hispanic Theology."

29. Alejandro García-Rivera, *The Community of the Beautiful: A Theological Aesthetics* (Collegeville, Minn.: Liturgical Press, 1999), 9.

the connection between Beauty and the beautiful, between Beauty's divine origins and its appropriation by the human heart."[30] García-Rivera notes that in addressing both the objective and subjective dimensions of Beauty and its reception, theological aesthetics attempts to address modern suspicions surrounding the experience of Beauty. Building on the unity of the transcendentals as found in Hans Urs von Balthasar's theology, García-Rivera understands the True, the Good, and the Beautiful in terms of communities. This construction allows for a relational understanding of the transcendentals that addresses the reality of difference. The aesthetic principle that emerges from this is the lifting of the lowly, a subversive aesthetic norm with ethical implications.

Roberto S. Goizueta contends that the role of aesthetics is integral and organic to Latino(a) theology. "If Tridentine Western theology stressed the fact that God is known in the form of the True (Doctrine), and liberation theology that God is known in the form of the Good (Justice), U.S. Hispanic theology stresses the fact that God is known in the form of the Beautiful."[31] Integral to his understanding of theological aesthetics, and his consequent critique of modern and postmodern discourses, is the relationship between form and content.

> One of the most devastating consequences of Western rationalism on Christian theology has been the divorce between theological form and content...the depreciation of preconceptual knowledge, now universally suspect because of its diffuse and hence "countless" character. In turn, the traditional forms of communicating such knowledge — symbol, ritual, narrative, metaphor, poetry, music, the arts — are necessarily marginalized as unacademic and unscholarly, that is, as pure (aesthetic) form without (conceptual) content.[32]

The separation of form and content has affected both the sources and norms of theology. This divorce leads to the privileging of the abstract over the concrete, as well as theoretical knowledge over "common sense" knowledge. Goizueta argues that unless scholars reject the separation of form and content, they will never truly understand the popular religious

---

30. Ibid., 11.
31. Roberto Goizueta, *Caminemos con Jesús: A Hispanic/Latino Theology of Accompaniment* (Maryknoll, N.Y.: Orbis Books, 1995), 106.
32. Goizueta, "U.S. Hispanic Popular Catholicism as Theopoetics," in *Hispanic/Latino Theology: Challenge and Promise*, 261–88.

practices of Latino(a) peoples. Through the eyes of the poor, one's eyes are directed to divine praxis. However, one cannot separate the reception of God's love from the sociopolitical embodiment of that love in social praxis. Theology must be understood as sacramental, with an incarnation sense of the intrinsic relationship between form and content. Revelation cannot be separated from its incarnated manifestation. This sacramental understanding bears witness to Christ's incarnation and the wounded bodies of the oppressed and marginalized.

Interestingly, the theologies of García-Rivera and Goizueta are both influenced by the theological aesthetics and theo-dramatics of Hans Urs von Balthasar. Both use von Balthasar as a starting point for their theological aesthetics. Why von Balthasar? He is arguably at the forefront of theological aesthetics in twentieth-century Roman Catholic theology. Building on the insights of these Latino(a) theologians, I turn to the contribution of von Balthasar as a methodological framework for understanding literature as theology. While Goizueta and García-Rivera have examined certain aspects of von Balthasar's aesthetics, there has not been a study of the importance of literature in his theology in light of Latino(a) theologies.

LITERATURE AS THEOLOGY

Roman Catholic theologian Hans Urs von Balthasar is one of the most significant, and often overlooked, figures in twentieth-century theology. His massive collection of theological writings covers a broad range of topics, from the classic theological loci of Christology and ecclesiology to pastoral concerns such as women's ordination. This Swiss-born theologian, educated by and for some time a member of the Society of Jesus, is the author of the most substantial theological aesthetics of the twentieth century.

Von Balthasar begins volume one of his seven-volume aesthetics, *The Glory of the Lord,* by placing Beauty at the forefront of his theology, at the same time mourning its "demise" in modern discourse. "We here attempt to develop a Christian theology in the light of the third transcendental, that is to say: to complement the vision of the true and the good with that of the beautiful *(pulchrum)*."[33] This is an attempt, in von

---

33. Hans Urs von Balthasar, *Seeing the Form,* vol. 1 of *The Glory of the Lord: A Theological Aesthetics,* trans. of *Herrlichkeit: Eine Theologische Äesthetik,* ed. Joseph Fessio, S.J., and John Riches, trans. Erasmo Leiva-Merikakis (San Francisco: Ignatius Press, 1989), 9.

Balthasar's words, "to restore theology to a main artery which it has abandoned."[34] Beauty has lost its relevance. For von Balthasar, when Beauty suffers, so do the other two transcendentals, the True and the Good, for they lose their appeal; the ethical and aesthetic are in conjunction. The Good must be attractive; it must be Beautiful.[35] Without Beauty, the True and the Good become obscured. Without Beauty, the Good ceases to be attractive, Truth stops being reasonable.[36]

A central aspect of von Balthasar's intellectual background that has profoundly marked his theology is his studies in literature. As noted by Edward Oakes, von Balthasar's training in literature colors his theological method. "What makes a study of Balthasar's work with the German classics so important is the issue of interpretation: for it was from his study of the German classics that Balthasar first received his training as a scholar and thus first came to his method of textual, and even theological, interpretation."[37] However, the significance of von Balthasar's use of literature goes well beyond his textual method; it offers an interdisciplinary theological contribution. For von Balthasar, literary sources are theological. He does not examine literature in order to find religious or theological themes therein. Instead, von Balthasar holds literature to be theological.[38] However, von Balthasar does not uncritically accept all literature as theology. For him certain literary figures are also theologians. His aesthetics offers an example of his use of literature as theology.

---

34. Ibid.

35. As Edward Oakes notes, "Here perhaps is the key that unlocks the whole point of the Aesthetics, for beauty is inherently attractive, meaning that it draws contemplators out of themselves and into a *direct* encounter with the phenomenon manifesting itself, and this beauty, the contemplator knows, testifies to itself in a way that the True and the Good cannot do. Although all three transcendentals, the Beautiful, the Good, and the True, in the traditional Platonic understanding, are all inherent aspects of the nature of Being, nonetheless, we may doubt, and often do, the inherent goodness and truth of the being of the world." Edward Oakes, *Pattern of Redemption: The Theology of Hans Urs von Balthasar* (New York: Continuum, 1994), 143–45.

36. "In a world without beauty . . . in a world which is perhaps not wholly without beauty, but which can no longer see it or reckon with it: in such a world the good also loses its attractiveness. . . . In a world that no longer has enough confidence in itself to affirm the beautiful, the proofs of the truth have lost their cogency." von Balthasar, *Seeing the Form,* 19.

37. Oakes, *Pattern of Redemption,* 73.

38. Alois M. Haas notes that von Balthasar would most likely be unaccepted by literary scholars and theologians. "The reason is simply that von Balthasar lets the whole fullness of literary, philosophical, and theological mythical formulations converge toward an explicitly Christian mythic, while contemporary literary theology clearly tends toward a philosophical mediation between religion and literature." Alois M. Haas, "Hans Urs von Balthasar's 'Apocalypse of the German Soul': At the Intersection of German Literature, Philosophy, and Theology," in *Hans Urs von Balthasar: His Life and Work,* ed. David L. Schindler (San Francisco: Ignatius Press, 1991), 46.

In his introduction to volumes 2 and 3 of *The Glory of the Lord*, Balthasar maps out his intent to give flesh to the abstract principles found in volume one through the study of twelve figures. "It will try to do this by presenting a series of Christian theologies and world-pictures of the highest rank, each of which, having been marked at its centre by the glory of God's revelation, has sought to give the impact of this glory a central place in its vision."[39] Von Balthasar selects his authors based on their historical significance and role in Christian culture. In terms of the aesthetic criterion, works are not chosen merely because they discuss the beautiful. "Rather, what is decisive for a theological aesthetic occurs most centrally in the heart, in the original vision and in the middle point where the basic forms crystallize."[40] Balthasar also notes that the scope of Christian aesthetics is not limited to the twelve he chooses to examine.

Volumes two and three of *The Glory of the Lord* are entitled *Clerical Styles* and *Lay Styles*. These titles emerge from von Balthasar's division of theological aesthetics into two eras: clerical, where Beauty had an official place in the church, and lay, where Beauty is found outside of the church. For von Balthasar, the chronological dividing line is 1300. After 1300, Christian spirituality became marginalized from theological discourse. The authors examined in *Lay Styles* are therefore found on the margins of the institutional church; their theologies were not that of the mainstream. By naming these authors "lay," Balthasar is emphasizing this marginalization. Two of the authors, Hopkins and St. John of the Cross, are clerics, yet for von Balthasar they are "laymen" in light of the church's dominant discourse. John of the Cross, for example, is depicted as a response to both the collapse of the Medieval worldview and a response to the Reformation.[41] Von Balthasar defines the theologians in *Lay Styles* as "someone who feels misunderstood and shunted aside from the central concerns of the church *precisely because* of this concern for beauty."[42] Within his theology of the laity, however, von Balthasar views the laity as the center of the church. Therefore, the theologians of "Lay Styles" are marginalized from the institutional church while simultaneously expressing the heart of the Christian message.

---

39. Hans Urs von Balthasar, *The Glory of the Lord: A Theological Aesthetics*, vol. 2, *Studies in Theological Style: Clerical Styles*, trans. of *Herrlichkeit: Eine theologische Ästhetik, II: Fächer der Stile, I Klerical Style*, ed. John Riches, trans. Andrew Louth, Francis McDonagh, and Brian McNeil, C.R.V. (San Francisco: Ignatius Press, 1989), 13.
40. Ibid., 14.
41. Ibid., 105–71.
42. Oakes, *Pattern of Redemption*, 180.

Among the twelve selected, one finds figures whose significant contributions have been seen primarily in the field of literature. However, they have to meet Balthasar's criteria. "A few representatives of the world of letters had to be selected, but only insofar as their literary work stands in an immediate relationship to the vision and exposition of the biblical revelation and there is a fluent transition from it to theology."[43] This is not a marginal aspect of his work, for as Jeffrey Ames Kay notes, "The greatest significance of Balthasar's theological method lies in his incorporation in systematic theology of literary sources and of the sources traditionally handled by spiritual and mystical theology."[44] For von Balthasar, literature and the arts reveal something about being, and for this reason are theological.

> Balthasar's theology is marked out, that is, by his own conviction that in the great works of art, literature and music we do indeed perceive something of the truth and reality of *being*. Thus it is clearly of great interest to enquire after Balthasar's own understanding of an indebtedness to the great figures of the German tradition of letters with which he is engaged.... It is not simply questions of the formal similarities between literature, art and music, and theological perceiving that interest Balthasar (though such questions do concern him in Vol. 1 of *The Glory of the Lord*) but of the *content* of such widely varied visions.[45]

The content of literature and the arts reveals something about being, in a similar fashion to theological elaborations. This view must be seen in light of von Balthasar's contention that through the incarnation, Jesus Christ transformed the very nature of human culture and cultural expression. Because all of human culture has been transformed, literature is a vital resource of human expression of divine Glory. The use of literature as a theological resource and conversation partner is a hallmark of von Balthasar's theology. Emerging directly from his background in literary studies, von Balthasar's incorporation of literature gives theology an interdisciplinary dimension in its very foundation.

---

43. Balthasar, *Clerical Styles*, 16.
44. Jeffrey Ames Kay, *Theological Aesthetics: The Role of Aesthetics in the Theological Method of Hans Urs von Balthasar* (Bern: Herbert Lang; Frankfurt: Peter Lang, 1975), 91.
45. John Riches, "Afterword," in *The Analogy of Beauty: The Theology of Hans Urs on Balthasar*, ed. John Riches (Edinburgh: T. & T. Clark, 1986), 182.

CONCLUDING COMMENTS

Understanding literature as theology can have substantial implications on how one conceptualizes a theological methodology. To embrace literature in such a fashion is to enter into the realm of theological aesthetics, placing Beauty as a central dimension of the theological task. This is not to diminish scholarship that examines literature as a theological source. The sociological, cultural, and religious dimensions revealed in literature are vital for theology. Latino(a) theologians, who claim to place the faith of Latino(a) communities at the center of the theological task, must turn to literature as a resource for approaching and describing the faith and lives of Latino(a) peoples. However, a methodology that embraces literature as theology poses a deeper question, for it challenges contemporary theologians to take the aesthetic voice as a serious theological dialogue partner and resource. By way of conclusion, I would like to explore three implications of this study for Latino(a) theologians. These three areas should be understood as future directions for a theology that embraces the literary voice as theological. They are: literature as an avenue of revealing the Hispanic imagination, the implications of theological aesthetics, and literature as an avenue for combating the isolation of academic theology.

Returning to the theological aesthetics of Roberto S. Goizueta, he sees the theopoetic as an avenue for uncovering the Latino(a) imagination. A central claim in Goizueta's work is that, "A theology that fails to thus move and motivate cannot claim to be speaking of the liberating God of the exodus or the crucified God of Calvary."[46] Building on the work of Amos Niven Wilder, who writes, "We speak about a theopoetic because the theme of divinity requires a dynamic and dramatic speech," Goizueta highlights the need to reassess the form of theology.[47] In his proposal of a theopoetic, however, Goizueta is not suggesting a rejection of rational thought. He does not privilege the aesthetic form over the theological content. Instead Goizueta seeks to unite form and content through praxis. "The tone of our words and the way we speak them must be consonant with their content, the reality about which we speak; our theological words and the way we speak them must be able to convey, or connote, the fact that the reality about whom we speak — that is, God —

---

46. Goizueta, "U.S. Hispanic Popular Catholicism," 262.
47. Amos Niven Wilder, *Theopoetic: Theology and the Religious Imagination* (Philadelphia: Fortress Press, 1976), 1–2, cited in Goizueta, "U.S. Hispanic Popular Catholicism," 262.

transcends all words and concepts."[48] Not only must theology engage them in the symbolic and metaphorical, but also privilege the expressions of Latino(a) communities. "A theology that truly reflects and expresses 'the Hispanic mind' will do so not only in content but also in form; a U.S. Hispanic theology cannot help but be, at bottom, a theopoetic discourse nourished by the symbols, rituals, and stories in which are embodied our profound faith in the living God."[49] This is clearly seen in the works of Latino(a) theologians engaging U.S. Latino(a) theological aesthetics.

As stated above, theological aesthetics offers exciting new avenues for contemporary theology. These include not only a broadening of what one understands as theology, but also ontological implications within the re-covery of the transcendental of Beauty. For Latino(a) theologians, who are influenced in particular by Latin American liberation theologies, this has implications for how one understands the role of ethics and aes-thetics. This was seen, for example, in the work of Roberto Goizueta. Within María Pilar Aquino's theology, the role of the "primacy of de-sire" represents an aesthetic accent. Emphasizing the primacy of desire, Aquino holds, is a means of contesting the possibility of a detached, decontextualized, and purely abstract rationality. The primacy of desire highlights the role of emotion and desire in theological elaborations. This has implications for the very form of theological writings and sources. Aquino writes, "Therefore the language of poetry, play, and symbol be-come an appropriate way of expressing the understanding and wisdom of the faith, because it is the means of expressing the human person's deepest and most genuine aspirations and desire."[50]

Aquino is not alone in her emphasis on desire within the theological task. María Clara Bingemer, whose work is foundational for Aquino, writes, "The cold circumspection of purely scientific inquiry must give way to a new sort of systematics springing from the impulse of de-sire that dwells at the deepest level of human existence."[51] Desire, for

---

48. Goizueta, "U.S. Hispanic Popular Catholicism," 265.

49. Ibid., 269.

50. María Pilar Aquino, *Our Cry for Life: Feminist Theology from Latin America* (Mary-knoll, N.Y.: Orbis Books, 1993), 111. As noted by Viladesau, "Because they relate to a transcendent object, many of religion's expressions are appropriately nonverbal, and a 'nega-tive' hermeneutic must be applied even to its verbal expressions. The latter are more related to the metaphorical speech of poetry, which addresses the existential human condition, than to the abstract concepts of science" (*Theological Aesthetics,* 17).

51. María Clara Bingemer, "Women in the Future of the Theology of Liberation," in *Feminist Theology from the Third World: A Reader,* ed. Ursula King (Maryknoll, N.Y.: Orbis Books, 1994), 311.

Bingemer, is in fact central to the theological task. In both Aquino and Bingemer there is an aesthetic turn in their theological writings, informing a broader change in the form of theological method. This aesthetic emphasis is understood as the only adequate means of expressing the human's deepest faith and sentiments. As Brazilian theologian Ivone Gebara notes,

> In other words, to some extent this procedure means returning the poetic dimension of human life to theology, since the deepest meaning in the human being is expressed only through analogy; mystery is voiced only in poetry, and what is gratuitous is expressed only through symbols. Purely rational concepts do not take into account the meaning, desire, flavor, pleasure, pain, and mystery of existence.[52]

Aesthetic form is the fullest expression of desire, emotion, and faith, which Aquino, Gebara, and Bingemer see as central to both the theological task and an understanding of the human. Purely rational concepts are not adequate vehicles for expressing the fullness of the human.

A third implication of this study is found in the ability of literature to help overcome the growing isolation of academic theology. This occurs on two levels. Linked to the first two implications, literature is a means of tapping into the Latino(a) imagination in a way that rational, systematic theology does not. This is not to say that aesthetic forms of theological expression are irrational. However, by opening theology to the emotional and the poetic, literature moves the reader in ways that academic theology does not. Second, and here I am echoing the concerns of Martin and Colín, incorporating literature into the discipline of theology expands the accessibility of theological reflection. Literature, unlike academic theology, is a more widespread means of theological discourse. In addition, this contests the academic elitism that is often associated with theological reflection. Last, in the growing interdisciplinary climate of the academy, literature and theology form a welcome collaboration.

I have explicitly withheld examining the question of criteria. In other words, to the question, "Which literature is theology?" I have not offered a concrete answer. All literature is not theology. I also hold that to be theological, literature must be grounded in theology. In other

---

52. Ivone Gebara, "Women Doing Theology in Latin America," in *Feminist Theology from the Third World*, 56.

words, literature that is descriptive of religion or religious practices is not necessarily theology. As a growing area within contemporary theology, literature and theology still have these and many other questions to thoughtfully pursue. In a sense, as the door is opened to new and exciting voices within theology, I am not quite ready to begin closing it quite so hastily. Only through the further study of literature, fueled by theological aesthetics, will this question and more continue to be grappled with in the arena of contemporary theology. The implications of this have substantial methodological implications for theology, not only in terms of sources and theological style, but also in a serious consideration of the place of Beauty in contemporary theology. Through the incorporation of aesthetics, theology is better able to speak to and from the human heart. As a theology that names and remains grounded in its context, giving a preferential voice to silenced and marginalized peoples in light of God's revelation, Latino(a) theology plays a significant role in this endeavor. Latino(a) theologians show us the faith of the people, the beauty and diversity of creation, and the possibility of writing a theology that allows itself to be touched by God's glory and its manifestation here on earth.

7

"Liberation" in the Latino(a) Context

Retrospect and Prospect

CHRISTOPHER D. TIRRES

Theology does not just incidentally bring about freedom because it reflects on certain symbols or doctrines in certain ways; theology does not necessarily result in freedom because it offers theoretical arguments as to the nature of freedom. As a form of social and religious therapy, theology anticipates freedom, calling into question the way things are, seeking out distortions, provoking a new way of being and doing in history. As part of its practical nature, theology is inherently involved with emancipation and enlightenment, and its form must be critical: uncovering, revealing, hearing, and enlightening.

— Rebecca Chopp[1]

One of the most central, yet naggingly implicit and ambiguous, terms within U.S. Latino(a) theology is the term "liberation." While it is clear that U.S. Latino(a) theology recognizes itself as a contextual articulation of the theology of liberation, there is no clear consensus as to what "liberation" and "liberative action" mean — or should mean — with the Latino(a) context. The crux of this ambiguity seems to revolve around U.S. Latino(a) theology's desire to distinguish itself from Latin American liberation theology on grounds that the former is primarily concerned with the "aesthetic" question of culture whereas the latter is

---

Parts of this essay were presented to the Latina/o Religion, Culture, and Society Group at the Annual Meeting of the American Academy of Religion in Toronto, Canada, on November 23, 2002. I am grateful to Arturo Bañuelas and Enrique Dussel for their comments on earlier drafts.

1. Rebecca S. Chopp, *The Praxis of Suffering: An Interpretation of Liberation and Political Theologies* (Maryknoll, N.Y.: Orbis Books, 1986), 143.

primarily concerned with the "Marxian" question of economics.[2] Thus, whereas "liberation" in the Latin American context has been identified with the idea of social transformation and revolutionary action, "liberation" in the Latino(a) context has been identified with the idea of cultural resistance, particularly in terms of cultural identity and popular religion.

While such a distinction may be valid on descriptive and contextual grounds, the bifurcation of revolutionary action and resistant action is specious on methodological and political grounds. Clearly, contexts differ: empirically speaking, Latin America suffers from greater material poverty than does the United States, while the cultural discourse about "Latino(a)" or "Hispanic" concerns is primarily a North American preoccupation. However, some important questions need to be asked about the purported differences between these two theologies of liberation: Should U.S. Latino(a) theology's methodological *approach* to the question of oppression be fundamentally different from that of Latin American liberation theology? Is the Latino(a) "preferential option" no longer for an oppressed *Other,* but rather, for a social *designation,* namely, Latino(a) culture? And need U.S. Latino(a) theology's turn to culture *necessarily* imply a methodological distanciation from a Marxian-based social theory?

If U.S. Latino(a) theology is to take the task of liberation seriously, each of these questions needs to be answered in the negative. In what follows, I underscore the important contribution that U.S. Latino(a) theology has made to the idea of liberation as "resistance," but argue that a more explicit link needs to be made with the idea of liberation as "social transformation" and "revolution." Toward this end, I begin with an assessment of two exemplary works that have sought to elucidate

---

2. Roberto S. Goizueta, *Caminemos con Jesús: Toward a Hispanic/Latino Theology of Accompaniment* (Maryknoll, N.Y.: Orbis Books, 1995), 102. Alejandro García-Rivera makes a similar distinction in "A Wounded Innocence: Sketches for a Theology of Art and Its Implication for a New Ecumenism," *Journal of Hispanic/Latino Theology* 9, no. 4 (May 2002): 7–9. In my estimation, Harold J. Recinos offers a refreshing alternative to these views. Recinos characterizes Hispanic popular religion as a " 'poetics of power,' in which religious institutions and symbols are resources for political action. Moreover, the cultural practices evidenced in Salvadoran popular religion are best viewed in relation to issues of class, capitalism, and power," 116. Harold J. Recinos, "Popular Religion, Political Identity, and Life-Story Testimony in an Hispanic Community" in *The Ties That Bind: African American and Hispanic American/Latino/a Theologies in Dialogue,* ed. Anthony B. Pinn and Benjamín Valentín (New York, London: Continuum, 2001), 116–28.

this fundamental link but have fallen short: Andrés Guerrero's *A Chicano Theology* (1987) and Roberto Goizueta's *Caminemos con Jesús* (1995). As I will show, Guerrero's book implies a connection between cultural symbols and "the idea of a new socialism" just as Goizueta's work suggests a tie between affective engagement and ethical-political action. Both of these texts are significant in light of their attempt to join their respective versions of resistance and revolutionary social action, yet both fall short in terms of their execution. I discuss some of the reasons as well as offer some suggestions as for how to best navigate this impasse. Specifically, I suggest — with the help of Latin American liberation theologians and critical Marxist philosophers alike — that "resistance" and "revolution" must be taxonomically couched within the larger concept of "integral liberation" and that both concepts can be considered "creative acts of liberation." Such steps would help U.S. Latino(a) theology better develop its *critical* function whereby it explicitly calls into question dominant structures of oppression and, in doing so, helps to craft a social reality that is more fully human.

ANDRÉS GUERRERO'S *A CHICANO THEOLOGY*

I begin with an assessment of Andrés Guerrero's *A Chicano Theology*, which in its own way sets out to make a link between resistance and revolution. In this groundbreaking text, Guerrero attempts to see resistance — Chicano self-knowledge as embodied in the idea of *la raza cósmica* and the symbolic power of *la Virgen de Guadalupe* — alongside one revolutionary form of liberation — what Guerrero repeatedly calls the "idea of a new socialism." This book is path-breaking not only because it is one of the very earliest and boldest articulations of what we now call "Latino(a) theology," but also because it identifies a problem that has yet to be sufficiently answered by Latino(a) theologians, Goizueta included.[3]

---

3. Special mention should be made of Virgilio Elizondo's *Galilean Journey: The Mexican-American Promise* (Maryknoll, N.Y.: Orbis Books, 1983), which is widely considered the foundational text of U.S. Latino(a) theology. Though it doesn't explicitly address the relationship between resistance and revolution, it does suggest an implicit "critical" hermeneutics in the sense that I develop later in this essay. Briefly, Elizondo not only espouses action as a form of *critical thought,* but also he shows an appreciation for *fulfilling, utopic action,* both of which are characteristic of the critical tradition since Marx. (Note, respectively, the pedagogical work of Freire and the "utopic" orientations of the Frankfurt School.) As I read him, Elizondo's appreciation for "critical thought" emerges in his discussion of the mestizo's *response to* conquest and assimilation (chap. 2) as well as the community's *confrontation with* Jerusalem, the

A *Chicano Theology,* published in 1987, begins with an urgent and honest claim. Guerrero argues that "traditionally, our church has been irresponsible in developing a native clergy and native leadership. Today we are millions of people with no representative voice in church or government. We are beginning to realize our situation of oppression and to look for ways to fight toward liberation."[4] Indeed, Guerrero's words were incisive for their time.[5] During this period of the mid- to late 1980s, groups like ACHTUS, Padres, and Hermanas — all interested in developing "a native clergy and leadership" — were either just being formed or still in their nascent stages.

Throughout his text, Guerrero seems to perceive a connection between cultural resistance, which is emboldened by cultural symbols, and revolutionary action. Guerrero writes, for example, of the "unifying strength" of the symbol of Guadalupe.[6] At the same time, Guerrero stresses the political character of Guadalupe and describes her as "more apt to choose some type of socialist government as an option for the poor."[7] Here, the parallel between a symbol of resistance and the idea of a new, revolutionary social order is striking, and is confirmed when Guerrero continues: "Guadalupe is a symbol of *resistance* against exploitative and unjust wages. She symbolizes *direct action* against the unequal destruction of resources and goods [emphasis added]."[8]

Although *A Chicano Theology* is extremely suggestive in what it implies between resistance and a new social order, the text remains incomplete insofar as it does not adequately address *how* cultural symbols may lead to a new socialism. It leaves the reader wondering how cultural resistance and political revolution are fundamentally connected. Ultimately, the reader is left with two implicit suggestions regarding their relationship, both of which deserve further scrutiny.

First, Guerrero seems to suggest that cultural symbols may lead to a new socialism based on a common group identity and a shared sense of mission. Throughout his book, Guerrero invokes the language of

---

symbolic center of power (chaps. 5, 8). Similarly, Elizondo points us in the direction of "fulfilling, utopic action" in his valuation of the culturally rich popular *expressions* of faith as well as the gospel promise of the fulfillment of *new life* (chaps. 6, 9).

4. Andrés Gonzales Guerrero, *A Chicano Theology* (Maryknoll, N.Y.: Orbis Books, 1987), 30.

5. Published in 1987, *A Chicano Theology* is based on Andrés G. Guerrero's Harvard Divinity School doctoral dissertation, completed three years earlier in 1984.

6. Ibid., 143.

7. Ibid.

8. Ibid.

"we Chicanos," which is, in actuality, a reflection of his interviews with nine prominent Chicano leaders. The fact that the nine people Guerrero interviews all have a clear sense of identity and mission is apparent. What remains to be seen, however, is if the identity of the Mexican American community at large embraces a particular group ideology and sense of purpose.[9] Seen in light of Guerrero's "idea of a new socialism," Guerrero's faith in "we Chicanos" is analogous to Marx's misplaced hope in the proletariat. Both Marx and Guerrero invoke the *idea* of a distinct group that purportedly shares a uniform ideology and mission. Just as Marx never empirically shows how alienated labor may give rise to a critical and revolutionary consciousness among the proletariat, Guerrero has difficulty moving from the general idea of "we Chicanos" to the reality of an extremely diverse community whose history, though shared, may not automatically lead to a common, shared sense of purpose.

Second, it seems that Guerrero attempts to make a connection between resistance and revolution by identifying the Chicano leader as the means by which symbols can be made revolutionary. While Guerrero is no doubt correct to highlight the importance of the organic intellectual in the process of liberation, it is striking that his concept of liberation seems to rest on the effectiveness of Chicano leaders. In a telling passage, Guerrero writes,

> A Chicano theology can emphasize the power of Guadalupe as a liberating influence provided that the people realize that the process of liberation is going on. If the people do not realize that the process

---

9. Having synthesized his conversations with the nine Chicano leaders, Guerrero writes: "We have faith as Christians that God exists, and we believe that Jesus Christ is God's only begotten Son. We also trust that these articles of faith are true because we have been taught that they are so by our leaders, by the tradition of the church, and by our parents who are part of a larger believing community" (105). While this is probably true for the vast majority of Chicano/as (and Latino/as, for that matter), it clearly is not true for all. Strategically speaking, Guerrero's often totalizing language of "we" could have been tempered by more inclusive language like, "in general, we believe x" or "oftentimes, we may do y" so as to account for the reality of an empirically diverse and plural Chicano community. Marcelo Suárez-Orozco offers two excellent studies on the empirical diversity of the Mexican and Latino(a) communities: *Crossings: Mexican Immigration in Interdisciplinary Perspectives* (Cambridge, Mass.: David Rockefeller Center for Latin American Studies, Harvard University Press, 1998), and *Latinos: Remaking America*, ed. Marcelo Suárez-Orozco and Mariela M. Páez (Berkeley: University of California Press, 2002). The question of how such diversity may be constructively theorized from within U.S. Latino theology is adeptly considered by Michelle A. González in "Nuestra Humanidad: Toward a Latina Theological Anthropology," in the *Journal of Hispanic/Latino Theology* 8, no. 3 (February 2001): 49–72.

is happening, then the symbol will continue to be used against them. If this is the case, then a Chicano theology urges that the Chicano leaders who recognize the process of liberation translate that message to their people. A Chicano theology insists that church leaders who read the signs of the times ought not to betray their people by keeping the liberating significance of Guadalupe from them.[10]

Such a passage not only seems to suggest a top-down view of the liberation process in which leaders discern the significance of a symbol and benevolently decide to pass on this knowledge to the people, but also it seems to miss the idea, articulated so well by Victor Turner, that symbols themselves function as performative "mirrors" of the people's own intrinsic agency.[11] In other words, the symbol itself is already a reflection of the people's "most salient opinions, imageries, tropes, and ideological perspectives," whether or not leaders recognize the symbol as significant or not.[12] Having said this, I do agree with Guerrero's more general insinuation that organic leaders can serve a useful function in their roles as intellectual critics who point, for example, to the potentially oppressive aspects of symbols. Such a view highlights organic leaders not as primary or privileged interpreters who are able to "keep the liberating significance of [symbols] from [the people]," but rather as critical interpreters among many.

Guerrero's *A Chicano Theology* stands as an important political-theological landmark at the dawn of the academic discourse of U.S. Latino(a) theology.[13] In spite of its failure to draw an adequate connection between cultural symbols and popular religiosity, on the one hand, and revolutionary consciousness and action, on the other, this text helped to set the agenda for what was to come in Latino(a) theology. In what follows, I consider in some depth another noteworthy, and philosophically more rigorous, foray in this direction: the work of Roberto Goizueta.

---

10. Guerrero, *A Chicano Theology,* 147.

11. Victor Turner, "Are There Universals of Performance in Myth, Ritual, and Drama?" in *By Means of Performance: Intercultural Studies of Theatre and Ritual,* ed. Richard Schechner and Willa Appel (Cambridge: Cambridge University Press, 1990), 8–18.

12. Ibid., 17.

13. As a self-identifying, intentional, and systematic body of scholarly work, "Latino(a) theology" has emerged within the last two decades. This being said, one must note that theological reflection *desde el margen Hispano* has, in actuality, been taking place for centuries, beginning with the dramatic and violent clash of cultures between the Spaniards, their African slaves, and the Amerindians in the 1520s.

ROBERTO GOIZUETA'S *CAMINEMOS CON JESÚS*

In his highly suggestive work, *Caminemos con Jesús: Toward a Hispanic/ Latino Theology of Accompaniment* (1995), Roberto S. Goizueta develops some of the same themes as Guerrero's *A Chicano Theology,* namely, the importance of popular religion, the cultural aesthetics of José Vasconcelos,[14] and the attempt to connect cultural expression with ethical-political action. As regards the latter, Goizueta puts forward a provocative reinterpretation of praxis in light of Hispanic experience and, in so doing, goes philosophically deeper than Guerrero in attempting to link everyday cultural expressions, embodied in popular religion, with socially transformative ethical-political action. This sophisticated reinterpretation of praxis deserves our further attention, scrutiny, and critique.[15] I will address this question both in this section and below in the section "U.S. Latino(a) Theology and Critical Social Theory."

In a number of articles and books,[16] Goizueta argues that the modern notion of "praxis" is latent with ambiguities.[17] A central problem is that

---

14. While Guerrero's and Goizueta's retrieval of an indigenous "American" philosopher is commendable, I find their choice of Vasconcelos more problematic than useful. Both have to backstep significantly in their appropriation of Vasconcelos. Guerrero writes that "Vasconcelos recognized the genius of [the] social phenomenon [of *La Raza*], which was unique to Latin America. *La Raza's* contribution was its concept of *mestizaje*. It was an inclusivistic model of social-racial integration" (*A Chicano Theology,* 123). Yet, soon thereafter, Guerrero is forced to concede that this model was not inclusivistic at all: "In trying to prove his point, Vasconcelos ran into trouble when he used the racist model of the eugenicists, with whom he was in dialogue. This model places the white first and the black last in its structure. By coming to our understanding of *La Raza* from the following analysis of our own perspective and within our own dialogue, we will, I hope, build a truer concept of our experience (with its nonracist model) than Vasconcelos, who was dialoguing with racist purists" (123–24). One is left wondering: Why begin with Vasconcelos at all?

15. Recently, Manuel Mejido has put forth a penetrating critique of Goizueta's "aesthetic turn," a critique with which I mostly agree. In this essay, I seek to add my own insights and clarifications to Goizueta's work so as to move the conversation forward. While I agree with Mejido that "one must wonder if [Goizueta] achieves the goal he sets for himself: the development of a more comprehensive notion of praxis that adequately balances the aesthetic, ethical-political, and poietic moments of human action," I am not so quick as Mejido to scrap the "aesthetic turn" altogether, given that this "turn," if approached correctly, can be made critically and with an eye to the political. See Manuel J. Mejido, "A Critique of the 'Aesthetic Turn' in U.S. Hispanic Theology: A Dialogue with Roberto Goizueta and the Positing of a New Paradigm," *Journal of Hispanic/Latino Theology* 8, no. 3 (February 2001): 18–48.

16. Goizueta, *Caminemos con Jesús;* "U.S. Hispanic Popular Catholicism as Theopoetics," in *Hispanic/Latino Theology: Challenge and Promise,* ed. Ada María Isasi-Díaz and Fernando F. Segovia (Minneapolis: Fortress Press, 1996), 261–88; and "Rediscovering Praxis: The Significance of U.S. Hispanic Experience for Theological Method," in *Mestizo Christianity: Theology from the Latino Perspective,* ed. Arturo J. Bañuelas (Maryknoll, N.Y.: Orbis Books, 1995), 84–103.

17. Goizueta seems to be drawing primarily on the work of Lobkowicz, Lamb, and Boff: Nikolaus Lobkowicz, *Theory and Practice: History of a Concept from Marx to Aristotle* (Notre

"praxis," which Goizueta describes as "communal or intersubjective action that has no external end or goal other than the action or relationship itself"[18] is often reduced to "poiesis," which he considers to be "an activity that seeks some end external to the performance itself."[19] In one sense, Goizueta's concern with a modern "reduction" of praxis is warranted given the dangers of modern technical rationality, which tends to value human action as a measurable "end" rather than a processual and interrelational "means." Furthermore, communal, affective exchange as "means" (and as principally embodied in the form of language) is indeed a necessary precondition of any teleological "end" and, in this sense, I would agree that it is correct to say that communal, intersubjective action is a foundational moment for human action.[20] But Goizueta takes the argument one step further and proffers that communal, intersubjective action has "no external end or goal other than the action or relationship itself." One must ask if, despite his best intentions, Goizueta puts forward an exaggerated and misleading abstraction of human action as "an end in itself."

Goizueta attempts to support his distinction between "praxis" and "poiesis" in terms of the perceived difference between humanistic "doing" and technical "making." For Goizueta, the former is captured in Aristotle, for whom living itself is the fundamental form of praxis, and the latter in Marx, given his stress on humankind's productive ability:

Dame, Ind.: University of Notre Dame Press, 1967); Matthew L. Lamb, *Solidarity with Victims: Toward a Theology of Social Transformation* (New York: Crossroad, 1982), 61–99, and "Praxis," in *The Dictionary of Theology*, ed. Joseph Komonchack, Mary Collins, and Dermot Lane (Wilmington, Del.: Michael Glazer, 1988), 784–87; and Clodovis Boff, *Theology and Praxis: Epistemological Foundations*, trans. Robert R. Barr (Maryknoll, N.Y.: Orbis Books, 1987). It would seem to me that the work of Bernstein and Chopp (both of whom Goizueta cites) would call into question the argument that Goizueta develops concerning "aesthetic praxis" as an end in itself. Richard J. Bernstein, *Praxis and Action: Contemporary Philosophies of Human Activity* (Philadelphia: University of Pennsylvania Press, 1971); Rebecca S. Chopp, *The Praxis of Suffering: An Interpretation of Liberation and Political Theologies* (Maryknoll, N.Y.: Orbis Books, 1986).

18. Goizueta, "U.S. Hispanic Popular Catholicism as Theopoetics," 264.

19. Goizueta, *Caminemos con Jesús*, 87.

20. Up to this point Goizueta's argument is akin to Jürgen Habermas's discourse ethics. See Jürgen Habermas, *The Theory of Communicative Action*, trans. Thomas McCarthy (Cambridge: Polity Press, 1986–89). One question that may be asked of both authors, however, is whether communicative action is a sufficient *critical* basis for emancipatory social action. For a good overview on the relationship between discourse ethics and political/liberation theologies, see Edmund Arens, "Interruptions: Critical Theory and Political Theology between Modernity and Postmodernity," in *Liberation Theologies, Postmodernity, and the Americas*, ed., David Batstone, Eduardo Mendieta, Lois Ann Lorentzen, and Dwight Hopkins (London and New York: Routledge, 1997), 222–42.

"If Aristotle identifies human life with praxis, inasmuch as life is always an end in itself, Marx identifies human life with productive labor that we actualize, or 'produce,' ourselves as persons."[21] One should note, however, that for Aristotle and Marx alike the distinction between praxis and poiesis is not so clear-cut. As one respected scholar of Aristotle points out, "commentators...often fail to face the real difficulty, that actions often or always *are* productions and productions often or always *are* actions."[22] Though the craftsman makes the stool for "technical" purposes (e.g., sitting), the stool may be finely constructed, and thus, aesthetically pleasing. Likewise, when the just man is paying off his debt *by* mending his neighbor's fence, "How...is one to understand the thesis that paying off a debt is an action but mending a fence is a production?"[23] As such examples show, praxis and poiesis may be seen as two sides of the same coin. While functionally distinct, they imply the same root action. As John Dewey reminds us, "It is no linguistic accident that 'building,' 'construction,' 'work,' designate both a process and its finished product. Without the meaning of the verb that of the noun remains blank."[24] In identifying poiesis with an "end in itself," Goizueta overlooks the possibility that poiesis may, in fact, encompass a "creative," praxic dimension.

One must similarly be attentive to the multiple notions of praxis within Marx's thought. Overall, Goizueta argues that Marx reduces praxis to poiesis insofar that Marx defines human praxis in terms of a human being's productive capacity through labor.[25] In doing so, Goizueta also critiques "some Latin American liberation theologians" who have been influenced by what he refers to as the "Marxian notion of praxis."[26] While Goizueta's interpretation of a reductionistic technical

21. Goizueta, "Rediscovering Praxis," 88.
22. J. L. Ackrill, "Aristotle on Action," in *Essays on Aristotle's Ethics,* ed. Amélie Oksenberg Rorty (Berkeley: University of California Press, 1980), 94.
23. Ibid., 94.
24. John Dewey, *Art as Experience* (New York: Perigree Books, 1980), 51.
25. To be sure, Goizueta takes an important step, at least in regard to Marx, in recognizing that Marx's interpretations of praxis are varied and multivalent. "It is only fair to note," writes Goizueta in a footnote, "that, while so-called orthodox Marxism came to interpret Marx in this reductionist manner, there are elements of Marx's thought, especially in his early writings, that would support arguments against such a reductionist interpretation." Goizueta, "Rediscovering Praxis," 99 n. 13, . See also *Caminemos con Jesús,* 85. Thus, to be fair to Goizueta, although the thrust of his argument tends to move toward a rejection of Marx, Goizueta does allow for the *possibility* that nonreductionist elements of Marx's thought may still be valuable resources for U.S. Latino(a) theological method.
26. Goizueta, *Caminemos con Jesús,* 82–88; "Rediscovering Praxis," 88, 99 n. 2, 99 n. 9.

making may capture well the spirit of orthodox or "vulgar" Marxism, one should note that the early Marx, especially, defines human action not in terms of productive labor, but more generally, in terms of "free-conscious activity" as it exists intersubjectively between people.[27] As with Aristotle, the separation of praxis from poiesis in Marx is once again not so facile and obvious.

At this point, Goizueta's attempt to distinguish praxis from poiesis may be both positively and negatively assessed. The positive contribution thus far is twofold: Goizueta is right to warn against the modern danger of reducing human action to a "mere" measurable and technical-rational end, and he is correct to underscore the communal dimension of human action as a fundamental precondition for knowledge and ethics. However, Goizueta's characterization of Aristotle's humanistic "doing" and Marx's technical "making" tends to be overblown. These poles become the straw men by which Goizueta invokes the idea of an action that has "no external end or goal other than the action or relationship itself."[28]

Unfortunately, this erroneous abstraction of praxis as an "end in itself"[29] is further enforced by Goizueta's appeal to the aesthetics of Mexican philosopher José Vasconcelos. Goizueta draws on Vasconcelos to highlight "the special pathos of beauty" by which "Vasconcelos means the 'empathic fusion' between subject and object that takes place in the aesthetic experience (i.e., the experience of beauty, or a work of art), wherein the person, or subject, loses him or herself in the experience."[30] This "aesthetic experience" is not only to be understood in terms of an

27. As I discuss momentarily, this insight has had a significant impact on the nonorthodox versions of critical, or cultural, Marxism that emerged after Marx, particularly various thinkers and schools attentive to the question of Marxist aesthetics. Mejido correctly points out that for Latin American philosopher Enrique Dussel, Marx's stress on person-to-person relationship figures so prominently that the essential relation in Marx is not the "subject's labor to the object of nature," but rather, the relation of "subject to subject" "as a practical, ethical relationship." And even though others, such as Jürgen Habermas, tend to read Marx as having a *tendency* to reduce "social praxis to one of its moments, namely work," we must accept the fact that social praxis as understood by Marx includes *both* "work" *and* "interaction." Enrique Dussel, *The Underside of Modernity: Apel, Ricoeur, Rorty, Taylor, and the Philosophy of Liberation*, trans. and ed., Eduardo Mendieta (Atlantic Highlands, N.J.: Humanities Press, 1996), 220. Jürgen Habermas, *Toward a Rational Society* (London: Heinemann; Boston: Beacon, 1970), quoted in Gajo Petrovic, "Praxis," in *A Dictionary of Marxist Thought*, ed. Tom Bottomore (Cambridge, Mass.: Harvard University Press, 1983), 388.

28. Goizueta, "U.S. Hispanic Popular Catholicism as Theopoetics," 264.

29. "Praxis is nothing other than human intersubjective action — that is, the relationships among whole human persons in community — as an end in itself," ibid.

30. Goizueta, *Caminemos con Jesús*, 91.

isolated event, as in the occasional appreciation of a work of art, but also in terms of the ongoing, lived experience of *mestizaje,* or cultural and biological fusion. In this sense, the highest form of empathic fusion, empathic love, refers not only to discreet *acts* of loving or "fusing," but also to the very embodiment of that cultural and biological fusion, the *life* of the mestizo his or herself. Thus, the parallel that is to be drawn is this: just as the work of art fuses subject and object, so too does the mestizo fuse the Spanish and the Indian. Both cases result in empathic love, which for the mestizo is the embodiment of life itself. Says Goizueta: "Life itself — understood as a verb ('living') rather than as an object of analysis — is never ethical or unethical, rational or irrational: life simply *is.*"[31] Furthermore, "Only the aesthetic sense allows us to live life itself, as an end in itself rather than as something to be understood or some set of acts with an ethical purpose. If life has no other purpose than to *be,* then the highest form of life — the only true and good life — is the life of enjoyment, the life of celebration and play."[32]

Here, Goizueta realizes that Vasconcelos's aesthetic theory is only worth retrieving up to a certain point given its painful ethical and political shortcomings. "Since Vasconcelos fails to systematically integrate the material and social dimensions of human into his aesthetics, his notion of mestizaje remains . . . idealistic and sentimentalized. . . . Mestizaje becomes an affective, emotional action which, as such, has superseded ethical-political action and, even more so, productive action."[33] Goizueta's assessment of Vasconcelos is absolutely correct here, and I could not agree more with the statement that "empathic fusion is mediated, not only by feelings but also by action, and not only by our physical bodies, but also by the political, economic, and social structures in which we participate."[34] What is incredibly ironic, however — and this is where the contradiction of Goizueta's own systematics becomes crystal clear — is that this statement is "so central to [Latin American] liberation theology," as Goizueta notes in a footnote.[35] Goizueta apparently wants to have it both ways: he critiques Latin American liberation theology for its tendency to reduce praxis to poiesis (insofar that it retains Marx's

---

31. Ibid., 93.
32. Ibid., 94.
33. Ibid., 122.
34. Ibid., 125.
35. "The insight, so central to liberation theology, remains inadequately addressed in European theological aesthetics, such as in the otherwise masterful work of Hans Urs von Balthasar," ibid., 125.

"ambiguous" use of praxis), yet he ushers in liberation theology when he
is in need of economic and political "mediation" (e.g., Marx's dialectical
approach, though Goizueta doesn't seem willing to admit this). One can
only ask: Why bring in Vasconcelos in the first place if ethical, political,
and social mediations — which are absolutely lacking in Vasconcelos —
are so central to a proper understanding of praxis?

In the final analysis, Goizueta is drawn to the chimerical, idealized
concept of praxis as an "end in itself," beauty "in itself," and empathic fusion "in itself." These abstractions would presumably require
no degree of teleological, poietic "making," and, thus, imply no sense
of teleology, given that they simply "are." In spite of his best intentions,
Goizueta's attempt to link the praxis of resistance, on the one hand,
with the poiesis of social transformation, on the other, falls short given
the internal inconsistencies of his argument. To be sure, there are two
other ways that Goizueta attempts to link resistance and revolution, and
I address these strategies at the end of this essay.

INTERPRETING "LIBERATION": TWO FRAMEWORKS

Both Guerrero and Goizueta highlight cultural resistance — Guerrero in
terms of the power of cultural symbols, Goizueta in terms of "aesthetic
praxis" — so as to draw a connection with the liberative aspects of social
transformation and revolution. However, both authors fail to make an
adequate connection between these two moments of liberation. In what
follows, I would like to consider two frameworks that may speak to
how this connection could be made more explicitly, thereby revealing
their common, organic roots.

First, Leonardo Boff's understanding of "integral liberation" inge-
niously highlights how revolutionary action and cultural resistance are
best understood as two *categorical subsets* of liberation among many.
Boff argues that an integral liberation theology, in whichever cultural
context it may arise, has "a variety of accents" though it has "only one
point of departure — a reality of social misery — and one goal — the
liberation of the oppressed." "There are different ways of developing
this basic experience [of liberation]," Boff writes, "and this is where a
variety of accents can be identified."[36]

---

36. Leonardo Boff and Clodovis Boff, *Salvation and Liberation*, trans. Robert R. Barr (Maryknoll, N.Y.: Orbis Books), 24–25. Boff puts forward the following nine accents: (a) liberation

U.S. Hispanic theology — if not North American contextual theologies at large — has articulated especially well two of these accents, namely, a people's potential for *resistance,* and the idea of the people as *agent* of their own liberation. As a response to a history of double violence — not only of "the obvious violence of the physical conquest, but also the deeper violence of the disruption and attempts to destroy the conquered's inner worldvision, which gives cohesion and meaning to existence"[37] — Latino(a) theology has emphasized in myriad ways the centrality of a people's agency and their ability to resist. Virgil Elizondo captures a core conviction of Latino(a) theology when he writes: "Despite all oppression, the people still [have] the strength to resist."

Yet, in light of the idea of integral liberation, Latino(a) theology can benefit from developing other "accents" of liberation. "Integral liberation" challenges Latino(a) theologians to continually reassess what is meant by "social misery" and "the oppressed." It urges Latino(a) theologians to consider social misery in its variety of forms, not only in terms of race and culture, but also in terms of the economy, the military, patriarchy, homophobia, and ecology. In short, integral liberation demands that Latino(a) theology be a public theology in its broadest and best sense.[38]

Boff undoubtedly provides U.S. Latino(a) theology with a useful taxonomy of liberation. Yet, a fundamental question may still be asked: What are the distinctive *qualities* of "resistance" and "revolution" that allow these concepts to be grouped under the rubric "liberation" in the first place?

---

spirituality ("the spiritual moment that gives rise to the theology of liberation. In contact with the poor, who constitute a whole exploited class, a person experiences a genuine encounter with the Lord and makes a commitment to justice, which is the prime characteristic of the kingdom of God"); (b) a liberative rereading of the Scriptures; (c) a rereading of the liberation content in theology ("All themes in theology have a social and utopian dimension, which, in a sociopolitical context [of oppression], must be recovered and placed in the service of the liberation process"); (d) theological reflection on an analysis of reality (which includes both a scientific analysis on the mechanisms that produce oppression as well as a faith interpretation of this analysis); (e) a people's potential for resistance; (f) the people as agent of their own liberation; (g) a popular pedagogy of liberation (which integrally links ideas of participation, democracy, and liberation); (h) rereading of history from the viewpoint of the defeated; and (i) the theory of the theology of liberation (which examines the methodological and epistemological scope and limits of the theology of liberation).

37. Virgil Elizondo, "*Mestizaje* as a Locus of Theological Reflection," in *Mestizo Christianity,* 10.

38. A notable step in this direction is Benjamín Valentín, *Mapping Public Theology: Beyond Culture, Identity, and Difference* (Harrisburg, Pa.: Trinity Press International, 2002).

In addressing this question, I find especially illuminating Hans Joas's philosophical work on the creative dimensions of action. Though Joas, a sociologist, is primarily concerned with the idea of creativity, his insights have direct bearing on the idea of "liberation" insofar that liberation already implies the "creation" of newfound forms of emancipation. Concepts like "new life" and "fulfillment," so prominent within liberationist discourse, for example, can speak equally to the idea of liberation as well as creation.[39] Given that liberative acts are, at their core, also creative acts, I would like to proceed by illustrating how various metaphors of creativity may speak to various shades of liberation. Joas identifies five metaphors — expression, production, revolution, the philosophy of life, and pragmatic intelligence and reconstruction — all of which speak to the "creativity of action." Given the concerns of this essay, I limit my comments to the first three metaphors — expression, production, and revolution.[40]

Expression is a metaphor that "circumscribes creativity primarily in relation to the subjective world of the actor."[41] Expression suggests novelty. One does not fully understand the significance of a vague idea until one expresses it, but when an idea is expressed, it may strike us as original and fresh. This theory of expression, as developed by Johann Gottfried Herder, highlights the creative self-expression not only of the poet, but of collectivities and cultures as well. Herder "conceived of cultural forms in terms of collective self-realization. Language, literature, religion, all the institutions of a people are themselves either a successful or an inappropriate expression of the life of that people."[42] This idea of

---

39. The parallel between human creation and divine liberation is a longstanding one, having its basis not only in the ancient Greek roots of Christianity, but also and especially in the debates of the early Renaissance about the creative ability of human beings themselves in light of the traditional understanding of *creatio ex nihilo*. Hans Joas, *The Creativity of Action*, trans. Jeremy Gaines and Paul Keast (Cambridge: Polity Press, 1996), 74. Also M. H. Abrams, *Natural Supernaturalism: Tradition and Revolution in Romantic Literature* (New York: Norton, 1971).

40. Although the focus of this essay is on these three metaphors, I do believe that the fifth metaphor — the pragmatic insight into "intelligence and reconstruction" — deserves Latino(a) theology's further attention. Briefly, the pragmatic model is useful insofar as it *encompasses* expression, production, and revolution in terms of habitual and self-corrective social action. In particular, I find John Dewey's aesthetics especially instructive, given Dewey's attention to everyday action, the functional significance of the means-end relationship, and the socially reconstructive character of aesthetics as the very "art of experience." One challenge in using the pragmatic model is keeping intact and making explicit the political dimensions it subsumes, namely, expression's emphasis on agency, production's insights into material preconditions and *praxis*, and revolution's utopic hope.

41. Joas, *The Creativity of Action*, 71.

42. Ibid., 82.

collective forms of self-expression as being the "life of a people" ties in with Latino(a) theology's understanding of *latinidad* as intimately linked with popular religion and the power of shared, cultural symbols. At its best, the symbol of Guadalupe, for example, is an expression of the life of a people, a collective articulation of the people's distinctiveness and originality.[43]

Second, the production metaphor "relates creativity to the objective world, the world of material objects that are the conditions and means of action."[44] While the expression paradigm highlights the creative act that we as individuals or as collectivities articulate, the production paradigm asks us to first consider the preconditions necessary for the possibility of this expression, such as the material objects that aid human acts of creation. These material objects can range from nature's raw materials that humankind subsequently refines, a canvas for a painting, a book that may open up imaginative spaces in our mind, or our very hands, limbs, and bodies, through which we continually "produce" and "reproduce" new realities.

Karl Marx is, of course, the great spokesperson for the production paradigm, which is often connected to another related metaphor, that of revolution. Revolution "assumes that there is a potential of human creativity relative to the social world, namely that we can fundamentally reorganize the social institutions that govern human society."[45] Here, emphasis is placed on the idea of replacing the current social and political order, which is captured in what Guerrero calls "the idea of a new socialism" and what Goizueta refers to as "social transformation." The revolution paradigm is also the paradigm that has, for better or for worse, often been associated with Latin American liberation theology.

Regarding the metaphors discussed thus far, it is clear that U.S. Latino(a) theology tends to work in the theoretical mode of expression, as seen especially in its articulation of popular religion and its symbols. As an oppositional force to dominant culture, popular religion "resists" cultural hegemony, and as a force of resistance, it "expresses" a people's agency. This is to say that by taking seriously the realm of

---

43. Whether one believes that the symbol "itself" offers new expression or that the social consensus gained around the symbol is the proper source for expression, what remains clear is that a new cultural vision — whether liberating or oppressive — is being conveyed, enunciated, and "expressed."

44. Joas, *The Creativity of Action*, 71.

45. Ibid.

culture, Latino(a) theology helps give voice, helps "press out" or, liter-
ally, "ex-press," the inner strength of a people. Without a doubt, this is
one of Latino(a) theology's greatest contributions.

This being said, however, Latino(a) theology has failed to grapple adequately with other liberation metaphors like "production" and
"revolution," which may strike some as "too Marxist" if not, by con-
notation, "too concerned with economics" and therefore "too Latin
American." In overlooking these metaphors, Latino(a) theology bypasses
some of the greatest philosophical contributions of the Marxian tradition, namely, Marx's insight into the creative dimension of human labor
(which, for Marx, refers to human action in general) and the philosophy
of praxis. Significantly, both of these contributions point to aesthetics,
which is one of the richest topics within Latino(a) theology today. Yet,
Latino(a) theology has yet to approach the expression paradigm and the
topic of aesthetics from within a production or revolution paradigm,
which leaves aesthetic acts of expression in danger of losing ties with the
political.

U.S. LATINO(A) THEOLOGY
AND CRITICAL SOCIAL THEORY

I have suggested that insofar as U.S. Latino(a) theology claims to be a *liberation* theology, it must understand its emphasis on cultural resistance
within the larger taxonomical framework of "integral liberation," which
demands the development of other accents of liberation as well. Toward
this end, U.S. Latino(a) theology must also consider how its emphasis on
cultural resistance may be approached from the perspective of the Marxian paradigms of "production" and "revolution." Goizueta, for one,
argues that Latino(a) theology should avoid any uncritical assimilation
of Latin American theological method. Such an uncritical appropriation would, in his words, "represent a failure to ground our reflection
in the experience of our own communities."[46] While I agree with Goizueta in principle, I would like constructively to engage him and others
as to what, exactly, Latino(a) theologians can and should appropriate
from Latin American theological method, particularly in regards to the
Marxian tradition.[47] The Salvadoran liberation theologian Jon Sobrino

---

46. Goizueta, "Rediscovering Praxis," 84
47. A notable step in bringing U.S. Latino(a) and Latin American theological method into
conversation is Gilbert R. Cadena, "The Social Location of Liberation Theology," in *Hispanic/*

suggests that whereas European theologies set out from the first Enlightenment (Kant, Rousseau, and Hegel), liberation theologies take as
their point of departure the second Enlightenment (Marx).[48] If indeed
Hispanic theology is a *liberation* theology, much more conversation is
needed regarding its understanding of Marx and his critical heirs.

Returning to Goizueta, I have noted that aside from a footnote,
Goizueta comes close to severing completely his view of praxis from
the Marxian tradition, thereby problematizing the very value of liberation as a worthwhile political "end." Alejandro García-Rivera and
Peter Casserella, both of whom share Goizueta's interest in the aesthetic dimensions of Latino(a) religiosity, make similar critiques of the
Marxian tradition without fully acknowledging how this rich and varied tradition can shed light on the political dimensions of aesthetics and
culture. To be sure, García-Rivera and Orlando Espín, who has written
the most extensively on Latino(a) popular religion, have drawn on the
work of Antonio Gramsci, but a host of other "critical Marxists" —
who, like Gramsci, shun orthodox Marxism's economic determinism in
favor of a more dialectical understanding of the relationship between
economic and cultural factors — await similar attention, including, for
example, Georg Lucáks;[49] Herbert Marcuse, Max Horkheimer, Walter
Benjamin, Theodor Adorno, and Jürgen Habermas of the Frankfurt
School;[50] Leszek Kolakowski, Gajo Petrovic, Mihailo Markovic, and

Latino Theology: Challenge and Promise, ed. Ada María Isasi-Díaz and Fernando F. Segovia
(Minneapolis: Fortress Press, 1996), 167–82.

48. Quoted in Eduardo Mendieta, "From Christendom to Polycentric Oikonumé" in
Liberation Theologies, Postmodernity, and the Americas, 264.

49. See especially, *History and Class Consciousness: Studies in Marxist Dialectics,* trans.
Rodney Livingstone (Cambridge, Mass.: MIT Press, 1971).

50. The following is a selection of some of the best-known works of the Frankfurt School,
all of which would directly speak to many of Latino(a) theology's concerns: Herbert Marcuse's
One-Dimensional Man: Studies in the Ideology of Advanced Industrial Society (Boston: Bea-
con Press, 1991), *The Aesthetic Dimension: Toward a Critique of Marxist Aesthetics* (Boston:
Beacon Press, 1978), and *Reason and Revolution: Hegel and the Rise of Social Theory* (Boston:
Beacon Press, 1960); Max Horkheimer's *Critical Theory: Selected Essays,* trans. Matthew J.
O'Connell and others (New York: Continuum, 1982); Theodor Adorno's *Aesthetic Theory*
(London: Athlone Press, 1997); Max Horkheimer and Theodor Adorno's *Dialectic of Enlight-
enment,* trans. John Cumming (New York: Continuum, 1999); Walter Benjamin's *Illuminations*
(London: Pimlico, 1999); and Jürgen Habermas's *Theory and Practice,* trans. John Viertel (Bos-
ton: Beacon Press, 1973), *The Philosophical Discourse of Modernity: Twelve Lectures,* trans.
Frederick G. Lawrence (Cambridge, Mass.: MIT Press, 1987), *The Theory of Communicative Action,* trans. Thomas McCarthy (Cambridge: Polity Press, 1986–89), and *Religion and
Rationality: Essays on Reason, God, and Modernity,* ed. Eduardo Mendieta (Oxford: Polity,
2002). Martin Jay provides an excellent intellectual history of the Frankfurt School in *The Dialectical Imagination: A History of the Frankfurt School and the Institute of Social Research,
1923–1950* (Berkeley: University of California Press, 1996).

others of the Yugoslavian Praxis Group, all representatives of East European Marxists;[51] and Latin American Marxists like José Mariátegui, Adolfo Sánchez Vásquez, and Enrique Dussel.[52] Such authors potentially offer U.S. Latino(a) theology a host of insights that speak to the relationship between resistance and revolution, culture and politics, including such insights as the relative autonomy of the superstructure;[53] the danger of the reification of humankind's creative acts into strictly measurable objective factors;[54] and, of course, the potential for social transformation through historical praxis.

As we have already seen, Goizueta has difficulty showing how, exactly, aesthetic praxis "involves" or "implies" ethical-political action given his enchantment with the idea of aesthetic praxis as "an end in itself."[55] As Goizueta would have it, these two instantiations of action are not related in terms of a shared teleology, since this would imply that aesthetic praxis connotes some degree of "making," and, thus, a working toward some "end." This is an unfortunate formulation for it fails to see the potentially *creative* aspects of "making." Yet, Goizueta appeals to two other grounds in order to explain the "mediation" between aesthetic praxis and ethical-political action: (1) the articulation of an "implicit" liberation in everyday, intersubjective action and (2) the recourse to a dangerous memory of suffering as a guard against a sentimentalized aestheticism. In what follows, I consider both.

---

51. For an overview of the East European Marxists see Arthur F. McGovern, *Marxism: An American Christian Perspective* (Maryknoll, N.Y.: Orbis Books, 1980), 68–82.

52. José Mariátegui, *Seven Interpretive Essays on Peruvian Reality,* trans. Marjorie Urquidi (Austin: University of Texas Press, 1971); Adolfo Sánchez Vásquez, *The Philosophy of Praxis,* and *Art and Society: Essays in Marxist Aesthetics* (New York: Monthly Review Press, 1974); Enrique Dussel, *Filosofía de la liberación* (Maryknoll, N.Y.: Orbis Books, 1985), *Ethics and Community,* trans. Robert R. Barr (Maryknoll, N.Y.: Orbis Books, 1988), *Las metáforas teológicas de Marx* (Estella, Spain: Verbo Divino, 1993), *Towards an Unknown Marx: A Commentary on the Manuscripts of 1861–63,* trans. Yolanda Angulo (London and New York: Routledge, 2001).

53. Culture and religion are "autonomous" in the sense that they may implicitly serve as liberating, counter-hegemonic forces to the status quo; "relative" in the sense that their liberating power is always put in check by the material preconditions and the dominant ideology of the time, in part, a reflection of these material preconditions.

54. This is precisely what Goizueta refers to as the negative "instrumentalization" of our affective dimensions of being, which is to say, a negative effect of technical rationality.

55. Recalling Goizueta's words, "praxis is inherently aesthetic, *involving* an affective engagement with an-other, and ethical-political action, oriented toward the liberation of other qua other.... 'Aesthetic praxis' *implies* an ethical-political commitment to the promotion of those relationships insofar as they foster the full humanity." Goizueta, "U.S. Hispanic Popular Catholicism as Theopoetics," 264.

Goizueta's first strategy is to articulate an "implicit" quality of liberation that he sees among Latino/as:

> My own experience in Latino communities...has led me to question...any emphasis on the social transformative dimensions of human action which would make this dimension itself foundational. In these communities, I have witnessed a type of empowerment and liberation taking place which, at least initially and explicitly, seems to have relatively little connection to any social or political struggles. Indeed, in many cases, empowerment and liberation are not explicit goals at all. Seemingly, the only explicit goals are day-to-day survival and, especially, the affirmation of relationships as essential to that survival. This affirmation is manifested in all those seemingly insignificant ways in which we love, care for, and embrace other persons. Central to the struggle for survival and relationships, moreover, is the community's life of faith, which also, at least on the surface, seems little related to social transformation.[56]

As I have remarked earlier, Goizueta's suspicion of any reification of the "social transformative dimension of human action" is an understandable one. Any liberation process can itself become a rigid type of orthodoxy, closing itself off to new voices and perspectives. From the castigation of popular religion by early Latin American liberation theologians to the initial unwillingness of middle-class Anglo feminists to seek out the perspectives of women of color, liberationist efforts have, in certain cases, appropriated the same totalitarian affinities that they initially sought to critique. At the very least, Goizueta is wise in offering us a general warning against such a vulgar instrumentalization of liberation.

However, Goizueta runs the risk of assuming that aesthetic praxis can, in itself, *suffice* for ethical-political action. As the above passage illustrates, Goizueta is content to linger in the affective, intersubjective, and day-to-day moments of liberation which apparently "have relatively little connection to any social or political struggles."[57] While it is clear that intersubjective, aesthetic praxis is always a necessary "component," "seed," "requirement," or "foundation" of any ethical-political

---

56. Ibid., 88.
57. Ibid.

act, what is not addressed is that the *quality* of this intersubjective action may vary greatly in respect to how it is integrated within a larger social theoretical framework. As a result, Goizueta's articulation of implicit liberation amounts to a "soft" critique of the present order. Popular religion is emancipatory in the Arnoldian sense, that is, insofar as it is a "counter statement to the world" or a "criticism of life."[58] As deeply communal, relational, and celebratory, popular religion figures as an implicit critique of Western rationalism. It is "critical" insofar as it exists and is reckoned with, that is, insofar as it *resists*.

In addition to putting forward an implicit critique of the status quo via Hispanic culture's expressive forms of resistance, U.S. Latino(a) theology is in need of putting forth an *explicit* critique of social structures of domination and a demystification of ideology.[59] Such an explicit critique does not preclude the liberating dimensions of resistance, but rather, is vital to it.

Critical social theory speaks directly to what Goizueta refers to as "day-to-day survival," or intersubjective actions, on at least two counts. First, by definition, critical *theory* "encompasses" and thereby situates

---

58. Very much like Goizueta, George Steiner defends aesthetic experience as having the ability to "break through" into our lives and challenge the everydayness of our experience. Steiner writes: "All serious art, music and literature is a critical act. It is so, firstly, in the sense of Matthew Arnold's phrase: 'a criticism of life.' Be it realistic, fantastic, Utopian or satiric, the construct of the artist is a counterstatement to the world....It says that things might be (have been, shall be) otherwise." As with Goizueta, however, I would qualify Steiner's use of the word "critical" as connoting a "soft" or "implicit" critique of the way things are. George Steiner, *Real Presences* (Chicago: University of Chicago Press, 1989), 11.

59. The basis of such explicit social critique is, of course, Karl Marx. Provisionally, I refer the reader to Richard Bernstein's characterization of Marx's notion of revolutionary praxis: "Marx's fundamental conviction, from beginning to end, is that the situation in which we find ourselves is not ultimately an ontological or existential one from which there is no escape. It is an historical state of affairs which while it has its 'own necessity,' is nevertheless the resultant of human activity and can be changed by revolutionary praxis. The more deeply we penetrate this situation, the more concretely and critically we understand the dynamics of our historical condition, the closer we can come to the real possibility of radical transformation. The reason why such critical understanding can be efficacious is because it speaks to man's deepest desires and needs — his search for liberation and emancipation where freedom becomes a concrete reality." See Richard Bernstein, *Praxis and Action: Contemporary Philosophies of Human Activity* (Philadelphia: University of Pennsylvania Press, 1971), 306–7. The philosophical foundations of what I am referring to as an explicit critique are considered in Seyla Benhabib, *Critique, Norm, and Utopia: A Study of the Foundations of Critical Theory* (New York: Columbia University Press, 1986). Martin Jay presents an excellent intellectual history of one important school of critical theory in *The Dialectical Imagination*. See also Jürgen Habermas, "The Tasks of a Critical Theory of Society," in *Jürgen Habermas on Society and Politics: A Reader*, ed. Steven Seidman (Boston: Beacon Press, 1989), 77–103; and John R. Pottenger, *The Political Theory of Liberation Theology: Toward a Reconvergence of Social Values and Social Science* (Albany: State University of New York Press, 1989), esp. 159–89.

and helps explain social phenomena, such as why popular religion is denigrated by Western rationalism to begin with. In this respect, "grounding our reflection in the experience of our own communities," as Goizueta says, must not only refer to a descriptive account of Hispanic experience, but also to a larger theoretical framework that helps explain why Hispanics (and other marginal groups) suffer in the first place. If aesthetic praxis — the embodiment of what Goizueta refers to as the "seemingly insignificant ways in which we love, care for, and embrace other persons"[60] — is indeed a fundamental source for liberative praxis, one would need also to examine the ways in which institutional structures of oppression — such as racism, capitalism, patriarchy, and homophobia — inhibit, thwart, and oftentimes deform aesthetic praxis. The influence of the mass media, the status and number of Hispanic (and black) dropouts and prisoners, and the institutional forms of heterosexual-male-supremacy are, for instance, never entirely separable from our day-to-day "intersubjective" actions. Rather, critical social theory holds that these realities impinge upon the very quality of our day-to-day communal exchanges. Market forces, racist sensibilities, and macho attitudes *pervade* the aesthetic praxic realm and continually threaten to undermine aesthetic expression as nonrational.

Second, *critical* theory helps unmask the ideological distortions of the "aesthetic-praxic realm." Popular religion, aesthetic praxis, and everyday living — as socially created, historically rooted practices — can never fully be goods, values, or ends "in themselves." Critical theory recognizes that "Tradition (whether 'popular' or not) is a source not only of truth but also of untruth, repression, and domination."[61]

Goizueta recognizes the possibility that tradition may be a source of domination, to which he states that a memory of oppression precludes a sentimentalized aesthetics. Goizueta's appeal to a Metzian "dangerous memory" that is embedded within Hispanic aesthetic praxis thus marks the second way in which Goizueta attempts to bridge the divide between aesthetic praxis and ethical-political action. For Goizueta, ethical stances within the Hispanic community emerge out of a sense of solidarity and compassion, which are born out of a memory of suffering. The very historical experience of Jesus' pain on the cross is important to U.S. Hispanics today, Goizueta argues, because by pointing out their own

60. Goizueta, *Caminemos con Jesús*, 88.
61. Elisabeth Schüssler Fiorenza, *Discipleship of Equals: A Critical Feminist Ekklesia-logy of Liberation* (New York: Crossroad, 1993), 62.

pain and suffering, "U.S. Hispanics record [their] own experience of violence and suffering, 'and by recording it point it out and thereby point to its end.' "[62]

Such a position places a great deal of weight on the subversive power of the Hispanic dangerous memory, about which one must be suspicious. Goizueta writes, "the memories of suffering expressed in U.S. Hispanic popular religiosity — the memories of a vanquished people — prevent us from romanticizing popular religious devotions, music, and ritual, as so often occurs when these are portrayed in the communications media of the dominant culture."[63] How can one be so sure, though, that a memory of suffering is a sufficient guard against a deformation of aesthetic practices? Although it is clear that aesthetic praxis, or "theopoetics" as Goizueta calls it elsewhere, may "[affirm] the victims' own beauty and dignity," how do we know that aesthetic praxis "is *always* empowering and liberating" (emphasis mine), as Goizueta suggests?[64] Is it is enough to say that aesthetic praxis is empowering and liberating "simply by virtue of the fact that it is, indeed, *theirs* [e.g., belonging to the victims]"?[65] This position, I would contend, does not go far enough. In affirming the value of aesthetic praxis and popular religion, Latino(a) theology must also consider the liberative *limits* of a memory of oppression. While I believe that Goizueta would not deny the importance of a critical hermeneutics such as I have been describing, I find that his tripartite strategy of (1) separating praxis from poiesis, (2) deemphasizing Marxist theory, and (3) valuing everyday, intersubjective actions as well as the Latino(a) memory of suffering as *sufficient* sources for critique leaves little room for such "explicit" critical mediations. While critical

---

62. Goizueta, "U.S. Hispanic Popular Catholicism as Theopoetics," 275. Goizueta goes on to quote Johann Baptist Metz: "Every rebellion against suffering is fed by the subversive power of remembered suffering.... The Christian *memoria* insists that the history of human suffering is not merely part of the pre-history of freedom but remains an inner aspect of *the* history of freedom." In light of Goizueta's work, my concern is that the *memoria* is functioning as the *sole* basis for liberation.

63. Goizueta, "Rediscovering Praxis," 93.

64. Goizueta, "U.S. Popular Catholicism as Theopoetics," 284.

65. Ibid., 284. The full quotation is as follows: "Indeed, we *ought* to be suspicious of the mystical and poetic when these emerge from within the history of conquest and domination, for then these lead to 'artificial and unnatural ideas about beauty which are dehumanizing and destructive.' But such aestheticism is alien to a theopoetics that, born from within the history of the victims, affirms the victims' own beauty and dignity. The theopoetics of the victims — insofar as it is truly theirs — is always empowering and liberating, simply by virtue of the fact that it is, indeed, *theirs*."

theory can never, in itself, suffice for an "integral," "final," or "fully realized" liberation, an engagement with it is desperately needed in moving Latino(a) theology — and more important, the Latino(a) reality — at the very least, in this general direction.

CONCLUSION

As I have repeatedly stressed, in one sense, Goizueta is right. Empiricist and functionalist schools in the social sciences have done much damage in reifying practical, measurable, and scientifically verifiable theory at the expense of all other theory, "including the insights of poets, philosophers, and theologians." As a result, faith-based communal expressions such as popular religion have been discounted as irrelevant.[66] Goizueta, Guerrero, and a host of other Latino(a) theologians make valuable contributions in demonstrating that popular religion and the human action that accompanies it are "supremely rational endeavors." In uncovering the foundational import of community and beauty, Latino(a) theology "expand[s] the scope of reason to include these...as intrinsic to [all] human praxis."[67]

There are, however, some potential traps in making — or better yet, in overstating — this important argument. One trap is polarizing praxic "doing" from poietic "making," thereby discrediting poiesis as "mere" instrumentalized making. Latino(a) theology must consider how praxis can positively be construed as a "creative poietic" act, at once aesthetic as well as socially transformative. U.S. Latino(a) theology must not hesitate to speak utopically of partial "goals" and transformative "making," while, of course, remaining suspicious of concrete, final, or total utopias.[68] Latino(a) theology must better develop what David Tracy

---

66. Goizueta, "Rediscovering Praxis," 94–95.

67. Ibid., 95.

68. If there is one strain within Latino(a) theology that has kept alive the stress on praxis as critically informed action rather than simply as intersubjective exchange, it is the feminist strain, and this is owing largely to its healthy hermeneutics of suspicion. Though I would contend that more explicit connections could be drawn between resistance and revolution within Latina feminism (as with Latino[a] theology in general), I do see the feminist contribution as a significant starting point in this direction. Unlike Goizueta's articulation of "empowerment and liberation" as having "relatively little connection to any social or political struggles" and which "in many cases...are not explicit goals at all," Ada María Isasi-Díaz states: "Solidarity with Latinas as oppressed people is a call to a fundamental moral option, an option that makes it possible and requires one to struggle for radical change of oppressive structures even when the specifics of what one is opting for are not known. As a matter of fact, only opting for a radical change of oppressive structures will allow the specifics of new societal structures to begin to

calls a "revisionist theory of praxis." At its best, such a revisionist theory of praxis not only takes into account the neoorthodox theological insistence that "the real power of Christian symbols in their full existential meaning" can illuminate and change the actual historical situation of humanity (to which Goizueta and Guerrero would agree), *but also* a revisionist theory of praxis takes into account the fact that Christian praxis must take seriously the critical relationship between theory and practice. Praxis, as distinct from everyday practice, must always relate to, in some form or other, "a critical theory applicable to all infra-structural and super-structural factors of human reality."[69] Without such a critical framework, Latino(a) theology risks valorizing popular religion and its symbols as somehow being self-sufficient, self-sustaining "ends in themselves." As I have suggested, it is not only *possible* for Latino(a) theology to engage revisionist Marxist theory without reducing "doing" to *mere* "production"; it is also vitally *necessary* that it utilize critical social theory as an instrument for liberation. If this term "liberation" is to refer to anything more than a strictly spiritual or gnostic "purification" or "absolution," then U.S. Latino(a) theology must wrestle with its Marxian roots. Latino(a) theology should not fall prey to the idea that the only liberative recourse left to humankind is that of resistance.[70]

At the very least, U.S. Latino(a) theology needs to clarify for itself what it means by "liberative action." In tackling this question, some fundamental questions need to be put on the table, such as: *From what* are we seeking liberation? How can we become *better aware* of that which oppresses? And what can we *do* in light of this oppression? Furthermore, how can engaged Christians and citizens — Latino/as and non-Latino/as alike — become participants in *building* and *creating* God's kingdom? These are very basic questions for any liberation theology, yet such questions need to be asked if U.S. Latino(a) theology continues to assume that it is indeed a *liberation* theology.

---

appear." As I read her, Isasi-Díaz demonstrates that a good degree of "poietic doing" (e.g., struggling toward the "goal" of liberation) is necessary if we are to know and live liberation, even if ever so partially. Goizueta, *Caminemos con Jesús*, 88; Ada María Isasi-Díaz, *En la lucha/In the Struggle: A Hispanic Women's Liberation Theology* (Minneapolis: Fortress Press, 1993), 42.

69. David Tracy, *Blessed Rage for Order: The New Pluralism in Theology* (New York: Harper and Row, 1988), 242–44.

70. Such a neoconservative leaning can be found in Lorenzo Albacete, "The Praxis of Resistance," *Communio* 21 (Winter 1994): 612–30.

In a sense, we end where we began — with an observation on the central, yet implicit, place that "liberation" plays within U.S. Latino(a) theology.[71] As Guerrero and Goizueta correctly intuit (yet fail to develop adequately), a profound connection exists between culture and social transformation, resistance and revolution, popular religion and liberation. In making this problematic explicit and in underscoring the merits of an *integral* and *critical* approach in addressing this connection, I have hoped to show that, indeed, much more work still needs to be done.

---

71. In the context of black theology, a parallel concern for the ambiguous meaning and usage of "liberation" is raised by Cornel West, who writes that if the social vision of black theologians is to equate liberation with middle-class status, Black theologians "should drop the meretricious and flamboyant term 'liberation' and adopt the more accurate and sober word 'inclusion.'" Cornel West, "Black Theology and Marxist Thought," in *Black Theology: A Documentary History, Vol. 1, 1966–1979,* ed. James H. Cone and Gayraud Wilmore, 2d ed., rev. (Maryknoll, N.Y.: Orbis Books, 1979), 413.

8

The Fundamental Problematic of U.S. Hispanic Theology

MANUEL J. MEJIDO

U.S. Hispanics are caught between two histories, the history of the industrialized center and the history of the underdeveloped periphery; between two cultures, the dominant Anglo-American culture and a marginalized Hispanic-American culture; and between two languages, the official English language and the ghettoized Spanish language. Similarly, U.S. Hispanic scholars are caught between two intellectual genealogies, one that can be traced back to Enlightenment-modernity, to that break with the Middle Ages that crystallized through the world-historical events of the Reformation, the "discovery" of the "New World," and the French Revolution, and another that can be traced back to the coming-to-terms with Latin America as the "underside" of Enlightenment-modernity, as the coming-to-terms with the "invention" of the Americas through the world-historical events of the conquest and colonization. In parallel fashion, U.S. Hispanic theologians are caught between two radically different understandings of theology: theology understood as a historical-hermeneutic science and theology understood as a critically oriented science, theology as understood by the dominant European and Anglo-American theological traditions and theology as understood by the Latin American theologies of liberation.

To the extent that U.S. Hispanic theology aims to grasp the theological *logos*[1] as it emerges from the experience of U.S. Hispanics, it must come to terms with this tension as what is most primordial to U.S. Hispanic

---

1. The theological *logos* is what mediates the finite and the infinite. It is what mediates the epistemological problem of the limits of theological knowledge and the ontological problem of God-as-limit. The trajectory of modern theology is the continuous coming to terms with the problem of the theological *logos* — that is, with the problem of the transcendentality of transcendence, with the problem of the limit, the theological limit.

theology. It must do so because, as the theological moment of a fragmented life, it is already there phenomenologically in the everydayness of
U.S. Hispanic reality. But, although U.S. Hispanic theology emerged in,
through, and because of this tension, it is becoming increasingly evident
that U.S. Hispanic theology is losing sight of this primordial dilemma,
not realizing that such a transformation undercuts its very conditions
of possibility. This is the fundamental problematic of U.S. Hispanic
theology. It can be grasped more specifically as an antinomy that has
exemplified the problem of knowledge since the end of the eighteenth
century when Immanuel Kant inverted the field of Western thought: On
the one hand, this tension can be grasped as the epistemological problem of the grounding of U.S. Hispanic theology, and, more specifically, as
the problem of the historical-hermeneutic reduction of the critically oriented theological sciences — a problem that today is taking the form of
the postmodernist eclipse of liberation. And, on the other hand, this tension can be grasped as the existential-empirical problem of intellectual
assimilation, particularly as the problem of the absorption of the liberation theologies of the periphery by the dominant theologies of the center
in and through globalization. In this second sense U.S. Hispanic theology
is understood as the theological moment of the general social process of
the assimilation of U.S. Hispanics into the Anglo-American mainstream.
But these two moments are in fact dialectically interlocked: For the epistemological problem of grounding can only be properly grasped as the
theoretical mediation of the existential-empirical problem of intellectual
assimilation, and the existential-empirical problem of intellectual assimilation can only be properly grasped as the sociohistorical mediation of
the epistemological problem of grounding. Thus it becomes the task of a
new generation of U.S. Hispanic theologians to retrieve the radical origins of U.S. Hispanic theology by coming to terms with the dialectic of
this tension, the fundamental problematic of U.S. Hispanic theology, as
the very (im)possibility of radically grounding U.S. Hispanic theology,
as the very (im)possibility of overcoming intellectual assimilation.

In the limited space I have available I propose to set in motion this
task: First, we elucidate the two moments of that primordial tension
that undergirds U.S. Hispanic theology — the epistemological problem
of grounding and the existential-empirical problem of intellectual assimilation. Second, in light of this tension, we reconsider one of the
fundamental concepts of U.S. Hispanic theology — *mestizaje*. As both a
critically oriented theological science of liberation and a set of scholarly

practices that reflectively resist assimilation, U.S. Hispanic theology can uncover its proper ground only by grasping itself as the theological moment of the history of U.S. Hispanic reality understood as the history of *mestizaje,* that is, the history of a fragmented life.

EPISTEMOLOGICAL TENSION:
THE PROBLEM OF THE HISTORICAL-HERMENEUTIC
REDUCTION OF THE CRITICALLY ORIENTED
THEOLOGICAL SCIENCES OF LIBERATION

From the point of view of the social theory–oriented theory of knowledge of the early Jürgen Habermas, particularly the idea of knowledge-constitutive interests, I argue that U.S. Hispanic theology has been caught between two radically different understandings of theology. These understandings are theology understood as a historical-hermeneutic science and theology understood as a critically oriented science. Never having reflectively grasped this tension for the most radical theological crisis of modern theology that it is,[2] U.S. Hispanic theology has systematically fallen captive to the historical-hermeneutic reduction of the critically oriented theological sciences of liberation. It has failed to realize that such a reduction undercuts the very possibility of U.S. Hispanic theology understanding itself as a theology that phenomenologically emerges from U.S. Hispanic reality and is a theological reflection on this reality, and as a theology that grasps the theological *logos* in the interest of the liberation of U.S. Hispanics from internal and external forms of compulsion.

Modern theology has for the most part understood itself within the limits of the historical-hermeneutic sciences to the extent that it has established theological knowledge through the interpretation of the meaning of the theological *logos* — a theological knowledge that is possible only within the horizon of an intersubjectivity between the self-understanding of theology and God-as-limit. Insofar as modern theology has posited this intersubjectivity as the very conditions of possibility for interpreting the theological *logos,* we say that it has labored under a

---

2. The movement of modern theology is the movement of theology as a theological enterprise that is perpetually struggling with the problem of the legitimation of both its point of departure and its fundamental concepts. But, it is also correct to say that, as crisis, modern theology provides the conditions of possibility for particular theological crises: those events that destabilize the self-understanding and fundamental concepts of theology such as to generate a discontinuity, a break with what we could call normalized theological science.

constitutive interest in the maintenance of the intersubjectivity of mu-
tual understanding. It has been subject to a practical cognitive interest.
And when theology has understood itself within these limits it has cau-
tiously borrowed from the empirical-analytic social sciences to engage
the problems of religion and modernity. This was the case during the
postwar era in Western Europe and the United States, for example, when
pastoral theology appropriated the sociology of religion to address the
challenges of secularization, urbanization in particular.[3]

But, in the late 1960s, theology for the first time understood itself as
a critically oriented science. This was the radicality of the Latin American theologies of liberation: that they are not satisfied with the practical
cognitive interest of the historical-hermeneutic sciences, and they are not
satisfied with the interpretation of the meaning of a theological *logos* that
is grasped through the restricted category of intersubjectivity. Rather,
the theologies of liberation sublate the practical and technical cognitive interests in an emancipatory cognitive interest that methodically
interlocks knowledge and interest: The theologies of liberation generate a theological knowledge that is interested in its own liberation — a
liberation achieved through the liberation of sociohistorical misery. In
other words, the theologies of liberation generate a theological knowledge that theoretically aims to grasp the invariance that exists between
God-as-limit — conceptualized through the idea of the Kingdom as a
this-worldly project — and the sociohistorical conditions of misery —
conceptualized as the anti-Kingdom — and that praxeologically aims to
overcome this invariance.

The radicality of these two different theological self-understandings,
these two different ways of negotiating the epistemological problem of
the limits of theological knowledge, becomes even more evident when
one considers their respective ontological and methodological correlates:

---

3. In Catholic circles, Jacques Maritain's *Humanisme Intégral* can be cited as the philosophical ground for the first theological appropriations of the social sciences usually associated with
the names of Jacques Leclerq, Gabriel La Bras, Joseph Henry Fichter, and François Houtart.
See, for example, *Conférence internationale de sociologie religieuse, Sociologie religieuse, science sociales: actes du IVe Congrès international* (Paris: Les Editions Ouvrières, 1955). Due
to its neo-Kantian roots, Protestant theology had greater affinities with the social sciences —
indeed, getting into a conversation that is substantially beyond the scope of this work, we can
say that Protestant theologians did not encounter the epistemological and methodological difficulties that burdened their Catholic counterparts. But we can nevertheless cite the names of
Ernst Troeltch and H. Richard Niebuhr as classic examples of the appropriation of the social
sciences by Protestant theology.

When theology has understood itself as a historical-hermeneutic science it has negotiated the problem of God-as-limit within an ontological horizon circumscribed by intersubjectivity — whether this horizon has been grasped as the Kantian consciousness-ideal correlate (e.g., Friedrich Schleiermacher and Joseph Maréchal); the Heideggerian analytics of being (e.g., Karl Rahner and Paul Tillich); modern evolutionary, existential, and social theoretical interpretations of the Hegelian idea of the sublation of becoming (e.g., J. B. Metz and Jürgen Moltmann); or the postmodern linguistic turn (e.g., David Tracy and Gordon Kaufman). However, when theology has understood itself as a critically oriented science, it has posited historical reality as the most primordial ontological category — a category that bursts the intersubjective restrictions on ontology through the idea of an intramundane metaphysics (Ignacio Ellacuría). As the most primordial ontological category, historical reality encompasses the other ontological horizons as moments or regions.

But with the methodological problem of the mediation of the theological *logos* the difference between the two theological self-understandings becomes most acutely pronounced: As a historical-hermeneutic science, theology has grasped the theological *logos* through the category of interaction. As a critically oriented science of liberation it has grasped the theological *logos* through the category of social labor understood specifically as the dialectic of labor and interaction. Thus the fundamental difference, the radical moment of this theological crisis is the category of social labor, or, more specifically, the poietic moment of social labor. This attempt by the theologies of liberation to come to terms with labor marks the radical theological break with not only the philosophy of consciousness, but with the idealism of Western philosophy in general. Indeed, the reality of labor, of *poiesis,* shatters the three moments of the historical-hermeneutic reduction of theology: the epistemological reduction of the theological enterprise to a science of interpretation; the ontological reduction of God-as-limit to an ideal, being, becoming, or language; and the methodological reduction of the mediation of the theological *logos* to interaction. Against the epistemological reduction, the theologies of liberation understand themselves as intellectual moments of the social history of the human species as this history takes form in social labor. Against the ontological reduction, the theologies of liberation now come to terms with the problem of the materiality of God-as-limit, and more specifically, the problem of the relationship between nature and history, praxis and poiesis, economics and culture. And against the methodological reduction, the theologies of liberation — grasping the theological *logos* through the category of social labor — now burst the idealistic restrictions on the question of the constitution of the theological *logos:* The constitution of the theological *logos* is now grasped, not as an asymptotic otherworldly ideal, the horizon of temporality, the sublation of becoming as eschatological hope, or the ultimate limit-symbol as otherness, but rather as salvation history which, as a physical reality, is grafted onto history.

Nevertheless the tragic legacy of liberation theology has been that, since its inception in the late 1960s, it has been grossly misunderstood. The theologies of liberation have often been accused of being a distortion of modern theology. This, however, is false, for liberation theology is in fact the coming to terms with the trajectory of modern theology. It is the coming to terms with the problem of what, drawing on Xavier Zubiri, we could call the substantivization of Divine reality.[4] In terms of the social theoretical idea of knowledge-constitutive interests, the emancipatory cognitive interest of the theologies of liberation have been misconstrued by the dominant theologies as a technical cognitive interest grounded in a vulgar materialism. In short, the dominant theologies have accused the theologies of liberation of reducing theology to an empirical-analytic science and of falling captive to the most dogmatic forms of dialectical and historical materialism. But this accusation is illegitimate and false: Illegitimate because, in marshaling this critique, the dominant theologies overstep the boundaries of their logical-methodological framework; it is rather the theologies of liberation that, through self-reflection, have achieved the right to critique. False, because it is the dominant theologies that are reductionistic — they reduce the mediation of the theological *logos* to interaction and theology to a science of interpretation. Geopolitical clashes, economic constraints, ecclesial castigations, censorship, and vulgar polemics have all contributed to this misunderstanding; and yet the most pernicious dynamic is still taking form today: namely, the postmodernist eclipse of liberation theology — for now it is no longer a question of marginalizing, of pushing to the periphery and covering-up, but rather of assimilating, perverting, and slowly eradicating. In the postmodernist scheme, liberation theology becomes but one among a community of particular, local, or contextual theologies. But this is

---

4. That is, the reduction of reality to this or that substantivity — space, time, consciousness, being, and the like. Xavier Zubiri, *Naturaleza, historia, Dios* (Madrid: Alianza Editorial, 1994), 15–16.

simply the latest moment of the historical-hermeneutic reduction of the critically oriented theological sciences of liberation.

All postmodern theologies are grounded on the linguistic turn that can be traced back to, for instance, Hans-Georg Gadamer's hermeneutics of language and Ludwig Wittgenstein's philosophy of language: God is posited as the *Other* and the theological *logos* is grasped as an intersubjective construction, that is as that ultimate religious reference generated through a constructive-dialogical process by an ensemble of historical particulars drawing on stocks of historically situated culturo-religious knowledge that exist ready-to-hand in the form of language. But, postmodern theologies, with all their talk of conversation, decentering, deconstruction, plurality, otherness, difference, and the like, fail to reflect upon the limits of theology as a historical hermeneutic science. This failure reappears dialectically as the ontological reduction of Divine reality to language, and the methodological reduction of the theological *logos* to interaction now understood — not in the traditional monological sense of an empathetic re-creation via the process of *Verstehen* — but in the dialogical sense of reaching understanding through communication. However, the emancipatory cognitive interest of the theologies of liberation shatters the epistemological, ontological, and methodological reductions of theology to the horizon of language.

This tension between theology understood as a historical-hermeneutic science — now specifically in its postmodern mode — and theology understood as a critically oriented science is the epistemological problem of the grounding of U.S. Hispanic theology. Again, we argue that U.S. Hispanic theology has systematically fallen captive to the historical-hermeneutic reduction of the critically oriented theological sciences of liberation, failing to realize that such a reduction undercuts the very possibility of U.S. Hispanic theology. It undercuts it to the extent that U.S. Hispanic theology understands itself as a theology that phenomenologically emerges from U.S. Hispanic reality and as a theology that grasps the theological *logos* in the interest of the liberation of U.S. Hispanics. We can now say that this reduction is the result of the following fundamental obfuscation: U.S. Hispanic theologians have methodically obfuscated the project of transplanting the critically oriented theological sciences of liberation in the U.S. context with the project of historico-hermeneutically reinterpreting these theological sciences of liberation. But these represent two radically different projects, and the second one leads inevitably to the eclipse of liberation. The theologies of liberation are not reducible to the sociohistorical conditions of Latin America; rather, it is more correct to say that the sociohistorical conditions of Latin America provided the conditions of possibility for the level of reflection that generated the theological crisis that is liberation theology.

EXISTENTIAL–EMPIRICAL TENSION:
THE PROBLEM OF INTELLECTUAL ASSIMILATION

Against the historical-hermeneutic reduction, U.S. Hispanic theology, grasping itself as a critically oriented theological science of liberation, uncovers the limits of the practical cognitive interest. Through the reflective power of the emancipatory cognitive interest, it can now understand itself to be an ensemble of socially situated intellectual practices: The epistemological subject is now grasped as a socially situated empirical subject with epistemological interests, and the epistemological problem of the limits of theological knowledge is now reformulated — from the perspective of what we could call the sociology of theological knowledge[5] — as the problem of the intellectualization of Divine reality. Now the epistemological tension between theology understood as a historical-hermeneutic science and theology understood as a critically oriented science becomes subordinate to the existential-empirical tension between the dominant theologies of the center and the liberation theologies of the periphery. The question of the relationship between knowledge and power emerges as a problem for theology, and with it the second moment of the fundamental problematic of U.S. Hispanic theology: namely, the existential-empirical problem of intellectual assimilation. More specifically, it is the problem of the absorption of the liberation theologies of the periphery by the dominant theologies of the center in and through neoliberal globalization. This is the problem of U.S. Hispanic theology as the theological moment of the general social process of the assimilation of U.S. Hispanics into the Anglo-American mainstream. This problem can be overcome only to the extent that U.S. Hispanic theology understands itself to be constructed by a set of intellectual practices in the context of an academic field that, dominated by Anglo-American interpretations of U.S. society, is already determined to be cut off from the phenomenological experience of U.S. Hispanics. As such, those U.S. Hispanic theologies that fail to critically come to terms with this state of affairs because they

---

5. Pierre Bourdieu, *Méditations pascaliennes* (Paris: Seuil, 1997).

draw on stocks of knowledge (such as text milieus, categories, technical language games, theoretical frameworks, and methodologies) that have their origins outside the phenomenological experience of U.S. Hispanic reality and religion will simply produce reified studies.

So now the epistemological problem of grounding appears as mediated through the existential-empirical problem of intellectual assimilation: For if U.S. Hispanic theology can properly ground itself only by overcoming the postmodernist eclipse of liberation theology, then the sociology of theological knowledge says that such overcoming can be achieved only through the intellectual practice of opening up a legitimate (institutionalized) space for U.S. Hispanic theology in the U.S. academy as a moment of the general struggle against the absorption and assimilation of the theologies of liberation by neoliberal globalization. Thus the struggle of U.S. Hispanic theology against intellectual assimilation becomes the struggle against the hegemonic fusion of liberalism and postmodernism, the struggle between the liberal belief in political correctness, identity politics, and the possibility of a harmonious multiculturalism equilibrated and adjusted via discourse, participation, and correct procedures, and the postmodern belief in the possibility of a community of diverse scholars which can, through communication and correct procedures, achieve a consensus on this or that interpretation, or, at least, agree to disagree.

U.S. Hispanic theology must see beyond this hegemonic fusion of liberalism and postmodernism. It must see beyond the myth that U.S. Hispanic reality is part of some inevitable harmonious synthesis of the Americas as most recently expressed through the idea of a "free trade area for the Americas" which the president of the United States of America, George W. Bush, at the Third Summit of the Americas (Quebec City, Canada, April 20–22, 2001) — making allusion to José Martí (!) — justified with the neoliberal jingle: "progress is found in pluralism; modernization is found in markets."[6] But, as we shall see below, far from being a moment of this mythical synthesis, U.S. Hispanic reality is in fact the mediation of the movement of violence and domination that is the dialectic of Anglo- and Hispanic America: Just as Hispanics in the United States are caught between two histories, the history of the industrialized center and the history of the underdeveloped periphery; two

---

6. "Remarks by the President at Summit of the Americas Working Session" (April 21, 2001), Office of International Information Programs, U.S. Department of State, *www.usinfo.state.gov*.

cultures, the dominant Anglo-American culture and a marginalized Hispanic American culture; and two languages, the official English language
and the ghettoized Spanish language — in this same way, U.S. Hispanic
theology is caught between two different understandings of theology —
theology as understood by the dominant European and Euro-American
theological traditions and theology as understood by the Latin American
theologies of liberation. These two theological understandings are part
of two intellectual worldviews that proceed phenomenologically from
that dialectic of violence and domination that is the history of Anglo-
and Hispanic America. Above we saw that, epistemologically, U.S. Hispanic theology is caught between two knowledge-constitutive interests;
now, existentio-empirically, U.S. Hispanic theology is caught between
two worldviews.

One worldview can be genealogically traced back to Enlightenment-
modernity. Like the movement of the Hegelian philosophy of history, this
first worldview emanates from Europe as center and today has found its
new form in Anglo-American liberalism, intellectually expressed most
recently through Michael Walzer's reflections on "terrorism" and, politically, by the already mentioned idea of a free trade area for the
Americas.[7] The second worldview, in contradistinction, can be genealogically traced to the coming-to-terms with Latin American reality as the
underside of the Enlightenment-modernity, that is, to the coming-to-
terms with the "invention" of the Americas through the world-historical
events of the conquest and colonization. This worldview, as we shall see
below, represents the latest movement of the history of Hispanic America as *mestizaje,* and most recently it has taken the form of the Latin
American philosophies and theologies of liberation, Porto Alegre, and
the Argentinean *cacerolazos.*

What distinguishes these two intellectual worldviews is their respective positions apropos neoliberalism. Thus, from here we name
one worldview *liberal,* as it either explicitly or implicitly supports the
liberal politico-economic project that emerged with the Enlightenment-
modernity and exists today as neoliberal globalization; and we name
the other worldview *liberationist,* as it is grounded in the idea that
only by liberating the human species from this liberal project can real
democracy, real equality, and real justice be achieved. Thus, on the

---

7. Michael Walzer, "Five Questions about Terrorism," *Dissent* 49, no. 1 (Winter 2002),
www.dissentmagazine.org.

one hand, there is the liberal worldview of the modernists and post-modernists: The modernists explicitly defend a variant of neoliberalism as the instantiation of the universal reconciliatory and emancipatory possibilities of reason.[8] The postmodernists, while they critique the universalism of the modernists, in the final analysis, because they fail to reflectively engage neoliberalism de facto accept the basic coordinates of neoliberalism. Richard Rorty's reflections on the U.S. left are perhaps the most evident example of the de facto liberalism of postmodernism,[9] although it is also present — as Slavoj Žižek has suggested — in the more radical *deconstructionist left*.[10] On the other hand, in contradistinction to the modernists and postmodernists, there is the liberationist worldview which takes as its point of departure the critique of neoliberalism whether elucidated ultimately through postcolonial or critical poststructuralist lines.[11]

Thus, caught between the liberal and liberationist worldviews, U.S. Hispanic theology must struggle against the liberalization of the liberationist worldview. But U.S. Hispanic theology will remain blind to this struggle so long as it remains caught in the snares of an intellectualized understanding of reality, a theorized understanding of social practices, that is perpetuated by the unconscious universalization of a particular vision of the social world associated with the specific sociohistorical and theoretical conditions of possibility of the scholarly disposition. Scholastic epistemocentrism does particular violence to those discourses on the social reality of minority groups as it suppresses the distortions produced by the internalization of the contradictions and tensions that suffuse a society, thus re-enforcing the oppression of that group, now in the academic realm. From this perspective, the task of U.S. Hispanic theologians that claim to expound a liberationist approach must begin with the unmasking of intellectual assimilation. Indeed, scholastic epistemocentrism

---

8. John Rawls, *Political Liberalism* (New York: Columbia University Press, 1996). Jürgen Habermas, *Between Facts and Norms: Contributions to a Discourse Theory of Law and Democracy* (Cambridge, Mass.: MIT Press, 1998).

9. Richard Rorty, *Achieving Our Country* (Cambridge, Mass.: Harvard University Press, 1998).

10. Slavoj Žižek, *Did Somebody Say Totalitarianism?* (London: Verso, 2001).

11. Homi Bhabha, *The Location of Culture* (London: Routledge, 1994), and Enrique Dussel, *Etica de la liberación en la época de la globalización y la exclusión* (Madrid: Trotta, 1998), are examples of the postcolonial tradition. Judith Butler, Ernesto Laclau, and Slavoj Žižek, *Contingency, Hegemony, Universality: Contemporary Dialogues on the Left* (London: Verso, 2000), and Michael Hardt and Antonio Negri, *Empire* (Cambridge, Mass.: Harvard University Press, 2000), are examples of what we call here critical poststructuralism. We cannot discuss here the differences that exist between these two perspectives.

has prevented even the most critical of U.S. Hispanic theologians from reflecting on the fact that scholarship is a specific type of social practices located in a specific social space — namely, the academic field — and as such it manifests the contradictions and tensions of a society. Intellectual production and the academic realm are not immune to the distortions and interests of social asymmetries and struggles, but rather they have to be understood as loci of this struggle.

Here the problem of the intellectualization of divine reality and the problem of intellectual assimilation interlock and bring forth the internal dialectic of U.S. Hispanic theology — that is, the dialectic between U.S. Hispanic theologians qua theologians and U.S. Hispanic theologians qua U.S. Hispanics: As theologians U.S. Hispanic theologians are situated in a dominant position among a fragmented people, and thus they run the risk of either eclipsing or intellectualizing the fragmented life that is U.S. Hispanic reality. But as U.S. Hispanics, U.S. Hispanic theologians are situated in a marginalized position in an academic sphere that is dominated demographically by Anglo-Americans and intellectually by the liberal worldview, and thus they run the risk of eclipsing its liberationist roots through assimilation. Only theology understood as a critically oriented science can resolve the internal dialectic of U.S. Hispanic theology. Indeed, only as a critically oriented science of liberation will U.S. Hispanic theology unmask the theologizing of Hispanic religion and struggle for the Hispanicizing of theology. And here we have the radical significance of popular religion: Popular religion is what mediates U.S. Hispanic religion and the academic field; it is what mitigates against the theologizing of U.S. Hispanic religion; indeed, it is the very possibility of the Hispanicizing of a theology that is dominated by Europe and Anglo-America. But popular religion can be properly grasped only within the horizon of *mestizaje*.

MESTIZAJE

As both a critically oriented theological science of liberation and a set of scholarly practices that resist assimilation, U.S. Hispanic theology will open a legitimate space for itself only by coming to terms with the fact that it is the theological moment of the history of U.S. Hispanic reality understood as the history of *mestizaje*. It is the history of a fragmented life as this fragmentation has taken form through labor and interaction. U.S. Hispanic theology's failure to understand *mestizaje* as fragmentation stems from the failure of reflectively understanding itself as *mestizaje* — that is, it stems from scholastic epistemocentrism, from the historical-hermeneutic reduction of liberation theology. However, it is clear from the epistemological problem of grounding and the existential-empirical problem of intellectual assimilation that U.S. Hispanic theology is *mestizaje* — intellectual *mestizaje* — as diremption, as tension. Only a phenomenology of *mestizaje* can bring this forth. Only a phenomenology of *mestizaje* can shatter the scholastic hubris.

Mestizaje came to be as the bastard of La Malinche — the absolute negation of the Amerindian civilizations by the Iberian conquest-colonialism, a negation that materialized through Indigenous and African slave labor. This was the Patronato regio, the Leyes de Indias, the Encomienda. These were the viceroyalties of Nueva España and Perú founded upon the ruins of Tenochtitlán and El Tawantinsuyo. This was the desire for El Dorado, the education of the Inca Garcilaso de la Vega, and the scholasticism of Juan Ginés de Sepúlveda. But, from the outset, as resistance, this negation was itself negated: This was the blood of the first martyrs — Hatuey, Cuauhtémoc, Manco Cayac, Túpac Amaru, Toussaint L'Ouverture. This was the prophetic voice of Bartolomé de las Casas.

Mestizaje would then become the *criollo* — the positivity of the struggles of independence as the repudiation of the *peninsulares,* the repudiation of Iberian hegemony. This was Simón Bolivar, José de San Martín, Miguel Hidalgo, Carlos Manuel de Céspedes, the Manifiesto de Cartagena, the Grito de Dolores, the Grito de Yara. But as the *criollo,* as the first affirmation of Hispanic America, *mestizaje* would perpetuate its positivity only through the negation of part of itself: This was the tyranny of *civilización* over *barbarie:* The negation of the autochthonous and the bucolic; the longing for the enlightenment of France and the pragmatism of the United States. This was Domingo Faustino Sarmiento — the project of a Europeanized and Anglo-Americanized Hispanic America; this was Buenos Aires over-and-against La Pampa, Caracas and Lima over-and-against Los Andes. But already Martín Fierro would negate the negation of the *bárbaro:* For the *gaucho* was not an impediment, but the very possibility of Hispanic America.

Mestizaje would next become the *raza cósmica* — the abstract and aestheticized synthesis of *civilización* and *barbarie* as the intellectualized recognition that a Hispanic America was possible only as a unified totality. This is the coming-of-age of *Ariel,* the repudiation of scientific rationalism, positivism, Yankee ingenuity — the repudiation of *Calibán*. Indeed, as the *raza cósmica, mestizaje* was the coming-to-terms with Anglo-American imperialism as the negation of *nuestra América*. But, like the overcoming of the diremption of *civilización* and *barbarie,* the negation of Anglo-America by aestheticized *mestizaje* was an intellectualized negation, a negation through interaction alone. This was the Generación del 98, Rubén Darío's *A Roosevelt* and José Martí's critique of the annexationists: "*Viví en el monstruo, y le conozco las entrañas — y mi honda es la de David.*"[12]

And *mestizaje* would then become the *raza de bronce,* the *revolucionario* — the coming-to-terms with the *raza cósmica* and *nuestra América* as sociohistorical projects, as tasks to be realized through interaction and labor. This was the Mexican Revolution of 1910: the sociohistorical concretization of the *raza cósmica* as embodied in the Constitution of 1917. This was the Cuban Revolution of 1959: the sociohistorical assertion of the autonomy of *nuestra América* through expropriation as the concrete negation of Anglo-American neocolonialism, and through the turn toward Moscow as the concrete negation of the hegemonic logic of the Monroe Doctrine and its Roosevelt Corollary. The difficulties and frustrations that have beset these sociohistorical projects are but an indication of the extent to which *mestizaje* as the *raza de bronce,* as the *revolucionario,* having concretely come to terms with its own fragmented reality and having attempted to overcome this fragmentation, has reached that point where forward-looking hope is negated by a fragmented history (i.e., conquest, colonialization, elitism, imperialism, underdevelopment) and becomes absurd. *Realismo mágico* is the literary expression of *mestizaje* as a Hispanic America that has come to terms with the limits of its own reality as absurd, as surreal: "*¿Qué es la historia de América Latina sino una crónica de lo maravilloso en lo real?*"[13]

At the limits of Hispanic American reality, *mestizaje* faces a fundamental choice: It can, with the moribund Cuban Revolution, the Ejército Zapatista de Liberación Nacional, the Foro Social Mundial, etc., continue to concretely struggle with its own fragmented reality. Or it can, with the new generation of *malinchistas* (i.e., the *MBA malinchistas:*

12. José Martí, "Carta a Manuel A. Mercado," Campamento de Dos Ríos, 18 de mayo de 1895, in *Obras Completas* 20 (Havana: Editorial Nacional de Cuba, 1963–66), 161.
13. Alejo Carpentier, *El reino de este mundo* (Barcelona: Seix Barral, 1979), prólogo.

Vicente Fox, Alejandro Toledo, Alvaro Uribe, etc.) and the new generation of *arielistas* (i.e., the *civil society arielistas:* Jorge Castañeda, Mario
Vargas Llosa, Ingrid Betancourt, etc.) — through the negative dialectic
that has been set in motion by neoliberal globalization deny its own
fragmented reality.

Thus, the phenomenology of *mestizaje* brings forth the history of Hispanic America as the history of a fragmented life as this fragmentation
has taken form through four dialectics: (1) Cortés and La Malinche,
(2) *criollo* and *peninsular,* (3) *civilización* and *barbarie,* and (4) Ariel
and Calibán. As a moment of the history of Hispanic America, U.S.
Hispanic reality is the mediation of Ariel and Calibán — *the mediation
of the dialectic between Anglo- and Hispanic America.* This is what is
most primordial to U.S. Hispanic reality: U.S. Hispanic reality is that
fragmented surplus that has been generated by that perpetual tension,
that logic of violence and domination that is the asymmetrical relationship between Anglo- and Hispanic America. The heterogeneity of
U.S. Hispanic reality — that is, its racial, gender, national, religious,
socioeconomic, political nuances — is subordinate to this movement of
violence and domination: Indeed, it can be said that the tension between Anglo- and Hispanic America is the transcendental condition for
U.S. Hispanic reality — U.S. Hispanic reality is U.S. Hispanic reality in
and through the dialectic of Ariel and Calibán. This dialectic has had
two movements, through which U.S. Hispanic reality has taken form:
(1) Anglo-America moves South (first as territorial expansion and later
as neoimperialism and neocolonialism), and (2) Hispanic America moves
North (as escaping its own fragmented reality).

In light of the phenomenology of *mestizaje* we can say that assimilation is the conscious or unconscious losing sight of this tension, of this
fragmentation as what radically constitutes U.S. Hispanic reality. Assimilation is the primary vehicle of intra-Hispanic violence understood as
a U.S. Hispanic reality which, caught in the nihilism of the particular,
has loss sight of its unity in and through the sociohistorical fragmentation that is *mestizaje,* and has turned against itself as East Coast vs.
West Coast, *mujerista* vs. *feminista,* left vs. right, rich vs. poor, dark
vs. light, Protestant vs. Catholic, Cuban vs. Mexican, etc. Thus, once
again, but from a different angle, we arrive at the fundamental problem
with political liberalism and postmodernism — they are both inherently
assimilationist: Both myopically perform an *epoché* on the dialectic between Ariel and Calibán and ahistorically grasp U.S. Hispanic reality as

a particular (i.e., a minority group) in community of particulars (i.e., a multicultural society) that will harmoniously integrate through pluralism and markets. That is, in other words, both liberalism and postmodernism are grounded in that narrative of the synthesis of the Americas. But the phenomenology of *mestizaje* invalidates such a narrative: U.S. Hispanic reality is not a concrete manifestation of the synthesis of the Americas; it is rather the concrete manifestation of the tension that is the dialectic of Ariel and Calibán.

•

Grounded in the phenomenology of *mestizaje* understood as the phenomenology of a fragmented life, indeed, reflectively grasping itself as intellectual *mestizaje*, U.S. Hispanic theology needs to reconsider its other fundamental concept — popular religion.

Mestizaje and popular religion are the two fundamental concepts of U.S. Hispanic theology: *Mestizaje* is the primordial category of U.S. Hispanic reality, and popular religion is the primordial category of U.S. Hispanic religion. Popular religion is subordinate to *mestizaje* to the extent that religion is grounded in reality; and theology is subordinate to popular religion to the extent that theology is an intellectual moment of religion — indeed, to the extent that theology wants to avoid what we called above the intellectualization of divine reality.

Thus I bring these reflections to an end with the following thesis for a future study on popular religion: U.S. Hispanic theology can shatter the reification of U.S. Hispanic religion only to the extent that it grasps the theological *logos* as it is mediated through U.S. Hispanic popular religion, that primordial religious moment of U.S. Hispanic reality that is always phenomenologically there as resistance and forward-looking hope in the face of fragmentation.

PART III

Agency, Community, and Religious Practice

9

On Tragic Beauty

ALEX NAVA

When asked to contribute an essay to this volume, I had planned on writing a standard academic essay beginning with a clear thesis statement (with common, often dull, stock formulas such as "I argue that..." "My thesis is..." or less modest expressions like "I prove that...") and then proceeding with the explanation and justification for my argument. Something happened, however, that interrupted my design for the paper. News of immigrants dying in the most desolate desert regions of my state of Arizona was being reported daily. In the months of June and July 2002 alone — when my attention turned in the direction of this essay — more than seventy desperate individuals, men and women, young and old, lost their lives, burnt by the sun and overcome by the unforgiving heat of the desert. And these numbers, or perhaps "numbers" is too cold of a term, these innocent lives tragically lost, are not too unusual a tally for the summer months on the U.S./Mexico border regions. Last year the horror of crosses in the desert was all too common, and there is no reason to think, especially considering current border policies, that these deaths will be the last ones we mourn.

Because of these events, I decided that I couldn't do justice to the subject matter of my essay by speaking abstractly and theoretically about the problem that suffering and evil pose to aesthetical theologies, about the oxymoron "tragic beauty." I decided that my writing — at least for this occasion — should be more narrative-like, more symbolic, passionate, plaintive, more personal. In confronting the reality of evil anyhow, as Paul Ricoeur's classic work *The Symbolism of Evil* explained,[1] thought faces something fundamentally unthinkable, something that is intractable to pure reason. If the experience of beauty has

---

1. Paul Ricoeur, *The Symbolism of Evil* (Boston: Beacon Press, 1967).

the ability to elicit a response of awe and wonder, the reality of evil leaves us at a loss for words, with a silence that is awe-ful and terrifying. In the face of evil, how can reflection be anything but metaphorical and allusive? Aren't metaphors and symbols more appropriate for communicating both the possibilities *and* limits of language than literal, logical concepts?

So my thoughts on tragic beauty begin with a consideration of the events occurring in the border regions of the United States and only then proceed to assess theologically the idea of "tragic beauty." While I remain convinced of the value and importance of theological reflection, I also firmly believe that intellectuals would be well served to keep in mind the maxim by Simone Weil, "Intellectual: A bad name, but we deserve it." Perhaps in recognizing the shortsightedness and self-isolation of much of academic thought, we might be led to the desert where God may speak to us if we are attentive to the face of the other, if we hear the Word crying out in the desert.

CROSSES IN THE DESERT

Anyone who has the opportunity to visit the desert regions of southern Arizona or Sonora, Mexico, can attest to the unexpected beauty encountered. If images of barren sand and flat, desolate terrain predetermine one's outlook of a desert, then perhaps the border regions of Arizona should be recategorized as something else. First-time visitors often respond with surprise at the verdant and mountainous surfaces of the desert. The deserts here are pregnant with life, home to a great diversity of animal and bird species (in fact, southern Arizona is one of the most popular destinations in the world for bird-watchers). Some of the rock formations in these areas are majestic and entirely unique. The cacti in these deserts — the Saguaros, the Organ Pipe, the Ocotillo — are remarkable and beautiful both because of their rarity in the world's ecology and for their proud and stubborn ability to survive even in the face of drought and cruel heat. No wonder, then, that the Tohono O'odham Indians consider this land sacred. Indeed, here in a cave on the sacred mountain Baboquivari dwells one of the traditional gods of the O'odham, I'itoi. In my work with several nonprofit organizations — Borderlinks, Humane Borders — I am brought to these areas often and in the midst of the deaths and suffering that I know occur in these lands, I often marvel at this contrast of ecological, earthly beauty and the tragedy of human suffering. Because many of these lands are national parks, there is great effort taken to preserve the fragile ecosystems — accompanied by invective against immigrants — while little to no attention is forthcoming on the fragility and vulnerability of human lives.

In my work with Humane Borders, while deploying water stations in these areas, I have come face-to-face with many immigrants beginning or in the midst of their journey to *el Norte*. On the Mexican side of the border, there is a small town that sees over one thousand immigrants per day ready to risk their lives for opportunities in North America. In addition to water stations, Humane Borders has distributed maps to many immigrants, warning them of the most desolate and dangerous parts of the desert. The first time I met a large group of immigrants about to cross the border, I was struck by the number of not only women, including mothers with their children, but also young girls not old enough to be admitted to a PG-13 movie. This very diverse group of individuals was united only by the vision of a better life and their uncompromising belief that their lives are in the hands of God. Needless to say, it has been deeply troubling for me to continue to learn, to never hear the end of the deaths occurring in this liminal territory that we call the border.

DESERT THEOLOGY

When Pascal exclaimed that "Jesus will be in agony until the end of the world," he spoke a truth that even a non-Christian might understand. The cry of Jesus on the cross is all too recognizable in history and society. I recall as an undergraduate student at the University of Arizona, I was immediately drawn to liberation theology because of its willingness to confront and oppose the forces of oppression and poverty, inequality and injustice. I saw in the theologians' work not a naive adaptation of Marxian interpretations of class struggle or the like — this is more a caricature than an identifiable feature of liberation theology. Their theologies resonated with me because they represented creative and faithful reflections on Christ crucified, not as an event of ancient history (as a historical critic or Christian fundamentalist might see it), but rather as an event that pervades our individual and collective histories. This is what Gustavo Gutiérrez saw in the great Dominican Bartolomé de Las Casas. For Gutiérrez, Las Casas recognized the passion of Christ in the world of his time: "In the face of the afflicted Indians of the Americas," Las Casas writes, "Jesus Christ is beaten, scourged and crucified not once,

but thousands of times."[2] While the deaths occurring along our border
with Mexico is not comparable to the decimation of the Indian population during and after the conquest, these border crossings and crosses are
becoming more frequent in our times. And the events and circumstances
of migration are urgent realities that are signaling the new and last dis-
covery of America.[3] It is these realities that are perhaps "postmodern,"
as Homi Bhabha writes.

> If the jargon of our times — postmodern, postcoloniality, post-
> feminism — has any meaning at all, it does not lie in the popular
> use of the "post" to indicate sequentiality — *after*-feminism.... The
> wider significance of the postmodern condition lies in the aware-
> ness that the epistemological "limits" of those ethnocentric ideas
> are also the enunciative boundaries of a range of other dissonant,
> even dissident histories and voices.... For the demography of the
> new internationalism is the history of postcolonial migration, the
> narratives of cultural and political diaspora, the major social dis-
> placements of peasant and aboriginal communities, the poetics of
> exile, the grim prose of political and economic refugees.[4]

No thoughtful person can deny that this new internationalism is changing our theologies and religious communities as surely as it is impacting
the social, economic, and political fabrics of our lives.

As a theologian, the fact and circumstances of these deaths have
not only demanded attention to the obstacles and suffering involved in
migration, but they have also led me to rethink some of the key narratives
of the Jewish and Christian Scriptures, especially concerning the attitudes
toward aliens and strangers as well as the Israelites' own struggles with
life and death in the desert.

The ethical injunctions of the Jewish and Christian Scriptures first
echoed in my mind. Deuteronomy, for instance, warns the Israelites (and
the contemporary reader) of the potential for forgetfulness. "Love the
stranger, for you too were once strangers in the land of Egypt." Justice here depends on a faithful memory and an awareness of a shared
human condition. Also, Matthew 25, that favorite text of the liberation

---

2. Gustavo Gutiérrez, *Las Casas: The Search for the Poor of Jesus Christ* (Maryknoll, N.Y.: Orbis Books, 1993), 62.
3. See Richard Rodriguez's extraordinary new book, *Brown: The Last Discovery of America* (New York: Viking, 2002). I discuss portions of this book below.
4. Homi Bhabha, *The Location of Culture* (London: Routledge, 1994), 4–5.

theologians, is unambiguous about the hospitality demanded toward the stranger. Indeed, Jesus identifies and is revealed in the face of the stranger and needy. "I was hungry and you gave me food, thirsty and you gave me drink, a stranger and you welcomed me." But the circumstances of the immigrant deaths raised other questions in my mind, questions that exceed these ethical considerations.

If the deaths along our border regions made me notice again the kind of hospitality due to strangers deriving from the religious traditions of the West, they also forced me to revisit the narratives of Exodus and the traditions of lamentations in ancient Israel. The plaintive cries and complaints of the Israelites in the wilderness began to take on a new, more immediate and haunting meaning. "Was it for want of graves that you brought us out of the land of Egypt.... Why did you bring us out of Egypt, to kill us and our children and livestock with thirst?" (Exod. 17:3). These anguished expressions tell of the suffering of this people who had endured slavery only to enter a land bereft of milk and honey, a land inhospitable to human needs. The faith in the "promised land" that Moses sought to instill in the Israelites proved to be precarious and fragile — like their lives — when tested in the unforgiving and death-dealing environment of the desert.

While Moses rebukes the Israelites for their doubts, does not Moses also begin to interrogate God, to possibly find some fault with God's promises? Distraught by the weeping of the Israelites in the wilderness, Moses complains to God, "Why have you treated your servant so badly? ... Where am I to get meat to give to all this people? For they come weeping to me and say, 'Give us meat to eat....' If this is the way you are going to treat me, put me to death at once" (Num. 11:10–15). Far from this expression being an exceptional moment of doubt, it seems that wrestling with God is a central characteristic of the faithfulness of the great Jewish prophets (as the name "Israel" suggests). Abraham has his complaints, Jacob wrestles with God, Job brings a lawsuit against God, Jeremiah wishes he was never born a man, and the texts of the Psalms, Lamentations, and the prophets all cry out in a voice of bewilderment at the seeming hiddenness of God from their lives.

Moses, furthermore, dies in the desert. He never makes it to the "promised land" (like that other great prophet who invoked this text, Dr. Martin Luther King Jr.). The hundreds of immigrants who every year meet their death in the wilderness of the U.S./Mexico border regions validate this struggle with God. These events are further outbursts of the words heard on the lips of Jesus, "My God, my God, why have you abandoned me?"

THEOLOGICAL REFLECTIONS ON TRAGEDY

These deaths, then, raise in my mind not only the prophetic injunctions to care for the poor, to welcome the stranger, but they provoke as well the need to consider the role of tragedy in theological reflection, to wrestle with the problem of evil. Confronted with the realities of innocent suffering, I don't see how it is possible to ignore this question. However important and indispensable the prophetic traditions remain, the cries and laments of the innocent present a challenge not fully faced by the great Jewish prophets. For the great prophets, it is typically (though not always) sin that is the target of their wrath. If the poor, the widow, and the orphan suffer it is because of the violence and selfishness, if not the apathy, of particular agents in history and society.[5] But how does this paradigm — however important and honest — account for the unthinkable, for suffering cannot be reduced to a clear and straightforward cause or explanation? Even if one, let's say, blames the failure of U.S. border policy for the deaths occurring along the border — a prophetic response that is accurate and necessary — does this exhaust the depth of the question concerning the loss of innocent lives? These losses, or so it seems to me, suggest a failure of any attempt to rationally construe or explain such tragedy. Even the prophetic tradition's explanations — that suffering is a consequence of disobedience, sin — finally proves to be unsatisfying. Perhaps, what the prophets and many great Christian theologians feared is unavoidable: wrestling with God.

This consideration of the problem of evil is noticeable in much of liberation theology as well as black and Latino(a) theologies. In the work of Gustavo Gutiérrez, for instance, one notices a shift in his later work (especially his work on Job and on Las Casas) to a more sustained reflection on the abyss of innocent suffering. Through his creative and profound reading of Job, he teaches us how close the poor and afflicted of the world are to this saint of the dung-heap. Job's wrestling with God is intelligible to anyone who has been "laid low by the blows of fate" (as

---

5. Michael Fishbane suggests that the classic prophet is the one who announces or proclaims the Word of God in the form of rebuke, exhortation, warning, or doom to the nation Israel. See "Biblical Prophecy as a Religious Phenomenon," in *Jewish Spirituality: From the Bible through the Middles Ages,* ed. Arthur Green (New York: Crossroad, 1994), 65.

Shakespeare once wrote) or to anyone for that matter sensitive enough to recognize the injustice reigning on the earth.

Simone Weil, however, was the first one who made me consider the question of tragedy. One of Weil's most original contributions to contemporary Christian thought is her insistence that Greek tragedy could be read vis-à-vis the passion of Christ. This is no light claim to make, and it is a claim that has very few precedents in the history of Christian theology. For Christian theologians, it was almost always the Greek philosophers and *not* the poets and tragedians who were sources of theological reflection. The most obvious reason for this philosophical predilection was the Platonic naming of the divine: the One or the Good. By contrast, the gods of the poets were human — all-too-human: plentiful in number, a-moral, capricious, violent, jealous, lustful. Why did Weil believe, then, that we can learn from the poets as much as we can learn from Plato (and, incidentally, there was very little, she believed in her own uncompromising way, that we can learn from Aristotle)? One of the keys to that question recalls in my mind the beginning line of the W. H. Auden poem, *Musée des Beaux Arts,* "About suffering they were never wrong, The Old Masters."[6]

Weil believed that the poets, the tragedians were not wrong about suffering, that suffering is misconstrued when reduced to a consequence of sin (of Adam and Eve), as much of Christian theology (beginning with Augustine) was inclined to do. In an honest manner, free of illusions and fanciful optimism, tragedy illuminated for Simone Weil the reality that no thoughtful person can deny: innocent suffering. Tragedy forced our attention to the horrors of history, to the cold and impersonal rule of violence and power in history (what she called "Force"). Tragedy illuminated these realities, according to Weil, by soliciting neither a condescending pity for the victims of Force, nor a rationale and explanation for their suffering. Instead, tragic poetry summoned a compassion that made evident that we all — we onlookers, we individuals far removed from their painful circumstances — share the same human condition, a fragile and vulnerable one to be sure. If chance had it otherwise, it would be us stealthily trying to cross the desert, fearing both human agents and the merciless elements of nature.

---

6. W. H. Auden, *Collected Poems,* ed. Edward Mendelsen (New York: Random House, 1976).

In comparing Homer's *Iliad* with the Gospels, Weil has this to say about love and justice in these two great traditions:

> The sense of human misery gives the Gospels that accent of simplicity that is the mark of the Greek genius, and that endows Greek tragedy and the *Iliad* with all their value ... for the sense of human misery is a precondition of justice and love. Anyone who does not realize to what extent shifting fortune and necessity hold in subjection every human spirit cannot regard as fellow-creatures nor love as one loves oneself those whom chance has separated by an abyss.... Only one who has measured the dominion of Force, and knows how not to respect it, is capable of love and justice.[7]

From a Christian theological perspective, then, Weil believed that the luminous nature of tragedy finally proved to be a more faithful reading of the passion of Christ — innocent suffering *par excellence* — and of human vulnerability or "misery" than found in much philosophy, or for that matter than much theology.

David Tracy is one contemporary theologian, however, who has creatively wrestled with the question of tragedy in light of Christian theology. His interpretation of "ambiguity," for one, calls to mind the strange mixture of extraordinary goodness and frightening evil in human history. Even the term "ambiguity" is too mild of a term, he writes, to name the startling beauty and the revolting cruelty in the human experience. How can events of great suffering be named at all? Consider his thoughts on the Holocaust:

> The genocide of six million Jews by the Nazis is — is what? *Shocking* seems an altogether inadequate adjective to apply to that enormity. Then what was it? Madness? Aberration? Sin? Or all these, and something more, something demonic and more radically interruptive of our history than we can imagine? ... None of us yet know even how to name it properly. This much, however, is clear: if we continue to talk about our history as if that *tremendum* event did not happen, then we are not truthfully narrating our history. And our century includes that and more. Witness the following litany of terrifying events: the Armenian massacres, the Gulag, Hiroshima, Uganda, Cambodia. We must recognize that

---

7. Simone Weil, "The Iliad or the Poem of Force," in *Simone Weil: An Anthology*, ed. Sian Miles (New York: Weidenfeld and Nicholson, 1986), 192.

Western humanist history includes the guards at Auschwitz who read Goethe and listened to Bach and Mozart in their spare time.[8]

Needless to say, theology cannot remain untouched by this (all too abbreviated) litany of tragic events. What does this all mean theologically?

Perhaps Tracy's most creative work on the question of tragedy and theology appears in his recent reflections on the "hiddenness of God" tradition. Calling to mind the laments from the Psalms, from Job, the Prophets, or the book of Lamentations he reflects on these outbursts in light of the history of Christian theology. Certainly his reflections on this topic emerge from the anguished expressions of anyone — especially the laments of those despised and oppressed others — who has suffered and who can empathize with the plea of the Hebrew Bible, "How long, O Lord, will you hide your face from us?"

But in theologically assessing the tragic, ambiguous face of history Tracy has been led to a well not fully exhausted, the sense of Divine hiddenness in Martin Luther. It should not be surprising that we might find in this anguished soul a theological direction to consider the problem of evil. For as Luther saw it, human history was at the end of its rope. From his vantage point, he was witnessing the events of the end times, when the rule of the wicked and the Antichrist would precipitate the messianic intervention of God. This apocalyptic construal of history is Luther's way of articulating in theological language the chaotic and unjust ways of the world. There is no order, no "great chain of being," no historical progress or evolution in this theological paradigm. The wicked thrive, the good suffer; the enemies of Christ appear victorious, the righteous and faithful fail; the Devil is visible, God is hidden.

Luther's theology of failure, however, is genius in this respect. Luther recognizes that the God revealed in the Old and New Testaments is after all a hidden God, a God revealed in cross and negativity, in death and the history of oppression. If one is to recognize the living God, look not in places of glory, in locations of power, wealth, worldly beauty; look instead in the direction one would least expect, in locations where God is seemingly most absent. The Crucified God, thus, shatters reasonable norms and expectations. The *Deus Absconditus* is revealed *sub*

---

8. David Tracy, *Plurality and Ambiguity* (San Francisco: Harper and Row, 1987), 67–68.

contrariis, in the filth of the world, in the *cloaca.*[9] Wisdom is obtained through folly, strength through weakness. And the poor and the suffering, not the educated and proud, are the people who often recognize these hard truths, who have eyes to see what is hidden from others.

This theology of the cross is clearly a dominant presence in much of liberation theology, only in this case God's hiddenness is revealed not merely in the alienated individual of existential philosophy and theology (e.g., in the *Anfechtung* or *Angst* of Luther and Kierkegaard). God's hiddenness is revealed *sub contrariis* in the "suffering of all those others whom the grand narrative of modernity has set aside as non-peoples, non-events, non-memories, in a word, non-history."[10] As the Jewish philosopher Levinas has insisted, the divine Other is impossible, inconceivable, unknown to human cognition or reason alone. If we are to recognize G-D then look to the face of the other.[11]

David Tracy's claim, however, is that there is a second dimension of Divine Hiddenness in Luther that brings us closer to the problem of evil. Luther daringly suggests that there is a hidden and inscrutable will of God that is different from the God revealed in the crucified Christ. If one face of God, the tender, redeeming face, is revealed in Jesus Christ, this other unknown face of God, Luther says, works both life and death, and all in all. It is this latter face of God that we can only fear and adore, Luther writes.[12] This second dimension of Luther's theology is so close to tragedy and is most daring in its wrestling with God over the problem of evil. Tracy's words on this issue are telling:

> At the very least, this literally awe-ful and ambivalent sense of God's hiddenness is so overwhelming that God is sometimes experienced as purely frightening, not tender: sometimes as an impersonal "It" of sheer power and energy signified by such metaphors as abyss, chasm, chaos, even horror; sometimes even as a violent personal reality.... It is Luther (here quite different from even Augustine and Pascal) who will not hesitate to reflect on what the ancient

---

9. Recall that Luther insisted that the Reformation breakthrough occurred on the toilet, the *cloaca.* Even if it actually occurred in the study above the toilet, the theological point is clear: God is strong where man is most weak and vulnerable. See Heiko A. Oberman, *Luther: Man between God and the Devil* (New Haven, Conn.: Yale University Press, 1989).

10. David Tracy, "The Hidden God: The Divine Other of Liberation," *Cross Currents* 8 (Spring 1996): 5–16.

11. See Emmanuel Levinas, *The Levinas Reader,* ed. Sean Hand (Oxford: Blackwell, 1989).

12. Martin Luther, *Martin Luther: Selections from His Writings,* ed. John Dillenberger (New York: Anchor Books, 1962), 166–203.

Greek tragedians named "fate" in ways Aeschylus and Sophocles would have understood. It is Luther's Hiddenness II which exposes the superficiality of so much modern talk about God (including Lutheran talk) — indeed any theological talk which refuses to face the radical hiddenness often present in both the biblical portrait of God and in much human experience of God.[13]

We would do well to underscore Tracy's suggestion that this sense of Divine Hiddenness, and the concomitant interrogation of tragedy, is a biblical portrait. Gustavo Gutiérrez recognizes this biblical dimension of the hidden God in his book *On Job*. Indeed, Gutiérrez notes that Job wrestles with divine ambiguity.

> It might almost be said that Job splits God in two and produces a God who is judge and a God who will defend him at that supreme moment; a God whom he experiences as almost an enemy but whom he knows at the same time to be truly a friend.... These are two sides of the one God. This painful, dialectical approach to God is one of the most profound messages of the book of Job.[14]

If we are forced to consider the question of God as surely as human experience in general from the perspective of "ambiguity," then the concept of "tragic beauty" may be more intelligible than at first glance. What else is this idea of "tragic beauty" but an oxymoron and a paradoxical *aporia*? The question remains, however, what is beautiful about all of this, about all this suffering and tragedy? Is there a danger in romanticizing suffering to the point of justifying it, to the point of masochism or even voyeurism? I certainly believe that these questions must be entertained to warn against the possible eclipsing of a prophetic spirit of resistance. Voices opposing suffering, repudiating injustice, and denouncing inequality and poverty must be litanies that resound from the mountaintops and that find a voice in contemporary theology.

Still, what is the attraction of theological aesthetics that seems to command the attention of many new voices in theology, including liberation and Latino(a) theologians?

---

13. Tracy, "The Hidden God," 10–11.
14. Gustavo Gutiérrez, *On Job* (Maryknoll, N.Y.: Orbis Books, 1987), 65.

THEOLOGICAL AESTHETICS

Part of the answer to the above question is apparent: beauty is, indeed, alluring and seductive. Any sensitive soul can attest to the startling, striking, even intoxicating impression of beauty. If revelation is the event or gift of God's self-manifestation, then beauty is a supreme form of revelation, originating not from the self but from the Other. And this event or gift is incarnated in a range of forms: in art and architecture, in symbol and image, in ritual and festival, in drama and music, and certainly through the grandeur and mystery of creation and the human body. As a spiritual revelation, beauty comes upon one suddenly, igniting the passions, seducing the soul, illuminating the mind. Attention, Simone Weil noted, is never more pure, more intense and alert than when inspired by beauty.

My own interest in Christian spirituality and mysticism has been related to their celebration of divine beauty. Taking their clue from Plato, the mystics suggest that truth is never achieved through pure cognition, through reason alone (indeed, it is not a human achievement at all). Instead, in certain graced moments — though brief and ephemeral — truth happens to one as beauty happens: truth is a manifestation, an epiphany, a moment in and out of time. T. S. Eliot called such experiences "unattended moments," "the moment in and out of time, the distraction fit, lost in a shaft of sunlight, the wild thyme unseen, or the winter lightning, or the waterfall, or the music heard so deeply that it is not heard at all, but you are the music while the music lasts. These are hints and guesses and hints followed by guesses. And the rest is prayer, observance, discipline, thought, action."[15]

If such moments are transient hints (a theological modesty in contrast to the more self-assured Eliot of the essays) they, nevertheless, are hints that are potentially transformational. Their message is unmistakable: "You must change." This spirituality is not of the self-help variety. This spirituality, if authentic and Christian, instigates a conversion from a self-centered existence to a way of being Other-centered. With beauty above me, with beauty below me, with beauty around me (Navajo chant), I am lost. This spiritual ecstasy (*ek-stasis,* to go outside of oneself) is nothing less than a loving communion. The theologian Hans Urs von Balthasar

---

15. T. S. Eliot, *The Four Quartets* (New York: Harvest Books, 1943), 44.

suggested that beauty is, thus, the glory and splendor of God seizing and enrapturing the human soul.[16]

James Joyce's character Stephen Dedalus, in *Portrait of an Artist as a Young Man,* allies himself with Aquinas (a poet himself, according to Stephen) on the understanding of beauty. Stephen suggests that three qualities constitute beauty: wholeness, harmony, and radiance.

> The instant wherein that supreme quality of beauty, the clear radiance of the esthetic image, is apprehended luminously by the mind which has been arrested by its wholeness and fascinated by its harmony is the luminous silent stasis of esthetic pleasure, a spiritual state very like . . . the enchantment of the heart.[17]

When the mind and heart are illuminated and arrested by an object of beauty, silence is the hallowed response to this disclosure of the "splendor of truth."

And as surely as in T. S. Eliot, Joyce describes mystical epiphanies jerking him clean-out of ordinary time and space.

> His thinking was a dusk of doubt and self-mistrust lit up at moments by the lightnings of intuition, but lightnings of so clear a splendor that in those moments the world perished about his feet as if it had been fireconsumed: and thereafter his tongue grew heavy and he met the eyes of others with unanswering eyes for he felt that the spirit of beauty had folded him round like a mantle and that in revery at least he had been acquainted with nobility.[18]

The hunger for beauty, suggests Joyce, is nothing else but an insatiable, erotic yearning for spiritual transcendence. In these moments, beauty overwhelms and has the effect of making anything else (including many modern philosophical and theological systems) seem so dull, prosaic, and trite.

In the world of theology, then, the attraction of aesthetics is intelligible in light of the spiritual void that was left in the wake of modern,

---

16. Hans Urs von Balthasar, *The Glory of the Lord: A Theological Aesthetics,* vol. 1: *Seeing the Form,* trans. of *Herrlichkeit: Eine Theologische Ästhetik,* ed. Joseph Fessio, S.J., and John Riches, trans. Erasmo Leiva-Merikakis (San Francisco: Ignatius Press, 1989).

17. James Joyce, *Portrait of an Artist as a Young Man,* ed. Chester Anderson (New York: Penguin, 1968), 213.

18. Ibid., 177.

transcendental, scholastic methods. The Enlightenment provided an insufficient spiritual diet (Weil), which proved to be the case in many modern theologies as well. One could not help wonder where spirituality was, where love was in this search for a more clear argument, for a more persuasive proof, a more rational theology.

TRAGIC BEAUTY

If we have a greater sense of why aesthetics is attractive to many contemporary theologians, we still haven't addressed the question that we established above: how to make sense of this expression "tragic beauty"?

While James Joyce offers us a desirable example of a form of thought that joins a tragic sensibility with the expression of beauty (recall his reading of history in *Ulysses:* "History is a nightmare from which I am trying to awake."), I would like to begin with Nietzsche on this topic, for very few others believed so passionately in the redemptive force of beauty ("Only as an aesthetic phenomenon is existence justified") and also offered such creative reflections on the birth and disposition of tragedy. This connection between beauty and tragedy should signal to us that for Nietzsche not any kind of aesthetics would do; an optimistic, cheerful aesthetics for a bored cultural and economic elite deserved the hammer, in his view. This iconoclastic philosophizing (with a hammer) distrusted any aesthetical vision that flinched from the hard and terrible. When successful, as with the ancient Greeks, tragedy accounted for tragic failure, for what is evil, troubling, problematic in existence.

But we must not be misled: this tragic sensibility, according to Nietzsche, is not world-denying. The Hellene — he who is most thoughtful and uniquely susceptible to the tenderest and deepest suffering — is saved by art, Nietzsche says. The secret of tragedy is that at the heart of the Greek's contemplation of the terror and violence of the human experience lies, in the words of Nietzsche, "joy, strength, overflowing health, excessive abundance."[19] And thus his thesis on the birth of tragedy: tragedy originates out of music, out of the chorus and the response to this in dance. If the chorus shares the suffering of the god Dionysus (the lord and master of tragedy), it does so musically, playfully, artistically.

It is as if in the beautiful expression of unjust suffering, suffering is made more endurable. Suffering is transformed into something less

---

19. Friedrich Nietzsche, *The Birth of Tragedy* (New York: Penguin, 1993), 6.

inscrutable, something more meaningful. The temptations of despair and cynicism are transformed into a lament of survival and resistance — and hope. What else were the spirituals and the blues in the African American traditions if nothing but an expression of tragic beauty? Through song and dance they voiced their refusal to be silenced, a small victory against the dehumanizing forces of oppression. Tragic beauty, then, is not all that tragic. The beauty of it is redemptive. When lost in the music, when enraptured by the drama, when affected by a piece of art, when the rhythm and harmony of the language allure you and nourish your soul, hope is resurrected even in the midst of great suffering.

With Simone Weil, likewise, it must be insisted that her fascination with tragedy did not divulge a life-negating cynicism. She is no Schopenhauer or Sartre. While she believed that tragedy illuminated the human condition without false consolations and illusions, she also believed that it did so in an aesthetical manner. And the experience of beauty was, in her view, a pure, unadulterated experience of joy. The rhythm of the form, the role of music, the performance of the drama, all were parts of the beauty of tragedy and produced in the participant a redemptive sensation. In one of the key experiences of her life, when she was in a small Portuguese village on the day of the festival of its patron saint, she observed a celebration that deserves the designation "tragic beauty."

> The wives of the fishermen were in procession making a tour of all the ships, carrying candles and singing what must certainly be very ancient hymns of a heart-rending sadness. Nothing can give any idea of it.... There the conviction was suddenly borne in upon me that Christianity is preeminently the religion of slaves, that slaves cannot help belonging to it, and I among others.[20]

If the ceremonial beauty of Catholicism seduced Weil — the rituals, the music, the art and architecture, the spiritual masters — it did so by its awareness of tragic beauty, by its luminous vision manifested not only in the official ceremonies of the church, but also in the lives and celebrations of the simple, poor, and uneducated. This dimension of Catholicism not only enchanted her, but came to possess her soul. It changed her.

---

20. Simone Weil, *Waiting for God* (New York: Harper and Row, 1951), 67.

TRAGIC BEAUTY IN LATINO(A) THEOLOGY

One element of contemporary religious thought that could shed further
light on our discussion of "tragic beauty" is Latino(a) theology, especially
the creative attention to the aesthetical dimension of popular religion.
In the view of Roberto Goizueta, for instance, aesthetics in the form of
liturgy and procession, or symbol, icon, and story, is at the heart of Hispanic religious traditions. For Goizueta, the wisdom of aesthetics leads
to a celebration of life as an intrinsic value in itself, not as a means to
an end, not as a utilitarian might understand human action. In an aesthetical framework, life has no other purpose than to *be*, as the mystical
poet Angelus Silesius once said about the rose. "The rose has no why, it
blossoms without reason, forgetful of itself, oblivious to our vision."[21]

Popular Catholicism, according to Goizueta, incarnates this aesthetical celebration of life. "The symbols and rituals of popular religion are
prime examples of the intrinsic value of beauty... for the goal of the
community's participation in the stories, symbols, and rituals of popular
religion is nothing other than that participation itself."[22]

Goizueta points to Vasconcelos to suggest that aesthetics honors love
beyond ethics. "In its highest form," writes Vasconcelos, "ethics is aesthetics, that is, service out of love, not out of duty; service with joy
and life, action as enjoyment, the final stage."[23] Celebration and liturgy,
then, is the human desire for aesthetic union with others and, no less, the
yearning for communion with the divine nature. Most interesting about
this celebration of love beyond good and evil in the work of Vasconcelos, however, is his reading of the process of *mestizaje* that occurs in
the New World. The miscegenation and hybridity that resulted was, in
this view, the effect of eros, "a healthy aesthetic instinct."[24]

Vasconcelos, Goizueta notes, says very little about the horror of the
conquest, however. Goizueta wants to turn to another figure, this time
a sixteenth-century Dominican priest, to attend to the laments of the
poor and oppressed, to heed a call for justice. In Las Casas we have
"a powerful illustration of the fact that, unless we attend adequately to
the ethical-political and economic mediations of aesthetic action... that

---

21. Angelus Silesius, *The Cherubinic Wanderer*, trans. Maria Shrady (New York: Paulist
Press, 1986), 54.
22. Roberto Goizueta, *Caminemos con Jesús: Toward a Hispanic/Latino Theology of
Accompaniment* (Maryknoll, N.Y.: Orbis Books, 1995), 102.
23. Ibid., 93.
24. Ibid., 99.

action will be distorted, unjust, fraudulent, hypocritical, and, in the case of religious worship, blasphemous."[25]

Among other Hispanic theologians, this refrain is consistent. An aesthetics that does not face the histories of suffering past and present does not merit the name "Christian." Orlando Espín, for one, notes that it is through popular religion that Latino/as deal with suffering. Religious images of popular Catholicism do not avoid the ambiguities of the human experience. Suffering is not veiled by illusions. "Anyone familiar with it (popular Hispanic Catholicism), writes Espín, "will recall that, among other elements, some that stand out are the emphasis placed on crucifixion scenes, on very graphic depictions of the suffering and bleeding Jesus, on devotions to crucifixes and crosses, and on particular Good Friday ceremonies recalling the torture, death, and burial of Jesus as well as the sorrows of his mother (*la Dolorosa*)."[26]

The work of Alejandro García-Rivera also considers theological aesthetics through the lens of cultural traditions and by attention to the ugliness of suffering. Indeed, if he is persuaded that beauty can prove to be elevating, that it can draw our soul upward to the divine (*anagogy*), "only a cultural aesthetics which can face up to suffering, even find its aesthetic force there, could adequately describe the Hispanic and Latin American experience."[27]

While none of these theologians suggest a consideration of "tragic beauty" per se, their interest in the aesthetical dimension of popular religion never silences the voice of protest, of lament and cry. While considering the role of beauty in Christian theology, and in Hispanic popular Catholicism in particular, they insist that attention to the face of the poor and afflicted other must never waver.

CONCLUSION

In concluding this essay on tragic beauty, I would like to return to the issue, and too often tragedy, of immigration that I began with. I would

---

25. Ibid., 125.

26. Orlando Espín, *The Faith of the People* (Maryknoll, N.Y.: Orbis Books, 1997), 23.

27. Alejandro García-Rivera, *The Community of the Beautiful: A Theological Aesthetics* (Collegeville, Minn.: Liturgical Press, 1999), 60. Another essay, by Sixto García, "The Sources and Loci of Hispanic Theology" in *Mestizo Christianity,* ed. Arturo Bañuelas (Maryknoll, N.Y.: Orbis Books, 1995), is an interesting exploration of sources of Hispanic theology, beginning with Scripture but including discussions of poetry, story, and myth, as well as contemporary Hispanic literature.

like to do so by briefly discussing the latest work of Richard Rodriguez, *Brown: The Last Discovery of America*. His work strikes me as a beautiful case of a tragic sensibility united to a passion for aesthetics, to a poetics of love. The extraordinary, complex, baroque form of the writing — so meditative, so allusive and paradoxical, so spiritual — is enough to warrant anyone's attention. This should especially be true for those who celebrate a brown theology.[28]

The passage that resonated with me as I sought to write this paper on "tragic beauty," fully aware of the deaths in the desert, is the following, moving, mystical-aesthetical description of the migration of Monarch butterflies in Pacific Grove, California.

There is a stand of eucalyptus in Pacific Grove, seventy miles, as the crow flies, from where I stand. Californians have for years gathered there to experience themselves as northerly, as spiritually related to Nature.... This grove is the meetinghouse, nay, nothing so plain; this grove is the cathedral of the Monarch butterfly. Every autumn, caravans of ragged wings propel themselves hence according to some fairy compulsion. It is a mystic site. We stand with our mouths agape; we look up, up, up — Look! *I see them!* — circling clouds of stained-glass wings descending in a gyre. Despite the surroundings, the beauty of them is so surprising, so silent, so holy as to be wounding to the soul, for they resemble what clouds of angels in baroque paintings resemble, what toccata and fugue resemble, or what galactic kaleidoscope resembles. I assume you know more about butterflies than I do. I experience awe, not expecting to, but do I misunderstand the thrall of instinct displayed to me? The solemnity is one of death, is it not, as much as of beauty?... These angels are several generations removed from ancestors who departed this grove last year; several generations removed from ancestors who will return next fall. They alight to hang like sere leaves upon the branches. As the sun turns its face from them, they quieten; some will die, fall, blow away, to catch with scraps of paper, gum wrappers, and twists of cellophane in the

---

28. While a discussion of the meaning of "brown" is beyond the scope of this paper, it is important to note that it does not simply refer to Hispanic culture and certainly not to any notion of race. "Brown" for Rodriguez is impurity, contamination, miscegenation, and hybridity; it is contradiction, conflict, paradox. It is also the subjection of the body and spirit to the passage of time, to decay and impermanence. It is the human condition. Adam and Eve, he writes, were brown.

crevices of logs. But others will gather strength, others will hoist sail to rise like windmills on torrents of air, to worship, I suppose; to submit once more to the same cruel engine, the same piercing joy that grinds the sea.[29]

More than being a dazzling, precise description of tragic beauty, this poem of migration produced echoes in my mind of human angels trespassing through the deserts of Arizona. Is this migrating pattern not, after all, something like the journey of brown bodies, transgressing borders, seeking something else ... something better, indefinable maybe, likely impossible, but certainly including the modest dream of work and food, shelter and water? Are the crosses in the desert parables of a truth that we urgently need to decipher?

I for one am certain that these strangers are parables of tragic beauty, of human fragility and impermanence — and no less of justice. These parables are misunderstood, confused, rejected by most Americans. If tragedy is a reflection on the problem of innocent suffering, on the irreducibility of evil to a consequence of sin, then to many Americans the deaths in the desert are not a tragedy at all: it is the result of a sin, the illegal trespassing of the border.

Did not Jesus, however, this master of irony and parable, liken the kingdom of God to the least of society, to the poor and the stranger (surely irony of great proportions)? But irony is often lost on those seeking a more obvious argument, a more visible proof, a sign. The face of the Other is the only sign Jesus (this hidden God) offers. "They have ears, but they do not hear, eyes but they do not see."

Of course, the deaths of immigrants are more tragic than the deaths of butterflies. One might even envy the butterfly who lived her full life-span, who made the journey and reached the "promised land" of Pacific Grove. But what of those who died in the desert before reaching their destination, like Moses, like Dr. King, like these immigrants? Were gravesites wanting in Mexico for these gentle souls? Why did their final breath have to be here in-between, in no-man's land? And this after pleading with God, after praying to *la Virgen,* after taking offerings to the "Three Kings" or to Juan Soldado. "My God, my God ... ?"

In considering these events in light of tragedy, I want to conclude with a last look at a Jewish tradition, that of the Jewish mysticism. For if in

---

29. Rodriguez, *Brown,* 189–90.

tragic poetry or in all great literature the harmony and dance of words is playfully celebrated, and a magic is conjured to inspire awe or provoke thought, then the Kabbalists stand apart in their intuitive understanding of the creative, magical power of letters and language. And these masters of the spirit knew as well the forces of conflict and death that threaten the spirit, that leave us at a loss for words, that make apparent the impossibility of naming the Unnamable. After all, wasn't it part of the allure of Kabbalah mythology for thousands of exiled Jews (post-1492) the daring theological hypothesis that God herself shares the exile of Israel, that God is to be found in-between, in the gaps and borders of history? Is the secret of these Jewish mystics — a secret that proved too strange, too heretical to orthodox traditions — the allusion that God, like humankind, is vulnerable, fragile, even broken? If the vessels that held the Sefiroth have shattered, then the world that results is always, already fallen, before first man and woman. This tragic vision — for here the fault is not with human sin — proved meaningful to the Jews forced again to wander, forced again into the desert of exile.

The hope of this anguished theology is the stubborn belief that the Israelites (and all homeless, exiled peoples) do not wander alone, that the hidden God is there. My own religious beliefs stand and fall with this faith in a hidden God invisibly present in the desolate circumstances of life and with the belief in a God who is crucified even here and now, in the desert.

The problem of evil and the question of tragedy raise, in my mind at least, such unorthodox questions. Surely there are no answers, no final solutions to the problem of evil. Explanations do not help. We are left with silence, with a silence wearing different masks: one awe-inspiring and wondrous, the other wounding and cruel. We are left with tragic beauty and with images of a hidden God at once awesome and alluring.

10

A Rereading of Latino(a) Pentecostalism

SAMUEL CRUZ

INTRODUCTION

The theory of deprivation has had a major influence in the sociological study of religion, particularly when studying religious movements on the fringes of society.[1] As a framework for understanding religious experience, sociologists have used deprivation theory to understand issues as different as alienation, material deprivation, psychological deprivation, and political powerlessness. In modern history, one of the earliest proponents of a theory of religion that suggests deprivation on the part of the religious believer was Karl Marx, who coined the now famous words, "religion is the opiate of the people." Subsequent to Marx, many have continued to use divergent forms of the theory of deprivation to examine the role of religion in understanding religious behaviors, beliefs, and choices not only of sects or religious movements on the fringes of society, but also of radical evangelical movements and Pentecostalism. Some important works in this area are those by Anderson, Glazier, Glock, and

---

1. The theory of deprivation and its application in the study of religion has its roots in the nineteenth-century philosophies of Ludwig Feuerbach and Karl Marx, as well as in the works of the twentieth-century psychoanalyst Sigmund Freud. These three thinkers understood religion to be an "opiate," meeting the needs of people who felt powerless in the face of suffering and more generally in their social and political lives. In the mid-twentieth century, sociologists of religion began to use this idea in a modified form. They began to understand the attraction of certain groups to cults, sects, and enthusiastic forms of religion (e.g., Pentecostalism) as being rooted in forms of economic, social, or political disenfranchisement and/or suffering. In this way, deprivation was taken to be the motivation behind certain kinds of religious commitment — although not for all religious commitment. In the late 1970s and 1980s, however, we witnessed the advent of types of neo-Pentecostalism in which highly educated, economically and politically established people began to join Pentecostal churches. This happening poses a challenge to the original assertions of deprivation theory. Although deprivation theory is questionable in light of the advent of neo-Pentecostalism, the theory unfortunately remains a key interpretive perspective in Pentecostal studies.

Poblete.[2] This framework, although helpful in the study of religion, can also be limiting in understanding the religious movements of the powerless in our society. In my study of Latino(a) Pentecostalism, I attempt to move beyond these theoretical approaches in search of more accurate insights into this religious phenomenon.

Our theoretical understanding of a religious group or, as Weber[3] would suggest, our understanding from the perspective of an *ideal type,* can be greatly challenged when we actually experience the worship practices and their repercussions in the daily life of the religious group at hand. This has been the case in my experience during field work involvement as a participant-observer with Latino(a) Pentecostal congregations in Newark, New Jersey, and throughout the New York tristate area. Theoretical conceptualizations, although at times helpful, are often inadequate in their overgeneralizations of social and religious reality.

Unproductive overgeneralizations seem to be dangerous when endeavoring to understand the foundational premises of Latino(a) Pentecostal rituals/beliefs as they pertain to Pentecostal notions of cultural, social, political, and theological realities. As a participant-observer, I encountered very unique manifestations of Pentecostal practices, which are often different from what is sometimes verbalized in Pentecostal discourses during worship services and from what religious scholars frequently assert.[4] The following example can illuminate this perspective: For many years, a commonly held view was that Puerto Rican Pentecostal churches did not emphasize cultural pride, but that they in fact discouraged it in favor of assimilation into the dominant cultural ideology. It has also been asserted that Pentecostals are apolitical.[5] My contention that Pentecostalism has provided a vehicle for acceptable political resistance and rebellion refutes this notion entirely. Perhaps the ways in which this

---

2. Robert Anderson, *Vision of the Disinherited: The Making of Modern Pentecostalism* (New York: Oxford University Press, 1979); Stephen Glazier, *Perspectives on Pentecostalism: Case Studies from the Caribbean and Latin America* (Washington, D.C.: University Press of America, 1980); Charles Y. Glock, "On the Role of Deprivation in the Origin and Evolution of Religious Groups," in *Religion in Sociological Perspective,* ed. Charles Y. Glock (Belmont, Calif.: Wadsworth, 1973). Renato Poblete, "Sociological Approach to the Sects," *Social Compass* 7, nos. 5–6 (1960): 383–406.

3. Max Weber, *From Max Weber: Essays in Sociology* (New York: Oxford University Press, 1967).

4. Michael Jackson, *Paths toward a Clearing: Radical Empiricism and Ethnographic Inquiry* (Bloomington: Indiana University Press, 1989).

5. See Anderson, *Vision of the Disinherited.*

political resistance and rebellion are manifested differ from that of Anglo culture in ways that have caused scholars to overlook this political activity completely.

As a participant-observer researching the religious practices within Pentecostal churches for the past several years, I have discovered that these assertions of apolitical values and pie-in-the-sky theology are not completely true. Although our research team (studying Latino[a] Pentecostal congregations in Newark) has discovered that there is a conservative cultural, social, and political dimension to these churches, as is the case with most churches, it has been noted that Latino(a) Pentecostals are less conservative in their practices regarding many social issues. One example is the role of women, who in most conservative or traditional denominations do not hold the same power as men, yet in Latino(a) Pentecostal congregations actually have more power than in the so-called progressive white liberal denominations. For more than sixty years now, women in Puerto Rican Pentecostal churches have been pastors, seminary professors, and leaders, holding key positions within the Pentecostal grassroots religious organizations.[6] The expressed value that Hispanic women, like women in other cultures, have clearly defined roles of being primarily homebound and raising children is contradicted by certain practices within Latino(a) Pentecostalism. In the Pentecostal religious ethos, serving God takes primacy over everything else, including family. This priority has allowed women to take on different tasks beyond those traditionally assigned to them. Particularly impressive to me is the great number of women who are Bible school professors.[7]

The teaching profession is one that has been dominated by women, but women holding these teaching positions have been mostly relegated to teaching lower-grade children rather than adults. However, within the Latino(a) Pentecostal movement, the female professors in the Bible schools are training many men for parish ministry.[8] Two Pentecostal women I interviewed put this phenomenon in their own words: Rev. Karen Hernández, an ordained Presbyterian minister whose religious roots are Pentecostal, said that the Pentecostal movement had a

6. Roberto Domínguez, *Pioneros de Pentecostés: En el mundo de habla hispana* (Miami: Literatura Evangélica, 1990).

7. Eldin Villafañe, *The Liberating Spirit: Toward an Hispanic American Pentecostal Ethic* (Grand Rapids, Mich.: Eerdmans, 1993).

8. José Caraballo, "A Certificate Program for Hispanic Clergy and Lay Persons in an Accredited Theological Seminary: A Case Study with Projection" (D.Min. thesis, Drew University, Madison, N.J., 1983).

tremendous impact on her as a young girl because of the female role models that she encountered in her church. She said that these women "taught me to believe that women were as capable as men; I learned passion in leadership, commitment, and consistency from them." On the negative side, she admitted that she had never considered pursuing ordained ministry, because at that time women were not allowed to be ordained in the Assembly of God church. However, Pastor Karen stated, "I think that the power unleashed among women in this movement created support among them, and led men to accept the eventual ordination of women."

Similarly, Rebecca Rodríguez, a former Pentecostal, who is currently a leader in the Reformed Church, stated that "Since the church was mainly made up of women, they (the women) had to take on what were considered traditional male roles such as preaching, positions as presidents on boards, and other church functions." Rebecca said: "These experiences have helped me in my professional life. I learned to be assertive, I acquired organizational skills, and became sensitive to the moods and characters of people." Although she admitted that the Pentecostal churches were far from perfect, Rebecca believes that they empowered women. In fact, the interviews I conducted with prominent male preachers within the Assembly of God church and throughout several independent congregations revealed, to my surprise, that many of these preachers mentioned women as their theological mentors. One interviewee, Rev. Félix, made special mention of Leonecia Rosado (also known as "Mama Leo"), a preacher and cofounder of the Iglesia Cristiana Damascus Concilio. In 1957, Leonecia pioneered in establishing drug treatment centers in New York City. Mama Leo was also a sought-after preacher, and she inspired a grassroots theology of women's liberation. Such accounts have inspired my research in the connections between Puerto Rican/Latino(a) leadership, in both secular and religious spheres, and Pentecostal churches.

The Latino(a) Pentecostal movement is primarily a religious organization of Hispanic congregations, whose goal is responding to the religious needs of its followers by providing theological answers to spiritual/religious questions about life and eternal matters. However, it seems to me that in many ways this form of religiosity, having been coopted by a great many number of Latino/as in the United States, has served as a vehicle for dealing with broader issues beyond the sacred, such as social, political, economic, and educational issues facing Latino/as. For the purposes of this study, particular attention has been focused upon the Puerto Rican community. My intention is not to suggest that Latino(a) Pentecostalism has become simply a social movement, but rather that it has gone beyond the obvious religious functions and has facilitated a community response to an array of social issues that have affected the Hispanic community in the northeastern United States.

In fact, when we look for political action groups within the Hispanic community, where traditional European and Euro-American political discourse would have us find them (i.e., unions, political parties, etc....), we might assume that very little political activism is taking place within Latino(a) communities. However, when we expand our conceptual scope of what constitutes political action and resistance to oppression, then we can begin to find some of this action and resistance activity occurring in places where we usually do not expect to find it, such as in Latino(a) Pentecostal congregations. Sociologists Kelvin Santiago-Valle and Angel Quintero-Rivera have correctly asserted that in Latin America and the Caribbean, traditional European approaches to dealing with societal problems via political organizations have not been popular. Unfortunately, not much attention has been paid to the alternative ways by which Latin American and Caribbean people have dealt with oppressive systems. Santiago-Valle discusses the lack of research in this area by examining capitalist exploitation, its effects on the Puerto Rican working class, and the responses of this particular community:

> There were a few paltry efforts to comb the archives and oral-history sources for traces of different countersystemic disruptions: on-the-job pilfering, odd-jobbing, the use of value-oriented reciprocal practices, and other early manifestations of the "informal economy."[9]

Quintero-Rivera in his analysis of Latin America and the Caribbean states, "In most countries what is considered the political has come to constitute elitist practices and organizations with increasing distancing from the daily life of most people."[10] This rejection of traditional

---

9. Kelvin V. Santiago, "The Discreet Charm of the Proletariat: Imagining Early-Twentieth-Century Puerto Ricans in the Past Twenty-five Years of Historical Inquiry," in *Puerto Rican Jam: Essays on Culture and Politics,* ed. Frances Negrón-Muntaner and Ramón Grosfoguel (Minneapolis: University of Minnesota Press, 1997), 100.

10. Angel Quintero-Rivera, "Culture Oriented Social Movements: Ethnicity and Symbolic Action in Latin America and the Caribbean" (Hunter College, N.Y.: Boletín del Centro de Estudios Puertorriqueños, 1991), 98.

political organization has resulted in the strong development of social and religious movements that have emerged in response to specific issues, and that often confront broad public issues.

Quintero views social and religious movements that primarily address particular issues as being simultaneously globalizing in their capacity.[11] He gives several examples, including that of the Bolivian coal miners' wives' movement, which began as a private gathering of miners' wives addressing personal common concerns, but through the process of their meetings and activities grew to encompass the miners' struggle more broadly than originally conceived. Similarly, I would suggest that Latino(a) Pentecostal congregations have evolved to respond to issues beyond the religious, though issues and concerns unique to their communities, to the extent of developing organizations that address vital issues in their communities from a Christian perspective. Another such example occurred in the 2001 New York City mayoral elections when an impromptu gathering of Latino(a) Pentecostal ministers was organized in an attempt to facilitate the election of what would have been the first Hispanic mayor. While this activity was overtly political, perhaps the more ambiguous resistance activities that take place throughout worship and other church activities go unnoticed or are not viewed as political. These more ambiguous political activities characterize the Latino(a) Pentecostal movement.

HISTORICAL OVERVIEW

The Pentecostal movement traces its history to the turn of the twentieth century, particularly to the Azusa Street Revival, which occurred in Los Angeles in 1906.[12] Latino/as have been part of this movement from its inception almost a hundred years ago.[13] As early as 1923, the influential Mexican preacher, Francisco Olazabal, founded the Pentecostal denomination called Concilio Latino-Americano de Iglesias Cristianas. Olazabal had originally been ordained a Pentecostal minister with the Assemblies of God denomination in 1918. As has been the case with other facets of Latino(a) history, such stories of the Pentecostal Latino(a) churches have not been fully told, least of all by scholars, who particularly seem to have lacked interest in studying the Latino(a) Pentecostal movement in

---

11. Ibid.
12. Walter J. Hollewenger, *The Pentecostals* (London: SCM, 1992).
13. See Domínguez, *Pioneros de Pentecostés,* and Villafañe, *The Liberating Spirit.*

urban centers within the United States. However, for the purposes of this discussion and my research, I focus attention on the movement's history and impact upon the Puerto Rican community (and vice versa). I specifically focus on the northeastern part of the United States, particularly New York City, New Jersey, and Pennsylvania. Though the Pentecostal movement originated in the United States, it was by way of Puerto Rico itself that the movement arrived in and had a significant impact upon the Puerto Rican *colonias* (enclaves) in New York. The Pentecostal movement arrived in Puerto Rico in 1916 via the preaching of the Puerto Rican preacher Juan Lugo, who had been converted in Hawaii. Intrinsic to the Pentecostal message was a sense of special calling, of being a chosen people with a special providential mission, a notion similar to that of manifest destiny found in nineteenth- and early-twentieth-century U.S. religion more broadly.[14]

In the mid-1920s surge of migration from Puerto Rico to New York City many immigrants joined the Pentecostal movement. With them came a sense of providential responsibility to bring the gospel not only to the newfound Puerto Rican *colonias,* but to what was understood to be a decadent U.S. society. In 1928 one of the first Hispanic Pentecostal congregations in New York was founded in Green Point, Brooklyn, and was called "La Iglesia Misionera Pentecostal."[15] This Hispanic congregation was founded many years prior to the formation of an official Hispanic ministry in the New York Catholic diocese, a ministry that resulted from the faithful leadership and commitment of Joseph Fitzpatrick. The Latino(a) Pentecostal churches have been an integral part of the Hispanic/Puerto Rican community throughout New York City from the beginning of the Community's establishment. In 1937, out of a total of fifty-five Latino(a) Protestant Congregations in New York City, twenty-five were Pentecostal.[16]

The first Bible school, indeed probably the first institution of higher learning founded for and by Latino/as in New York City, was the Spanish American Bible Institute founded in 1935. This school eventually grew to have twenty-three different sites throughout the city. These accomplishments occurred during a period both when economic and political

14. Daniel Rodríguez, *La primera evangelización norteamericana en Puerto Rico 1898–1930* (Mexico, D.F.: Ediciones Borinquén, 1986).

15. Caraballo, "A Certificate Program for Hispanic Clergy and Lay Persons."

16. Frederick Whitman, "New York's Spanish Protestants," *Christian Century,* February 7, 1962, 161–65.

resources were scarce and in the midst of increasing racism toward new incoming Latino(a) immigrants. Presently, there are well over eight hundred Latino(a) Pentecostal congregations in New York City alone, scores of Bible schools, over fifty Pentecostal-based drug rehabilitation centers, and countless Christian bookstores.[17] These figures do not include the churches and Bible schools found in New Jersey, Connecticut, and Pennsylvania. In Newark, N.J., the Latino(a) Pentecostal congregations research team (part of the Newark Project) has found sixty-seven Latino(a)/Brazilian congregations in one year and expects to find many others, many with unique characteristics.

LEADERSHIP DEVELOPMENT

In researching the connection between the development of Puerto Rican leadership and Latino(a) Pentecostal congregations, I interviewed many Hispanic leaders in order to attain a more meaningful understanding of the correlations involved in this phenomenon. One unexpected interview that I conducted happened during a walking census in Newark, and gave me information of what I would call *the development of leadership by fire.* During this walking census of Newark I came across a church called Templo Ebenezer located on Montclair Street. As I was writing down the name and address of the church, one of its parishioners, a middle-aged Latino man named David, approached me. I asked him how long the church had been there. He responded that the church was established in Newark in 1950, but that it had been in its present location since 1960. David proceeded to tell me that during the time the church has been in its present location the neighborhood has been predominately Italian and there was a great deal of racial tension in Newark. In the early 1960s the Italian, community exhibited this tension and hostility toward the new Latino(a) congregation in their neighborhood by constantly shattering the windows of the temple. The police did not offer much help.

David reported that the minister at that time, Rev. Ricardo Tañón, was extremely frustrated with the community response as well as with the lack of police response, and that he subsequently attempted to gain a deeper understanding of the political, and especially the racial, situation in Newark. He discovered that the racial situation was egregious, and that African Americans were likely to be hated more than Hispanics.

---

17. Caraballo, "A Certificate Program for Hispanic Clergy and Lay Persons."

Rev. Tañón therefore went about two miles across town to speak to the pastor of a Holiness black congregation. This Holiness congregation had a large choir, and Rev. Tañón offered the opportunity to use his temple free of charge. When the black congregation began to use the temple, the leaders of the Italian community began to question what was going on, and Rev. Tañón told them that, as a result of the broken windows, they were contemplating donating the church to this African American congregation. Several days later the Italian community leaders came to the pastor's home and guaranteed that his windows would no longer be broken if the church did not give the temple to the African Americans. This crisis led this minister to become involved in the racial and political issues within his church's community. He did not approach the dilemma with prayer alone, but tackled it in a very sophisticated manner. Although his solution seems somewhat harsh to the black community, he evidently knew that the blacks were disliked more than the Hispanics and that the possibility of having a black congregation in the neighborhood would force the Italian community to take a less hostile approach to having a Hispanic church there.

EFRAÍN FÉLIX, DAVID ANGLADA, AND LUIS PÉREZ

In 2000, I had a phone interview with the Rev. Efraín Félix, who had been a Pentecostal and Reformed church pastor in Brooklyn, New York, for over thirty years. As soon as I explained to him the purpose of my call, he immediately conveyed to me his pleasure in having someone attempt to tell the story of Puerto Rican Pentecostalism in New York City and its surrounding areas. He proceeded to say, "Despite some of the flaws found among Latino Pentecostal congregations and its leadership, it is the only institution in the New York tristate area which has offered a *continuous service* to the Puerto Rican/Latino community for the last fifty to sixty years." He went on to say that, when no other institution cared about or knew how to respond to the massive political, economic, and social problems being confronted by Puerto Ricans, Cubans, and other Hispanics, the Pentecostal church was meeting these challenges by creating a squadron of leadership and supportive social programs to address the dire needs of the community.

During my interview with Rev. Félix, he gave an autobiographical sketch of himself: how when he came into contact with a storefront

congregation in Manhattan, he lacked self-esteem, could not read, and
could barely communicate verbally because of his lack of education. He
told me that his pastor felt that he would be a good leader and urged him
to attend the Instituto Bíblico (Bible School). In order for him to attend
this school he would have to learn how to read and write, and therefore
literate women and men within the congregation taught him until he
attained the necessary skills to make it possible for him to attend classes
at the Bible School. Rev. Félix shared that hundreds of men and women
were trained to become pastors, missionaries, and Christian educators as
well as to assume other roles of leadership in these grassroots schools.
In fact, he pointed out to me that these schools, which even provide
college-level courses, have been so successful in their retention rate and
percentage of Hispanic graduates that some philanthropic foundations
were funding studies to try to discover the reasons for such high success
and to emulate this system in traditional colleges. Rev. Félix emphasized
that the Latino(a) Pentecostal churches were instrumental in promoting
the leadership of women in religious and secular circles. He stated that
most, if not all, of the Bible schools that he knew were very receptive to
having women as their students.[18]

During the last thirty years, the leadership formed within Pentecostalism has expanded into many different spheres of social, religious,
political, and economic life. Interestingly, throughout the different interviews that I have conducted, the theme of leadership skills and the
importance of dealing with certain cultural and political issues were discussed as directly attributable to this religious tradition. This was evident
in another of my interviews conducted with Rev. David Anglada, the assistant bishop for the New York and New Jersey Synod of the Evangelical
Lutheran Church. Rev. Anglada provides counsel to the bishop on Hispanic issues. He views his job as that of an advocate in Lutheran parishes
for Latino/as and for the Hispanic community at large. Rev. Anglada
made it clear to me that he believes he acquired the most needed skills
to perform this task while a seventeen-year-old youth minister in the
Assemblies of God Pentecostal church under the mentorship of the Superintendent Rev. Adolfo Carrion. He stated that Rev. Carrion taught him
how to build coalitions and how to lobby people who would support his

---

18. Rev. Félix made it clear to me that he did not want to romanticize this issue because he
believes women undoubtedly suffered discrimination, but he maintains that their opportunities
were unusually good within Latino(a) Pentecostalism.

leadership and agenda within the religious spheres as well as in secular domains.

Rev. Anglada shared that the skills he acquired were not only useful in his church work, but also in his secular career as a special advisor to the superintendent of the New York City Board of Education. His skills also facilitated his active role in political organizing. Rev. Anglada shared that, in particular, the ability to communicate effectively and the art of persuasion that he learned in the church were instrumental in his political and community organizing. He told me that despite the fact that Pentecostal congregations and their theologies were mostly concerned with spiritual matters, there were several issues that, though not of a religious nature, became very important to Pentecostal leaders. One such issue was the preservation of the Spanish language. For many pastors, the defense of the Spanish language became a serious matter. One of the reasons was that, early on in the movement, the ministers of these churches in Puerto Rico had experienced the forced imposition of English throughout the island. Rev. Anglada explained that many pastors went on to create a theological discourse which asserted that Spanish was a heavenly language. Though the ministers did not necessarily believe this in a strict sense, they wanted their constituencies to take the defense of their language very seriously. Teaching young children Spanish became part of the curriculum in many Pentecostal Sunday schools.

According to Rev. Anglada, church leaders were also keenly aware of the leadership and influence that they had upon a great number of people in their community. When asked if he thought that his Pentecostal theological roots were present in his ministry within the Lutheran Church, he responded that, though he considers himself to be theologically Lutheran, his preaching style and liturgical approach are directly attributable to his Pentecostal roots. He even acknowledged that his theology of healing, although expanded to include emotional and psychological healing as well as physical, has its origins in his Pentecostalism. Though tamed by his academic theological training, he stated that his views on the spirit world are much more open than that of traditional Lutherans.

A similar experience was shared by Rev. Wilfredo Laboy, deputy superintendent of District 15 in the New York City Board of Education. Rev. Laboy expressed his views about the role of Latino(a) Pentecostalism very emphatically, saying that, "Unfortunately few people know about the important role that this church has had in our community."

In his perspective, only thirty years ago very few places were seriously trying to address the needs of the Hispanic communities, but the Pentecostal Hispanic churches were actively seeking solutions and trying to establish the leadership to do so.

Another interesting example of the impact of Pentecostalism on leadership in other areas of secular and religious life is that of the Reformed Church in America (RCA). The RCA is the oldest continually active denomination in the United States and was formerly called the Dutch Reformed Church. This denomination started a Hispanic ministry approximately thirty years ago, and the influence of Pentecostalism via Latino(a) leaders trained in that tradition has been great. I interviewed the Rev. Luis Pérez, who is the national secretary of the Hispanic Council of the Reformed Church in America; he attributes most of his leadership skills, such as "organizational development," "public speaking," and "community organizing" to his formative years in the Pentecostal church. Interestingly, though he denies that his current theological views are Pentecostal in nature and stated on several occasions that he was Calvinistic in his theology, when asked about his beliefs on divine healing, speaking in strange tongues, prophecy, eschatology, and liturgy, the views he expressed are theologically Pentecostal. Despite the fact that his leadership in the Reformed Church might not have had the intent of the Pentecostalization of the Reformed Church, in many respects this has been the result; of fifty-five Hispanic ministers in the Reformed Church, forty-seven were originally ministers within the Pentecostal movement and maintain Pentecostal beliefs. In visiting several of these congregations, I could have easily assumed that they were Pentecostal congregations had I not known their stated religious affiliations. Theologically and culturally, these churches differ greatly from traditional RCA congregations in their worship styles.

CULTURAL RESISTANCE OF DOMINANT CULTURE

Religious practice has been an integral part of U.S. sociopolitical culture, as was evident when the U.S. military arrived in Puerto Rico in 1898. The legal and political understanding of the separation of church and state was not realized from a practical perspective. Just as when the natives and blacks were forcefully encouraged to affiliate with Spanish Roman Catholicism, so Puerto Ricans were pressured to affiliate with the newly introduced Protestant churches. As a result of the new U.S. political and judicial system, in particular its notions of the separation of church and state, the already fragile Roman Catholic Church virtually collapsed.[19] A great number of individuals who needed institutional religion for such things as marriage, baptism, and funerals were left to depend upon the newly arrived Protestant churches.[20]

The religious political ethos of the Puerto Rican people was disrupted, causing religious dislocation for many. This religious anomic situation became even more acute for those immigrants who began to arrive in New York City during the 1920s, searching for a better quality of life. The Roman Catholic church was not very receptive to the new Spanish-speaking Puerto Rican immigrants; in fact, many church leaders looked upon the new immigrant group as a problem rather than as an opportunity for growth and service.[21] Therefore, they took little interest in providing for the spiritual, social, or economic needs of these new immigrants. The mainline Protestant denominations had begun to establish themselves among the Puerto Rican community without much success.[22] Apparently, the rationalistic, Anglo-centered worship styles and theological approach did not provide a comfortable arena for the development of popular religious expression that is so vital in Caribbean religiosity.

Within this sociohistorical, religious, and political context, Pentecostalism entered the Puerto Rican religious arena. For the first time in over four hundred years the Puerto Rican people experienced a religious movement that fit with the dominant cultural understanding of acceptable religious practice while at the same time maintaining Puerto Ricans as key religious players. Symbolically and concretely, this situation created a sense of empowerment. Although Pentecostalism is considered Protestant, several divergent characteristics distinguish it from other Protestant denominations and make it much more attractive to Puerto Ricans, as David Martin states:

> Caribbean culture is one which is spoken and sung rather than written down. It is also informal, spontaneous, flexible and infinitely varied. Clearly such characteristics offer a potential harvest to a

19. Samuel Silva-Gotay, *Protestantismo y política en Puerto Rico 1898–1930* (San Juan, P.R.: Editorial de la Universidad de Puerto Rico, 1997).

20. Nélida Agosto Cintrón, *Religión y cambio social en Puerto Rico 1898–1940* (Río Piedras, P.R.: Ediciones Huracán, 1996).

21. Ana María Díaz-Stevens, *Oxcart Catholicism of Fifth Avenue: The Impact of Puerto Rican Migration upon the Archdiocese of New York* (Notre Dame, Ind.: Notre Dame Press, 1993).

22. Caraballo, "A Certificate Program for Hispanic Clergy and Lay Persons."

religion which is oral, informal and constantly splitting in order to adapt. What is above all most evident is the capacity of Pentecostalism simultaneously to conform and to transform. It finds out the morphology and shape of the local society and participates in the life of people.[23]

This characteristic appears to allow groups from diverse backgrounds to assimilate the movement to their traditions, and furthermore, to find within it traits easily grasped as similar to their specific cultural traditions.

The comments of Joseph Murphy regarding the fertile ground that Catholicism provided for Santería seem to be comparable to Protestantism and Pentecostalism in the Caribbean. He states:

> The more symbolically austere traditions of Protestantism did not have this panoply of sacred objects for Africans to identify and interpret. Catholic symbolism provided a haven for the orishas, symbolic building blocks to recreate the new way of the orishas in the New World.[24]

Pentecostalism, with its emphasis on the spirit world, divination, healing, and spirit possession, offers a panoply of sacred beliefs with which Puerto Ricans could identify and which they could reinterpret. With an affinity with African cultural and religious characteristics found in the Caribbean, these Pentecostal traits have provided a vehicle for the revitalization, on the one hand, of the Afro-Caribbean sacred worldview among the Puerto Rican masses, and on the other, of the anti-assimilation resistance that the movement has fostered within the Puerto Rican community in the diaspora. In a society where rational, stoic behavior seems to be the example to follow as the norm of proper behavior, Caribbean culture has definitely found itself at odds.

The acute presence of the sacred in all aspects of daily life is central for Puerto Ricans. Requesting personal healing and guidance and desiring a sense of the future from God are very common practices for Puerto Rican and Caribbean people, but are religious expectations not commonly found among Euro-American Protestant churches. Therefore, in order to belong to one of these churches, a certain degree of spiritual

---

23. David Martin, *Tongues of Fire: The Explosion of Protestantism in Latin America* (Cambridge: Basil Blackwell, 1990), 133.

24. Joseph Murphy, *Santería: African Spirits in America* (Boston: Beacon Press, 1992), 114.

oppression had to be accepted. The Pentecostal movement provided the church with many characteristics similar to other Protestant churches, but also embodied many traits that held an affinity with Afro-Caribbean religious traditions. Puerto Rican Pentecostals have been able to conform to U.S. Christianity while simultaneously expressing their heartfelt spiritual convictions. The structural composition of spirit-led churches also provided for the empowerment of Puerto Rican leadership which, for the first time, created a situation in which Puerto Rican people could achieve a degree of control over their religious trajectory. This ability to hold religious power would be critical in providing cultural and religious expression to the Puerto Rican community.

After so many years of being subjected to foreign forms of religious practice, Puerto Ricans experienced a relatively great freedom of religious expression without completely abandoning U.S. mainline religious behavior and beliefs. In Pentecostal churches the sacraments are practiced and the Bible is used; all the major Christian teachings are taught as in other Christian churches. But Pentecostalism also offers a wealth of opportunities for the development and growth of Afro-Caribbean religious practice. I would contend, for example, that the syncretism of Haitian voodoo and Santería with Catholicism, which provided opportunities for religious, cultural, and political expression for Cubans and Haitians, has also occurred for Puerto Ricans through Pentecostalism.

CONCLUSION

Sociologists of religion have not yet begun undertaking many new approaches to the study of Pentecostalism and other enthusiastic forms of religiosity. However, promising work in this regard is being conducted by scholars such as Mariz, Neitz, and Warner.[25] They and several others have been providing new frameworks from which scholars and researchers can begin to explore and offer different hypotheses about this very important twentieth- and twenty-first-century religious phenomenon. When applied to the study of Puerto Rican/Latino(a) Pentecostalism, this new perspective offers great possibilities for discovering

25. Cecilia Mariz, "Religion and Poverty in Brazil: A Comparison of Catholic and Protestant Communities," *Sociological Analysis* 53S, supplement (1992): 63–70; Mary Jo Neitz, *Charisma and Community: A Study of Religious Commitment within the Charismatic Renewal* (New Brunswick, N.J.: Transaction Books, 1987); R. Stephen Warner, "Work in Progress toward a Paradigm for the Sociological Study of Religion in the United States," *American Journal of Sociology* 98 (March 1993): 1044–93.

the profound impact this movement has had in the various Latino(a) communities. As I have attempted to demonstrate in this analysis, the contributions of the Pentecostal Latino(a) congregations in the areas of culture, politics, religion, and leadership development are currently largely unexplored territories for research and would benefit from better understanding. One such research trajectory that I am pursuing is investigating the contributions of Latino(a) Pentecostals in the preservation of indigenous music, rituals, and other religious practices.

Leadership development within political organizations — including elected officials, leaders in universities, and those of other historical denominations beyond that of the Reformed Church — have roots that can be traced to Pentecostalism. Preliminary investigations into these areas are proving to be fertile for research. I hope that a more complete picture of Latino(a) Pentecostalism and its contributions to Latino(a) communities in the northeastern United States and beyond will begin to unfold as different scholars continue to conduct research into these areas. As the views about what constitutes political activity, resistance, and cultural preservation continue to expand and become further informed, we as researchers can reach more meaningful insights regarding such religious phenomena.

11

Transformative Struggle

The Spirituality of Las Hermanas

LARA MEDINA

> Años de un caminar que se hace historia,
> de mujeres valientes que han tomado
> con decisión, firmeza, fe y anhelo
> las riendas de la vida junto al Pueblo. . . .
>
> Años de lucha, huellas que no se borran
> Páginas de una historia que libera
> Años de lucha, mujeres que se entregan
> A plantar en la tierra la justicia.[1]

As songwriter and community activist Sister Rosa Martha Zárate Macías sang this composition in 1991 at the twentieth anniversary of Las Hermanas (The Sisters), two hundred women in attendance remembered the long, hard struggle that had brought them to this moment. Many of the women had been with Las Hermanas since its inception in 1971, when fifty primarily Chicana women religious or sisters gathered in Houston to discuss how they might better serve the needs of Spanish-speaking Catholics in the United States.[2] Their plans for more effective service resulted in Las Hermanas, a thirty-year-old national religious-political feminist organization of Latina Roman Catholics. For three decades Las

---

Originally published in the *Journal of Feminist Studies in Religion* 17, no. 2 (Fall 2001): 107–26.

1. Years of a journey that make history, / a journey of valiant women who travel / with assuredness and faith, longing to take / the reins of life together with the people. . . . / Years of struggle, footprints that cannot be erased, / pages of a history that liberates; years of struggle, women who devote themselves / to planting justice in our land. Translation by author.
2. "Women religious" and "sisters" are used interchangeably in this essay.

Hermanas has provided a counter-discourse to the patriarchy and Eurocentricism of the U.S. Roman Catholic Church by creating an alternative
space for Latina Catholics to express a feminist spirituality and theology.

Through their direct involvement in the Chicano(a) movement of
the 1970s, Las Hermanas brought the ethnic and gender struggles for
self-determination into the religious realm. Their activism expanded the
ministerial role of the church by bridging religious needs and the struggle
for civil rights. In the process, Las Hermanas expressed a spirituality
and a theology rooted in the Mexican, Cuban, and Puerto Rican Roman
Catholic faith, but shaped by their experiences as feminists and fused
with their politically informed ethnic identities. Las Hermanas provided
the inspiration for the internationally recognized *mujerista* theology first
articulated by Ada María Isasi-Díaz and Yolanda Tarango in *Hispanic
Women: Prophetic Voice in the Church* (1988).[3] As a theology based on
praxis or reflective action in making justice a reality, *mujerista* theology
reflects a commitment to the self-determination of Latinas held by Las
Hermanas.[4]

In this essay I first present an overview of the social factors influencing the mobilization of Las Hermanas and the challenges and goals in
its first two decades. Second, I note how the group's spirituality is narrated through conferences, liturgies, and artistic expressions. I argue that
"transformative struggle" grounds its spirituality and empowers grassroots members to confront adversity to make justice a reality. Sources
include in-depth interviews, participant observation, archival research,
and the literature of *mujerista* theology. Such a methodology of first placing the subject within its broader sociohistorical context offers insight
into how Latino(a) theology and the study of Latino(a) religions remains
grounded in concrete social realities. For Latino/as, to *do* theology means
to act *in the world* out of a commitment to the liberation of Latino/as
and other oppressed communities. To understand Las Hermanas within
its historical context and then to examine the actions by which it has
met the challenges of its time is to grasp how Latino/as *do* theology.
Relying on the voices of the subjects "to tell their stories" and to enrich
one's interpretive analysis is vital to representing Latino(a) theology and

3. Ada María Isasi-Díaz and Yolanda Tarango, *Hispanic Women: Prophetic Voice in the
Church* (San Francisco: Harper & Row, 1988; reprint Minneapolis: Fortress Press, 1992). The
link between Las Hermanas and *mujerista* theology is developed further in this essay based on
interviews with Tarango and Isasi-Díaz.
4. *Mujerista* theology is further developed by Ada María Isasi-Díaz, *En la Lucha:
Elaborating a Mujerista Theology* (Minneapolis: Fortress, 1993).

Latino(a) religions. Examining the material expressions such as rituals, songs, and poetry for their underlying spirituality is to access Latino(a) theology at its most humane level.

Las Hermanas is an organization of primarily grassroots women. Its history offers a model for how Latinas live in the intersection of the sacred and the political. Its spirituality of transformative struggle defies dualistic attempts to separate the sacred from everyday life. For Las Hermanas and for Latino(a) theologies, making social justice a reality is of ultimate concern. Further exploration of this epistemology could enrich our study of Latino(a) religiosity.

SOCIOHISTORICAL CONTEXT

Influenced by the renewal represented by Vatican II, American Catholic feminism, the black and Chicano(a) civil rights movements, and Latin American liberation theology, Las Hermanas organized to fight the overt discrimination within the church *and* society toward Chicano(a) and other Spanish-speaking communities. The invitation to unite Mexican American sisters came from Gregoria Ortega, a Victorynoll sister, and Gloria Gallardo of the Sisters of the Holy Ghost. Ortega had been transferred out of the diocese of Abilene, Texas, where she had opposed the severe abuse of Chicano(a) youth by teachers, police officers, and judges. Gallardo worked as a community organizer and catechist in San Antonio, among Chicano/as suffering chronic unemployment, inadequate health care, and malnutrition.[5] Together they decided to organize Chicana sisters "who have tried to become more relevant to our people and because of this, find themselves in 'trouble' with either our own congregation or other members of the hierarchy."[6]

In planning for the initial meeting, the two women contacted bishops throughout the country asking for the names of Mexican American sisters. While some bishops responded, others refused to cooperate. Unwilling to give up, the organizers contacted the Leadership Conference of

---

5. In San Antonio of the late 1960s, 26.8 percent of the Spanish-surname families lived below the poverty level. This exceeded the national average of 20.4 percent. *1970 Census of Population, Characteristics of the Spanish Surname Population by Census Tract, for SMSAs in Texas: 1970*, PC(S1)-61.

6. Circular letter to prospective members from Sister Gloria Gallardo, S.H.G., October 20, 1970. Las Hermanas Collection, St. Florence Library, Special Collections, Our Lady of the Lake University, San Antonio, Texas. Hermanas member Sister María Carolina Flores must be credited with archiving the records of Las Hermanas.

Women Religious (LCWR), who willingly supplied them with the names of major superiors in charge of the various religious communities. Their efforts resulted in fifty women attending the first gathering. While this might seem like a small number of participants, religious life in the early 1970s still placed very restrictive limits on travel other than for spiritual retreats. According to Sister Yolanda Tarango, "Just the fact that these women strategized to get there was tremendous. Some went with their superiors as they were not trusted."[7]

The sisters attending the first meeting had joined religious life prior to Vatican II or shortly thereafter, and embodied various levels of political and ethnic consciousness. The majority of them shared the experience of having to deny their ethnicity once they entered the convent. Many of them also shared frustration and anger over being prevented from speaking Spanish and ministering in their own ethnic communities. Tarango shares her experience:

> At that time you were supposed to leave behind your past as it was not desirable to work with one's people. I experienced much racism. . . . We were forbidden to speak Spanish even in hospitals, schools, not even to the janitors. . . . It was a violent tearing away from our pasts.[8]

Their stories revealed the trauma that many Chicana sisters underwent in religious life. Sister María de Jesús Ybarra shared the following example that took place even after Vatican II:

> One sister was a daughter of farm workers. She was working along the route that her parents traveled to pick the fields. She did not allow her parents to stop and visit her because she was ashamed of them. She told me, "I lived in fear for constant years that my order would discover that I was Mexican."[9]

The call to unite and the opportunity to "tell their stories" enabled the women to recognize the similarities, identify the elements of oppression, and "realize it was not just my order or my life but that we were in a widespread situation. In the coming together we raised each others' consciousness."[10]

7. Interviews with Yolanda Tarango, June 2, 1990, and August 23, 1996.
8. Interview with Yolanda Tarango, June 2, 1990.
9. Interview with Sister María de Jesús Ybarra, April 10, 1997.
10. Interview with Yolanda Tarango, June 2, 1990.

Mobilizing as Mexican American sisters proved to be an emotionally charged event. Sister Carmelita Espinoza expressed the following:

> Most of us had been pretty brainwashed or repressed. Coming together at the first conference was a call to action and a personal call to our own identity and that of the struggling Hispanic community.... We realized we needed to all go back to our orders and demand to work with the Hispanic community.[11]

Experiencing institutionalized patterns of discrimination within the church composed only a portion of the women's concerns. At their first conference, the women gave unanimous support to four goals for more effective service in Chicano(a) communities. These women desired (1) to activate leadership among themselves and the laity, (2) to effect social change, (3) to contribute to the cultural renaissance of La Raza, and (4) to educate their Anglo-dominant congregations on the needs of Spanish-speaking communities.[12]

The decision to form a national organization quickly took root, and those present chose "Las Hermanas" as the official name as well as the motto, *Unidas en acción y oración*.[13] In reflecting on their choice of name, Las Hermanas representatives wrote in 1975:

> Our title signifies the common vision and purpose of the first members. In our native language, the term "sisters" means much more than a blood relationship. Its more profound meaning is a relationship of sisterhood which demands a certain identity with and sharing of the total self with the whole of humanity.[14]

The need to express "a certain identity" led to the decision to limit full membership with voting rights to "NATIVE Spanish-speaking sisters... Puerto Ricans, Cubans, Mexicans, Spaniards, Mexican-Americans, and any other Latin Americans."[15] The few Anglo sisters present who had been ministering in Spanish-speaking communities either chose not to return or remained as associate members with limited privileges. Teresa

---

11. Interview with Carmelita Espinoza, April 1996.
12. Las Hermanas Historical Background, July 5, 1971. Las Hermanas Archives.
13. "United in action and prayer." A hierarchical leadership model was chosen with a president, vice-president, and secretary, but in 1972 this structure was replaced with a team government consisting of three national coordinators holding equal status and power to represent the organization.
14. "La historia de Las Hermanas," privately printed, 1978, 9. Las Hermanas Archives.
15. Circular letter dated April 21, 1971. Las Hermanas Archives.

Basso recalls: "There were some Anglo sisters who were very hurt by this decision and never came back . . . but we felt that this organization was going to allow us to develop our own leadership abilities. That would not happen if the Anglo sisters had [a] vote."[16] A follow-up letter soon after the conference clarified further the need to be exclusionary: "At this particular time there is a greater need . . . to help ourselves with our own self-identity problem and to better establish ourselves among La Raza."[17] These women realized that they had to reclaim their identities on their own terms and in their own spaces.

By the time of their next assembly eight months later on November 25–27, 1971, in Santa Fe, New Mexico, attendance quadrupled with close to two hundred sisters present. The first issue of *Informes,* the organizational newsletter, in September 1971 stated, "Our current 'membership' is over 900, giving HERMANAS members in 25 states, Mexico, Guatemala, Bolivia, Ecuador, and Peru."[18]

The added presence of Puerto Rican and Cuban women at the second conference enriched and broadened the organization. Sister Rosamaría Elías, the first Puerto Rican woman to join Las Hermanas, recruited other Latina sisters such as María Iglesias and Dominga Zapata. The attendance of these women reflected a commitment to solidarity among Latinas that the Chicanas had envisioned for the organization. In reflecting on her reception, Elías recalls, "the Chicanas gave us such a warm welcome, they really wanted us there. I remember feeling so important . . . they were hugging me and I really felt at home."[19] A strong sense of being *hermanas* and being rooted in the people's struggle, as well as the confidence that the Chicanas projected, attracted other Latinas. Tess Browne, originally from Trinidad, found the native-born women of Las Hermanas extremely helpful as "they understood how this country worked more than I did."[20] María Iglesias, of Cuban and Puerto Rican ancestry, describes the cross-pollination that took place among the women. "In building solidarity with the women, we also built solidarity with each other's causes, and we gained from each other a real solid focus that we needed to be advocates for our people."[21] Over the years

---

16. Interview with Teresa Basso, March 8, 1997.
17. Circular letter, April 21, 1971. Las Hermanas Archives.
18. *Informes* 1, no. 1 (September 19, 1971): 2.
19. Interview with Rosamaría Elías, May 20, 1997.
20. Interview with Tess Browne, May 20, 1997.
21. Interview with María Iglesias, March 2, 1997.

Chicanas would remain the majority of Las Hermanas, but the influence and leadership of Latinas would significantly shape the organization.

In spite of the tremendous pain that many of the sisters had experienced in religious life, they recognized the symbolic power they held as religious women and their access to a degree of power within the institutional church. In Latino(a) Catholic communities, sisters and the priests traditionally hold a place of honor, with "sanctified" authority. While male clerics with the powers of ordination obviously hold greater status within a patriarchal religion, women religious also hold "sacred status" among the community and are often more closely connected to the everyday lives of the faithful.

Acknowledging their "unique resources as Spanish-speaking religious women," the members of Las Hermanas dedicated their individual and collective purpose "to enable each other to work more effectively among and with the Spanish Speaking People of God in bringing about social justice and a truly Christian peace."[22] Teresa Basso elaborates, "It was the beginning of Hispanic women [religious] coming together to respond to the voice of the people and to work as agents of change within the church because we knew that we did have some power there."[23] Seeing themselves as "agents of change" and making a commitment to service for the sake of social justice reflected a radical transformation of the use of power within the institutional church.

By 1975, membership extended to Latina laity, initiated by the fact that many of the women chose to leave religious life as their consciousness was raised through Las Hermanas. Sister María Iglesias explains:

> We had to accept the lay women as equal members because some of the founders of the organization could no longer stay in their congregations who would not honor their desire to work among their own people.... We couldn't turn our backs on them. It was a painful decision because we knew we would polarize and lose people.[24]

For some members, feelings of rage toward the institutional church erupted as they came to terms with the racism they had experienced.

---

22. Sister Gloria Gallardo, letter to Leadership Conference of Women Religious (LCWR), November 17, 1971. Las Hermanas Archives.
23. Basso interview.
24. Iglesias interview.

88888888888888888888888888888ref8888

For some, leaving religious life proved to be the best alternative. Others chose to remain in their religious communities and fight the battle from within.

Moving to a membership that included laity meant a change in identity for the organization. Some members felt that broadening the membership would diminish the organization's status within the hierarchical and clerical structure of the church. For Sister Ybarra the move proved too radical and influenced her departure from the organization. "I felt like somebody took over the organization."[25] Despite the tremendous loss from the departure of such key members as Sister Ybarra, the move to a lay organization reflected, for many, "a sign of vitality." As Teresa Basso articulates, "Las Hermanas's identity developed with the people."[26] Membership over the years would fluctuate. In the early 1990s, approximately seven hundred women belonged to the organization, with an average of two hundred attending the annual conferences, or *asambleas*.[27]

Besides U.S. Latinas being denied access to their cultures, home language, and community involvement, women religious from Mexico often labored for meager wages as domestics in U.S. seminaries and rectories and in virtual isolation from Latino(a) communities, as a Las Hermanas survey showed, which identified fifty-nine such sites.[28] The survey raised the consciousness of concerned Catholics and resulted in scholarship funds for several of the women.

A lack of ethnic representation at various levels of the church hierarchy exacerbated the concerns of Las Hermanas. As examples, Latinas represented less than 1 percent of women religious while Latino/as represented 28 percent of the U.S. Catholic population. Latinos represented only 3 percent of the priesthood.[29] Before 1970, only one Mexican American, Fr. Patricio Flores, in the history of the U.S. Roman Catholic Church had been named bishop. In contrast, Irish Americans composed 17 percent of the U.S. Catholic population but with a representation of

---

25. Ybarra interview.
26. Basso interview.
27. *Asamblea* or assembly is often used in archival materials to refer to the annual conferences. I use the terms interchangeably.
28. María de Jesús Ybarra, *Reporte Sobre Trabajo Hecho de Proyecto Mexico*, August 25, 1974, Las Hermanas Archives.
29. Gilbert Cadena, "Chicano Clergy and the Emergence of Liberation Theology," *Hispanic Journal of Behavior Sciences* 11 (1989): 107–21.

56 percent among Catholic bishops and 36 percent among all priests.[30] This extreme underrepresentation of Latino/as in positions of ecclesiastical authority had created an absence of culturally relevant and sensitive ministries.[31]

In secular society, issues of underemployment, poor education, little political representation, overt discrimination, and the Vietnam War compelled a generation of Chicano/as and Puerto Ricans nationwide to respond to the injustices with a nationwide "politics of mass protest."[32] Fundamental to the movement was a quest for cultural identity, self-determination, and civil rights. Chicano(a) activists challenged the Catholic Church with pleas for institutional support.

Throughout most of the 1970s Las Hermanas collaborated with PADRES (*Padres Asociados por los Derechos Religiosos, Educativos, y Sociales,* or Priests Associated for Religious, Educational, and Social Rights), an organization of Chicano clergy formed in late 1969 in San Antonio, Texas. PADRES, too, had mobilized to challenge discriminatory practices toward Chicano/as within the church and society; however, PADRES remained a clerical organization, and in the mid-1980s it ceased to exist.[33] It was Fr. Edmundo Rodríguez of PADRES who introduced Sister Ortega to Sister Gallardo in Houston, as he knew they both had similar frustrations and aspirations about their vocations. Within a short time, the two organizations represented the emerging Chicano(a) leadership within the church as they joined forces in an entire movement for change.

During the 1970s, Las Hermanas and PADRES influenced the policy decisions of major ecclesial bodies, including the United States Catholic Conference/National Conference of Catholic Bishops (USCC/NCCB), the Leadership Conference of Women Religious (LCWR), and the Secretariat for Hispanic Affairs of the United States Catholic Conference.

---

30. Andrew Greeley, *The Catholic Priest in the United States: Sociological Investigations* (Washington, D.C.: United States Catholic Office, 1972).

31. For an overview of Mexican Americans and the Catholic Church, see Jay P. Dolan and Gilberto M. Hinojosa, *Mexican Americans and the Catholic Church, 1900–1965* (Notre Dame, Ind.: University of Notre Dame Press, 1994).

32. "Politics of mass protest" refers to resistance and strategic community mobilization that demanded change of the status quo. See Carlos Muñoz Jr., *Youth, Identity and Power* (New York: Verso, 1989), 171.

33. See Timothy Matovina, "Representation and the Reconstruction of Power: The Rise of *PADRES* and *Las Hermanas,*" in *What's Left? Liberal American Catholics,* Mary Jo Weaver, ed. (Bloomington: Indiana University Press, 1999).

Together, they lobbied successfully to increase the number of Chicano/
Latino bishops, and worked to establish Latino(a) ministry programs
and offices. They cofounded the Mexican American Cultural Center
(MACC) under the leadership of Virgilio Elizondo as the first national
pastoral training center for Chicano(a)/Latino(a) ministries. Las Hermanas and PADRES representatives sat on the first steering committee
and taught MACC's initial courses. They also played an integral role
in the first two national Hispanic pastoral *encuentros* held in 1972 and
1977 in Washington, D.C.[34] The *encuentros,* or gatherings, brought together for the first time on a national level Chicano(a)/Latino(a) laity and
religious leaders to discern and articulate their concerns to the wider
church.[35] Las Hermanas and PADRES also established significant ties
with Latin American liberation theologians, including Gustavo Gutiérrez
and Juan Luis Segundo. Influenced by liberation theology, the organizations contributed to the beginning discourse on "*raza* theology," later to
be named U.S. Latino(a) theology.[36]

Composed of strong and vocal women, Las Hermanas was not immune to institutional and intraethnic attempts to marginalize their
voices. Las Hermanas refused to be the traditional helpmate or subordinate member of a movement for change. Its collective struggle with
PADRES encountered the same obstacles and challenges plaguing "secular" Chicanos and Chicanas. Yet Virgilio Elizondo spoke very frankly
about the impact Las Hermanas had on the transformations taking place:
"In honesty, we were not used to women coming into their power. We
welcomed it but at the same time we were threatened by it.... We did
not know how to do it.... also the barrier of the ordained priest is
a structural obstacle."[37] Working within an ecclesial institution that,
by its very nature, carries an aura of sanctification made the struggle
against patriarchy perhaps even more arduous. As Ana María Díaz-
Stevens points out, "The power to govern the institution derives from

---

34. A third *encuentro* was held in 1985, but is beyond the scope of this paper.

35. The *encuentros* ultimately resulted into the *Plan National Hispano de Pastoral,* approved
by the U.S. Catholic bishops in 1987. For an extensive discussion of the development of the *encuentros,* see Moises Sandoval, "The Organization of a Hispanic Church," in *Hispanic Catholic
Culture in the U.S.: Issues and Concerns,* ed. Jay P. Dolan and Allan Figueroa Deck (Notre
Dame, Ind.: University of Notre Dame Press, 1994).

36. *Raza* theology was the chosen term at the two joint organizations' joint conference
in 1978.

37. Interview with Virgilio Elizondo, February 17, 1997.

Holy Orders, which is a sacrament reserved to men. Thus, Catholicism can be considered a patriarchy par excellence."[38]

When asked why Latina feminists would bother with the Catholic religion, Las Hermanas members Isasi-Díaz and Tarango have responded: "The church sanctions — justifies — patriarchy in society by being itself a patriarchal structure.... If the church were to denounce patriarchy, it would be an important moment in the process of the liberation of women."[39] A commitment to the empowerment of grassroots Latinas combined with faith in a God of justice, and with reluctance to leave their religious tradition, convinced Las Hermanas to continue the struggle inherent in the church structure. As one Hermana member shared, "If the boys want me to leave, they are going to have to carry me out, because it is not their church."[40]

Las Hermanas also developed national and international alliances with the National Association of Women Religious (NAWR), Sisters Uniting, Women's Ordination Conference (WOC), and the Latin American Conference of Religious Congregations (CLAR). Members participated in all arenas of the Chicano(a) movement, including student protests for educational rights, community organizing, and the farm labor movement under César Chávez and Dolores Huerta.[41] They responded to these struggles out of the desire to serve their people authentically.

Initially, Las Hermanas did not focus explicitly on a feminist agenda. Its concern for its ethnic communities reflects what historian Vicki Ruiz calls "a community-centered consciousness" among Chicana activists.[42] Furthermore, the type of leadership that would evolve among these women reflects "one of the basic themes of Chicana feminism," that is, "a leadership concerned with empowering *others,* not a hierarchical kind of leadership."[43] In reflecting on the early consciousness of Las Hermanas, Yolanda Tarango recalls:

---

38. Ana María Díaz-Stevens, "Latinas and the Church," in *Hispanic Catholic Culture in the U.S.,* 245.

39. Isasi-Díaz and Tarango, *Hispanic Women,* x.

40. Browne interview. The length of this paper prohibits me from the detailing the specific attempts to silence Las Hermanas. I refer readers to my forthcoming book, *Las Hermanas: Religious-Political Activism, 1971–2000* (Philadelphia: Temple University Press).

41. Ibid., for further detail on these activities.

42. Vicki Ruiz, *From Out of the Shadows: Mexican American Women in Twentieth-Century America* (New York: Oxford University Press, 1998), 100.

43. Rosie Castro, cited in ibid.

When we first started it was more of a dormant feminist consciousness. Through our involvement in the Chicano movement we
began to translate that analysis to the church and name the racism
that we saw there. We wanted to create an organizational basis
to challenge the church. It was not specifically a women's agenda
but the women's version of advocating for rights of Latinos in the
Church."[44]

This "dormant feminist consciousness" transformed into a clear agenda
focused on women by 1976. While some members never claimed a
"feminist" identity, others proudly use the term. According to Margarita Castañeda, a feminist herself, "This is the reality in Las Hermanas
and the Catholic Church. You have those who believe in feminist issues and those who don't."[45] Over the years, Las Hermanas has been
able to make room for the spectrum of Chicanas and Latinas just as in
the broader Chicano(a) movement. As Ruiz points out, "Chicanas have
articulated ... a recognition of differences as they live amidst the 'swirls
of contradictions.' "[46]

Since 1980, Las Hermanas has focused specifically on issues affecting
grassroots Latinas, including moral agency, reproductive rights, sexuality, domestic abuse, and women's ordination. Their second decade
marked a significant shift from a primarily community-based focus to
that of women's empowerment as members recognized "the indifference
of the Church towards women."[47] Overall, the two concerns are not
mutually exclusive; Las Hermanas understands that the empowerment
of women is directly tied to the empowerment of Latino(a) communities. Its activism during the last two decades can be characterized as
"feminist discursive politics" aimed at articulating a counter-discourse
to the status quo, which excludes women from primary spheres of
influence.[48]

---

44. Interview with Yolanda Tarango, August 23, 1996.
45. Interview with Margarita Castañeda, March 15, 1997.
46. Ruiz, *From Out of the Shadows,* 100.
47. Carmen Villegas, "Informes y Análisis de la Reunión de NAC," *Informes* 2, no. 1 (March
1987): 5 (author's translation).
48. Mary Fainsod Katzenstein, "Discursive Politics and Feminist Activism in the Catholic
Church," in *Feminist Organizations: Harvest of the New Women's Movement,* ed. Myra Marx
Ferree and Patricia Yancey Martin (Philadelphia: Temple University Press, 1995).

A SPIRITUALITY OF
TRANSFORMATIVE STRUGGLE

By 1980, the spirituality of Las Hermanas was clearly grounded in
a struggle for transforming personal, social, and political constraints.
While *spirituality* can be an elusive term, as Western thought has traditionally separated spirituality from more tangible and physical concerns,
my use of the term emphasizes the multiple ways people relate to the
world around them, to their source of life, and to themselves.[49] For
Latinas immersed in the everyday struggle to survive and prosper spiritually, culturally, and economically, the manner in which they relate to
this struggle is key to understanding their spirituality. Relating to the
struggle in a transformative way rather than in a passive mode or with
a victim mentality is fundamental to the spirituality of Las Hermanas.
Embracing struggle for the goal of making justice a reality is seen as life-
giving.[50] Keeping in mind class differences, Yolanda Tarango explains
further:

> Hispanic women do not envision themselves apart from the struggle.
> The challenge is in transforming that struggle so that it has, not
> only a redeeming but, an energizing effect.... The transformation
> [of struggle] is critical for the liberation of Hispanic women... for
> assuming control over one's life.... *La vida es la lucha* implies the
> struggle we must embrace and learn to love in order to survive in
> the present and envision life with dignity in the future.[51]

Transformative struggle and its foundational role in the spirituality of
Las Hermanas helps to explain the group's determination to keep going
amid the most challenging obstacles.

Vital to embracing struggle as life-giving is a deep faith in a divine presence desiring justice for *el pueblo*[52] and for women. This
"sense of the divine" illuminates the manner in which members of Las

---

49. I have been influenced by numerous feminist writers to arrive at this definition, including
Anne E. Carr, *Transforming Grace* (San Francisco: Harper & Row, 1988); Audre Lorde, "The
Power of the Erotic," in *Weaving the Vision*, ed. Judith Plaskow and Carol P. Christ (San
Francisco: Harper & Row, 1989); and Yolanda Tarango, "La Vida es la Lucha," *Texas Journal
of Ideas, History and Culture* 2 (Spring–Summer 1990): 11.

50. Tarango, "La Vida es la Lucha," 11.

51. Ibid., 9–10.

52. *El pueblo* translates as the people, the community of Latino/as.

Hermanas respond to life. As Isasi-Díaz and Tarango point out, it is this "sense of the divine in their lives that gives them strength for the struggle — a struggle that is not part of life but life itself."[53] Furthermore, faith in women's creativity, inherent power, and nurturing relationships over generations enables Las Hermanas to express a spirituality and a theology beyond the boundaries of the institutional church.

Transformative struggle emerges most clearly through Las Hermanas conferences, women-centered rituals, newsletters, public speeches and protests, songs, and *mujerista* theology. These venues create the space in which to articulate issues integral to the daily lives of Latinas and their strategies for change and empowerment. The physical, artistic, and literary spaces stand in sharp contrast to the silence of the ecclesial hierarchy on matters of gender, race, class, and sexuality. I focus on the spirituality narrated through the theology, annual conferences, women-centered rituals, and poetry. An overview of the theology emerging from Las Hermanas helps obtain a deeper grasp of the underlying spirituality. The first articulation of what would later become known as *mujerista* theology is now a little over ten years old and continues to offer insight into the theological praxis of Latina Catholic feminists.

As previously stated, Hermanas members Yolanda Tarango and Ada María Isasi-Díaz coauthored the first publication articulating a U.S. Latina feminist theology, *Hispanic Women: Prophetic Voice in the Church*. The two theologians synthesized the religious understandings of grassroots Latinas following several small-group retreats organized by members of Las Hermanas. Financial support from numerous women's religious congregations, individuals, and organizations including the Center of Concern, Quixote Center, National Assembly of Religious Women, and the National Coalition of American Nuns enabled the authors to dialogue with Latinas in various parts of the country.[54] According to Tarango and Isasi-Díaz, Las Hermanas provided "a real link" and "the seedbed" for the production of *mujerista* theology.[55] Sylvia Vásquez, a former member of the organization, comments on the role that Las Hermanas and *mujerista* theology played in her own educational and spiritual development:

53. Isasi-Díaz and Tarango, *Hispanic Women*, 103.
54. A complete list of contributors is provided in *Hispanic Women*, vii. Included are many of the religious communities with which members of Las Hermanas are affiliated.
55. Interviews with Tarango and Isasi-Díaz, August 1996.

The work of Ada María and Yolanda has been to extrapo-
late what goes on in Las Hermanas and put it into theological
language . . . our ability to articulate our experience of God. This
has far-reaching implications. It helped me to understand that theology is everybody's. *Mujerista* theology gave me an affirmation
and a validation. . . . It freed me.[56]

When Isasi-Díaz developed the theology further, in her second book,
En la lucha, she returned to several of the women connected to Las
Hermanas that she and Tarango had interviewed.

Influenced by Latin American liberation theology, these Latina theologians emphasize "doing theology" as a praxis rather than an intellectual
exercise. As feminist theologians, they challenge traditional theology
that ignores the experiences and perceptions of women, particularly
women of color. Tarango and Isasi-Díaz place theological authority in
the hands of grassroots Latinas, whose faith and lived experience inform their beliefs and actions. The goal of this theological enterprise is
to maintain Latino(a) cultural values, with a commitment to the struggle
against sexism in all its manifestations, and to reach "not equality but
liberation . . . [from] socio-political-economic oppression."[57]

A four-part methodology intrinsic to this theology includes "telling
our stories, analyzing, liturgizing and strategizing."[58] These interrelated
"parts" describe *how* the transformation of struggle takes place. Through
telling our stories, Latinas engage in self-reflection that gives importance to their experiences, reveals shared experiences, and leads to the
recognition that the "personal is political"; and that structural forces
impact individual and communal lives. Deeper inquiry (analysis) into the
forces of oppression is required in order to make the connections among
oppression's different manifestations. *Liturgizing* enables Latinas to design "how best to represent the divine"[59] in their lives and negates the
sense of unworthiness or absence often experienced in patriarchal rituals.
Strategizing seeks to find ways emerging from the community to change
oppressive structures by transforming a domineering use of power into an

---

56. Interview with Sylvia Vásquez, August 23, 1996. Vásquez went on to become an
ordained minister in the Episcopal Church.
57. Isasi-Díaz and Tarango, *Hispanic Women,* xii.
58. Ibid., chap. 5.
59. Ibid., 101.

enabling and creative use of power — "all in the context of a community and its common good."[60]

These movements do not operate in isolation but intertwine in developing critical consciousness and praxis among Latinas. Praxis, or "critical, reflective action based on questions of ultimate meaning" means to act in the world out of a commitment to the liberation of Latinas and other oppressed communities.[61] The struggle for liberation means not only the struggle for self-determination, but also for the ability to survive and prosper physically, economically, and culturally as active agents in the making of justice for all. This struggle requires a redefinition of power that Las Hermanas has addressed consistently at their national conferences.

The issue of power held primary attention at the 1989 national conference in San Antonio. Defining power as enablement, creativity, and the ability to act rather than to control and dominate set the framework for the participants to examine their own concepts of power; how they use their power in their daily lives; and what social forces, including religion, attempt to keep women powerless.[62] Using the women's own experiences as a starting point validated grassroots Latinas "who have never been taken seriously, [who have] not been taken into account."[63] Portraying power within the individual, between companions in the struggle for liberation, and in the desire to make a difference in one's life gave the women a deep sense of their own personal power.[64] Conference participant Teresa Barajas describes best the impact that redefining power had on her life:

For me and I believe for many of us, the conference opened up a wider perspective of the meaning of the word *poder.*[65] I saw in many of us that the word awakened a fear . . . because we have always associated it with oppression, violence and absolute control . . . that many of us have experienced since we were little. . . . We learned that power is something very good in us if we know how to

---

60. Ibid., 102.
61. Ibid., 1–2.
62. "Special Issue! La Mujer Hispana: Poder, Lucha y Esperanza, LAS HERMANAS 1989 Conference," *Informes* 4, no. 3 (December 1989).
63. Ada María Isasi-Díaz, in ibid., 4.
64. Synopsis of presentation by María Antonietta Berriozabal, in ibid., 5.
65. *Poder* translates as power.

use it. . . . We also saw that we often use our power without even knowing it.[66]

And as another participant stated, "From now on I will not have [fear] and I will have the power to continue going forward."[67]

Many of the women attending the conference shared stories of abusive power from the actions of priests, bosses, husbands, children, and the government. But as Rosa Martha Zárate pointed out, "These women also shared experiences of resistance, of struggle, of contestation, of liberation. This was an assembly of hope!"[68] Discussing issues of power, *machismo,* and the limitations of traditional gender roles imbued many of the women with the knowledge that they were not alone in the struggle for liberation. As one participant remarked, "Together we have the ability to plan and act — therefore WE HAVE POWER."[69] Solidarity among Latinas, relative autonomy from the institutional church, and a striving for justice in all aspects of life characterizes the spirituality of Las Hermanas.

Liturgizing or ritualizing contributes immensely to the process of transformative struggle and is another key example of how this spirituality is narrated. My own participation in Las Hermanas rituals in 1997 and 1999 provided a deep sense of how these women envision the divine in their lives as a transformative presence, one fully, but not exclusively, represented and present in the image and likeness of women.

The theme of the 1997 conference, "Celebrating 25 years of Las Hermanas," included a ritual designed primarily by Carmen Villegas and Sister Juanita Morales in consultation with numerous other Hermanas members. Drawing on the home-altar tradition of many Latinas, the participants created a communal altar in the center of the ritual space to claim and mark the gathering area as sacred. Pictures and statues of significant and holy women important in participants' lives decorated the altar, along with candles representing offerings to the divine and the spiritual presence of each Hermana member.

66. Teresa Barajas, "Reflexiones desde San Antonio," *Informes* 4, no. 3 (December 1989): 2 (author's translation).

67. Ibid. (author's translation).

68. Rosa Martha Zárate, "Encuentro Nacional de Las Hermanas," *Informes* 4, no. 3 (December 1989): 3.

69. María Inez Martínez, "Empowerment, Enablement, Hope," *Informes* 4, no. 3 (December 1989): 1.

Sitting in a circle around the altar emphasized egalitarian relationships and the unity of the women present. Songwriter and singer Rosa Martha Zárate serenaded the group with her music of liberation. One of the facilitators passed out small rectangular pieces of colored paper and asked the participants to write on them words describing experiences or persons that limited their self-determination. The women then joined the pieces of paper, forming a long paper chain. Standing in a circle and holding the paper chain enabled the women to visualize the shared experience of bondage. As each woman called out her personal oppression, she broke the chain and symbolically destroyed its source. The women then turned to each other and blessed one another using words of their own choosing.

Such language, symbols, and actions strongly reflect the women's cultural, political, and feminist sensibilities and their ability to create "a counter discourse in response to the words, rituals, and symbols that emanate from the Vatican."[70] The emphasis on women's power, solidarity, and commitment to liberation are themes uncommon to traditional Catholic services. Las Hermanas liturgies, however, articulate a shared historical project of personal and social change. Defining and deciding for themselves what images, rituals, and myths express their deepest values, the women express "a language of defiance and ultimate resistance."[71]

Through the ritual actions and symbols employed, the women create a sacred reality that sanctifies and legitimizes their ability to shape their own religious practices; these practices, in turn, reflect their particular social and political concerns. In the creative process, they construct a "redemptive reinterpretation of the hegemonic order."[72] Traditional Roman Catholic liturgy — with its strict gender roles, austere use of symbols, and silence regarding the everyday struggles of Latinas — becomes relativized. The Las Hermanas ritual itself becomes a political act as it stands "as a critique and a denunciation of institutional liturgies,

---

70. Katzenstein, "Discursive Politics and Feminist Activism," 48.
71. Virgilio Elizondo, "Popular Religion as the Core of Cultural Identity in the Mexican American Experience," in *An Enduring Flame: Studies on Latino Popular Religiosity,* ed. Anthony M. Stevens-Arroyo and Ana María Díaz-Stevens (New York: Bildner Center, 1994), 116.
72. Catherine Bell, *Ritual Theory, Ritual Practice* (New York: Oxford University Press, 1992), 196.

which whether consciously or not, function mainly to maintain the good order of patriarchy."[73]

The total experience of a Las Hermanas conference including self-reflection, dialogue, and ritual has inspired numerous other creative acts such as poetry, altar making, and songwriting. As one example, Enedina Cásarez Vásquez, an artist, writer, and teacher from San Antonio, remembers returning from her first Las Hermanas conference in 1989 and deciding to form a writing group for Chicana poets.[74] Naming themselves *Mujeres Grandes,* they have since published two anthologies of poetry and continue to meet regularly to discuss their writings.[75]

The late 1980s and early 1990s witnessed a downslide in the organization resulting from overextended leadership and limited financial resources. With only 140 paid members and seven corporate members, the national coordinator at that time, Sister María Carolina Flores, reluctantly asked the looming question, "Do we still need LAS HERMANAS?"[76] Responses to a questionnaire sent to approximately 745 readers of *Informes* testified to members' desire to keep the organization functioning. In 1995, the national coordinating team stabilized and was composed completely of lay women. Surviving under a precarious financial situation did not alter the women's belief in the organization. "Sheer will" and "an unwillingness to let go" characterized their defense against a serious financial battle. Paying their own travel expenses to attend national board meetings reflected their determination to keep Las Hermanas active.[77]

While a weak financial base continues to cause difficulties, some members interviewed also expressed frustration over lack of a specific national agenda, other than national conferences and the now-sporadic publication of *Informes.* For a few long-term members, a lack of "a radical political vision" shaping the agenda for the twenty-first century causes concern. In their opinion, the early political activism deeply influenced by liberation theology and the Chicano(a) movement, has faded.[78]

73. Ada María Isasi-Díaz, "Rituals and Mujeristas' Struggle for Liberation," in *Mujerista Theology* (Maryknoll, N.Y.: Orbis Books, 1996), 193.

74. Interview with Enedina Cásarez Vásquez, August 1996.

75. *Mujeres Grandes Anthology 1,* ed. Angela de Hoya (San Antonio: M&A Editions, 1993); *Mujeres Grandes Anthology 2,* ed. Angela de Hoya (San Antonio: M&A Editions, 1995).

76. See insert titled "Special Report," *Informes* (October 1994).

77. The personal expense, however, does keep some board members from attending all board meetings, which weakens leadership endeavors.

78. Interview with Rosa Martha Zárate, Sara Murrieta, and Alicia Salcido, July 26, 1997.

According to Rosa Martha Zárate, "We don't have a political analysis or a concrete vision of the kind of society we want to create. We need a critique of liberal capitalism."[79] While justice remains an integral part of the organizational goals, concrete ways to achieve justice on a broad scale have in the last decade become more elusive.

Amid differing opinions lies the awareness that there will be no return to what the organization was like in the 1970s. The aging of many original members calls for "new blood, younger blood with fresh ideas" to contribute to future directions.[80] Most of the women interviewed agreed that the organization must critically reevaluate itself in order to advance in the twenty-first century. The theme, "Envisioning the Future," chosen for the 2001 conference in El Paso, Texas, indicates that the leadership is taking action.

With an increasingly conservative papacy, the need for Las Hermanas as a conscientious voice of dissension remains high. As Isasi-Díaz points out, "Las Hermanas has the potential to develop further a three-prong purpose. To be prophetic through protest, to be priestly by ministering to Latinas, and to educate through consciousness raising ... to radicalize each other."[81] The role that Las Hermanas has played — providing Chicanas and Latinas a space to raise critical issues regarding women in the church *and* in society — is unique among national organizations of Latinas in the United States. While successful Chicana/Latina organizations exist, such as the Mexican American Women's National Association (MANA) and Mujeres Activas en Letras y Cambio Social (MALCS), they do not focus on the intersection of politics and religion. For example, at the 1999 Las Hermanas conference held in Denver, two hundred participants learned of the global economy and its effect on less technologically developed countries. Questions following the discussion required the women to reflect on their own participation in the economy and possible localized solutions.

The distinctive mixture of spirituality and activism for which Las Hermanas has become known continues to mark its contribution to diverse strategies challenging ethnic, gender, and class oppressions. As Ana María Díaz-Stevens suggests, "Despite its shortcomings, Las Hermanas represents, to date, the most creative and successful effort for solidarity

---

79. Ibid.
80. Castañeda interview, March 15, 1997.
81. Isasi-Díaz interview, August 1996.

in a diverse U.S. Latino reality."[82] The spirituality and theology emerging from Las Hermanas offers affirmation to Latinas concerned with the marginalization of their ethnic communities. Immigrant bashing, censures of affirmative action, legislation directed against bilingual education, and unfair wage differentials exemplify ongoing attempts to halt Latinas' self-determination. In addition, many of the church issues from the 1970s continue to face Latino(a) Catholics: underrepresentation, insensitive ministries, inadequate services, and limitations on women. In the words of Yolanda Tarango, "All of our experiences with the official church and social institutions create the urgency to say, 'No, we have a different perspective and we are going to give it a public voice.'"[83] At the center of this perspective, at the center of the legacy of Las Hermanas, lie the critical, creative, and prophetic voices of Chicanas and Latinas, "describing, analyzing and expressing their own historical and cultural subjectivities."[84] The struggle continues, and transformation remains the ongoing challenge.

The decision of Las Hermanas to remain a decentralized, autonomous organization for women only allows freedom to create a new form of being church. This new form is necessary for Latinas needing more than what the "official" church allows or offers. Las Hermanas's commitment to a woman's sphere in which religious and moral agency can be discussed and exercised, and to living in the intersection between religion and politics, has contributed to its longevity. The lack of substantial financial resources, however, continues to pose serious obstacles. Yet, Las Hermanas offers a legacy to Chicanas and Latinas forging paths toward greater self-realization for themselves and their communities.

---

82. Díaz-Stevens, "Latinas in the Church," in *Hispanic Catholic Culture*, 268.
83. Interview with Yolanda Tarango, August 23, 1996.
84. Antonia Castañeda, "Women of Color and Western History: The Discourse, Politics, and Decolonization of History," *Pacific Historical Review* 61, no. 4 (November 1992): 522.

12

The Predicament of *Neplanta*

Chicano(a) Religions in the Twenty-First Century

RUDY V. BUSTO

The defining characteristic of Chicano(a)/Latino(a) (and Filipino American[1]) religions is that of predicament. First, as *Webster* coldly defines it, a "predicament" is a "difficult situation bringing perplexity about [the] best procedure for extrication, sometimes with lack of freedom to do what one would prefer"; and second, "predicament" can be understood in the etymological sense of having been predicated or categorized and classified by others, be they scholars or church officials. The term *neplanta*, "or middle place," as I am using it here, comes from a well-known anecdote recorded by Diego Durán about a Christianized Indian caught in the middle (*neplanta*) between the loss of the old Mesoamerican religious system and the insistence of Iberian Christianity in colonial Mexico. Durán noted, "Since the people were not yet well rooted in the [Christian] Faith, they were governed by neither one religion nor the other," and he offered an example:

> Once I questioned an Indian regarding certain things. In particular
> I asked him why he had gone about begging, spending bad nights
> and worse days, and why, after having gathered so much money
> with such trouble, he offered a fiesta, invited the entire town, and

Originally published in *Perspectivas*, the Hispanic Theological Initiative's Occasional Papers Series, no. 1 (Fall 1998): 7–21.

1. I would argue that Filipino Americans share religious and historical similarities with U.S. Latino/as in that they are also primarily Roman Catholic, have a homeland previously under Spanish and American colonialism, and their presence in the United States is marked by racism, violence, and labor exploitation.

spent everything. Thus I reprehended him for the foolish thing he
had done, and he answered, "Father, do not be astonished, we are
still *neplanta* ... " [Durán continues] ... or better said, they believed
in God and also followed their ancient heathen rites and customs.[2]

I would like to consider the idea of *neplanta* religion as a way to illuminate the predicaments that have dogged U.S. Latino(a) cultures and
religions ever since the ink dried on the Treaty of Guadalupe Hidalgo in
1848 and the Treaty of Paris in 1898. Like the now-familiar metaphor
of the borderland, and the fancier postcolonial formulation of hybrid
cultures, *neplanta* brings to specifically Chicano(a) traditions both the
aspects of *place* [technically "in the middle of some things"] and the
process of transformative interaction between religions, ideological systems, and cultural identities (as the root element — *nepan* — conveys a
sense of mutuality or reciprocity).[3] *Neplanta* thus accounts for the multi-
tude of "syncretisms," popular and vernacular religious practices (those
beliefs and practices beyond "orthodoxies" described by Latino[a] scholars or religion like Otto Maduro, David Carrasco, and others[4]) and the
shifting subjectivities of a people whose identity is nevertheless tied to a
series of realities. I am referring to the mythical geographies of Aztlán,
to the diasporic realities of secondary segmented labor migrations which
have historically occurred along the beetfield routes from South Texas to
Michigan, to the journey into the underworld of copper miners in Southern Arizona, to the movement of agricultural and factory labor into the
South and southeastern United States, and to the quiet and invisible
domestic and factory labor of women throughout the country.

Where, then, does the predicament of *neplanta* religion lead us when
we view the trajectory of Chicano(a) religions at the close of this
Christian millennium? Where are those hints of how the dilemma of
Chicano(a) spirituality expresses a distinctly "Chicano(a)" presence in
the contemporary recalibration (some would say contestations) over

---

2. Diego Durán, *Book of the Gods and Rites and the Ancient Calendar*, ed. and trans.
Fernando Horcasitas and Doris Heyden (Norman: University of Oklahoma Press, 1971), 410–
11.
3. Francis E. Karttunen, *An Analytical Dictionary of Nahuatl* (Austin: University of Texas
Press, 1983).
4. See Otto Maduro, "Reassessing Religious Rims: Hispanic Hierophanies," a paper
presented at *Re-constructing Time and Borders: Latino/a Religious/Cultural Change and Identities Symposium,* Duke University, March 28, 1998. See also the essays in Anthony M.
Stevens-Arroyo and Andrés I. Pérez y Mena, eds., *Enigmatic Powers: Syncretism with African
and Indigenous People's Religions among Latinos* (New York: Bildner Center for Western
Hemisphere Studies, 1995).

the character and cartography of American religions? Let me offer two examples of how the predicament of *neplanta* compels agency and innovation in Chicano(a) religions as it forces us to ask difficult questions about the very identity and process of Chicano(a) religions and cultural identity by examining briefly the writing of two visionaries, José Arguelles (unknown in the university classroom or textbook) and Cherrie Moraga, Chicana poet, dramaturge, and troublemaker. In these writers we can begin to explore the outer boundaries of the discomforting *neplanta* position within the context of grand overarching themes or objects of study like "Latino(a) religions," "the church," or the separation of the Americans into North, South, or Central. I present Arguelles and Moraga as two particular examples because what they have to offer us in the study of Latino(a) religion are alternative ways of thinking about our past, our spirituality, and our relationships to various types of knowledge that are not so obvious to the social scientist looking for quantifiable verity, or to the architecture of the systematic theologian.

THE INNOVATION OF THE INDIGENOUS PAST: JOSÉ ARGUELLES

Scarcely anyone in the academy remembers the day the universe shifted on August 16 and 17, 1987. According to José Arguelles's calculations, on the evening of August 16 through to the next day, the sacred calendar of the ancient Maya, the 260-day Tzoikin (or "long count"), returned its great wheel of days back to the beginning of its 52×52-year Calendar Round cycle. At the exact same time, the solar calendar, the 365-day Haab, completed a turn of its 52×52-year cycle of days. When these two ancient calendar wheels simultaneously clicked "back" into their beginning positions, the "Harmonic Convergence" of the moment would see not only the return of the great Mesoamerican god, Quetzalcoatl, bursting out from beneath a large tree in Oaxaca, Mexico, but also a worldwide transformation of humanity resulting from the "resonance frequency shifts" in the cosmic "morphogenetic field" of what Arguelles, in his new age revisioning of the Age of Aquarius, called the "Mayan Factor," "that is, a complicated synchronicity involving ancient Mayan prophecy, biochemistry, astrophysics, art, and the I-Ching."[5] Whether or

5. José Arguelles, *The Mayan Factor: Path beyond Technology* (Santa Fe, N.Mex.: Bear & Co., 1987), 144.

not Quetzalcoatl did in fact reappear from beneath the Mexican earth, I have not heard. Nevertheless I recall the general hum of expectation in Berkeley where I was a graduate student at the time, and I recall hearing about a sharp peak in airline reservations to "power spots" around the world as believers gathered to greet the new era. According to Arguelles (in case the reader missed the previous "Harmonic Convergence"), we are again poised for a "Galactic Synchronization" beginning in 2012 C.E., which he describes as "synchronization with the beyond." ETs, UFOs, the "space brothers" — these are not alien entities, but for Arguelles, emanations of *being* itself. He concludes:

> The great return of Harmonic Convergence, then, is an awakening from cultural trance. It is the opportunity for all to engage the Mayan Factor, and, in a word, to receive the galactic imprint. Though at first we do not appear to be Mayan, by the time we reach the moment for galactic synchronization our way of life shall be in every regard a modeling after the lifestyle of the Maya who preceded us in Central America. Only we shall find ourselves as planetary Maya, possessing a brilliantly simple and sophisticated technology based on the matching of solar and psychic frequencies which harmonize the "ration of the sense fields."[6]

There is more to Arguelles's singular worldview and vision of the future than space allows. Suffice it to say that hardly anyone knew (or perhaps cared) that the new age prophet of the Harmonic Convergence event was a Mexican American with a Ph.D. from the University of Chicago; that he had taught at Princeton, the University of Colorado, Evergreen, the Naropa Institute, and other places; that he had written seven books, and, while at the University of California at Davis, had organized the first Whole Earth Festival in the 1970s; that he was raised in Mexico and Minnesota to a "Mexican father with strong Communist leanings and a romantically inclined German-American Lutheran Mother."[7] In his book *The Mayan Factor*, Arguelles details his lifelong search for the meaning behind Mayan calendrics, modern science, and his own genealogy as a descendant of Mesoamerican philosophy and religion. Although "we" would no doubt consider Arguelles "outside"

6. Ibid., 173.
7. Marilyn Ferguson, *Surfers of the Zuvaya: Tales of Interdimensional Travel* (Santa Fe, N.Mex.: Bear & Co., 1989), 9–11.

the realm of normative or historically prefigured definitions of Latino(a) religious thinkers, I would argue that in Arguelles we can locate the innovation of *neplanta* religion in the negotiation and pursuit of religiosity beyond the "predicate" of what normatively constitutes religion or Chicano(a) cultures. That is, is it enough that Arguelles's genealogy and his interest in ancient Mesoamerica qualify him as a Latino(a) religious innovator? Or must there also be other, more tangible and compelling political or geographical shibboleths that must be met? Can we "claim" Arguelles and his work as "Chicano(a)" religion, even if he never speaks of Aztlán, the Virgin of Guadalupe, or the beloved Mother Church? Does the fact that he is mestizo raised in the (relative) comfort of Midwestern suburbia outside of Aztlán somehow disqualify him from our reading list in Chicano(a)/Latino(a) religions? Is his "new age" eclecticism any less "Latino(a)" than, say, Gloria Anzaldúa's borrowing from Jung and her complete rewriting of ancient Mexican history in her celebrated work *Borderlands/La Frontera*? And if we admit Arguelles, can we not also "reclaim" the colorful and mysterious Marie de Souza de Canavarro, "the first woman, and second person of European descent naturally to profess Buddhism on American soil [in 1897]"[8] (although her father was probably Mexican, her first language Spanish, her first religious identity Roman Catholic, and her childhood spent in Texas and California)?

This predicament of catalogue and classification of what constitutes specifically Chicano(a), or even broadly, "Latino(a)" religion(s), I am arguing, needs to be questioned for underlying essentialisms of culture, identity, and nationalisms that may in fact prohibit the understanding of the richness of our "object" of study. On the other hand, the predicament of *neplanta* must continually force us to negotiate the boundaries of what constitutes Latino(a) tradition and culture if we are to stave off the dangers of assimilation. But, even within the supposedly "safe" *fronteras* of Chicano(a) cultures, the dilemmas of finding oneself "between things" can be equally troubling. Here, the recent work of Cherrie Moraga gives us the best example of "betweenness," even when one is presumably on the "inside" of the Chicano(a) canon.

---

8. Tom A. Tweed, "Inclusivism and the Spiritual Journey of Marie de Souza Canavarro (1919–1933)," *Religion* 24 (1994): 44.

CHERRIE MORAGA:
THE IRRUPTION OF THE SACRED FEMININE
IN THE *SEXTO SOL*

In her startling and raw collection of essays and poems, *The Last Generation,* Cherrie Moraga abrades the "1,950-mile long open wound" of Chicano(a) culture that Anzaldúa described as the border between Mexico and the United States.[9] Transgressing the boundaries of sexuality, assuming an essentialist indigenous Chicano(a) identity, and realizing the power of prophetic voice, Moraga laments the passing of Chicano(a) culture:

> I write with the same knowledge, the same sadness [of the Aztec sages faced with the destruction of their gods and codices], recognizing the full impact of the colonial "experiment" on the lives of Chicanos, *mestizos* and Native Americans. Our codices — dead leaves unwritten — lie smoldering in the ashes of disregard, censure, and erasure. [This book] emerges from those ashes. I write against time, out of a sense of urgency that Chicanos are a disappearing tribe, out of a sense of this disappearance in my own *familia....* My *tio's* children have not taught their own children to be Mexicans. They have become "Americans." And we're all supposed to quietly accept this passing, this slow and painless death of a *cultura,* this invisible disappearance of a people. But I do not accept it. I write. I write as I always have, but now I write for a much larger *familia.*[10]

Moraga also understands that she is caught between the universality of writing to reach the widest audience possible and the paradox of being a Chicana writer whose universality nevertheless depends upon her cultural specificity.[11] Her other worry is that in the 1990s, without the backing of a strong cultural and political Chicano(a) movement, Chicano(a) expressive culture (text, art, music, performance) risks being swallowed up by the commodifying and appropriating mainstream culture. In composing her Chicano(a) "codex," Moraga operates in the interstices — the *neplanta* — between ancient Aztec myth and prophecy, and the decay or even death of modern Chicano(a) politics and identity;

9. Cherrie Moraga, *The Last Generation: Prose and Poetry* (Boston: South End Press, 1993). Gloria Anzaldúa describes this *herida abierta* [open wound] in her book, *Borderlands/ La Frontera: The New Mestiza* (San Francisco: Aunt Lute, 1987).
10. Moraga, *The Last Generation,* 2.
11. Ibid., 59.

she is also pulled between the defiance of her Chicana lesbianism and queer *raza* culture on the one hand, and the patriarchy and rigidity of Chicano(a) cultural nationalism on the other. In reading her book it is clear that she struggles as well with the unresolved desire for an authentic indigenous identity and her distance from lived Indian cultures.[12]

I want to comment on Moraga's innovation in her use of Meso-american myth and prophecy to underscore the point about how *neplanta* religion resolves the discomfort of liminality. One example: In her essay, *En busca de la fuerza femenina,* Moraga searches for "a portrait of *la Mechicana* before the 'Fall,' before shame, before betrayal, before Eve, Malinche and Guadalupe; before the occupation of Aztlán, *la llegada de los españoles,* the Aztec's War of Flowers . . . [a portrait of womanhood] more than the bent back in the fields, more than assembly-line fingers and the rigid body beneath the bed, more than the veiled face above the rosary beads."[13] She finds her answer at the top of a pyramid in Tepotzlán, Mexico, witnessing a total eclipse of the sun: "*El sol fue co-mido por la fuerza femenina*" [the sun was consumed by female power] she explains, "But we women were not afraid, accustomed as we are to the darkness." Moraga writes:

> In public we mouthed the shapes of [the words of the Conchero priest in Aztec regalia who] mourned the loss of light, and in secret we sang praise to She Who Went Unacknowledged, She Who Re-mains in Shadow, She Who Has the Power to Put Out the Sun's Light. Coyolxauhqui, the moon, reduced in newspapers to the image of a seductress, flirtatious coquette, merging coitus with the sun. Later, we women, lesbianas from all parts of America Latina, would offer sacrifice, burn *copal,* call out her name.[14]

Realizing for the first time in her life the eclipsing power of the female force, she accepts the interpretation that the sun's return in a "second dawn" after the eclipse has marked the end of the *Quinto Sol,* the current era, according to Aztec myth. This dramatic passing of the epoch, she

---

12. According to Anthony Stevens-Arroyo, no one is selling "certificates of authenticity," as is occurring among the "Northern" Tainos in New Jersey. See his "Baroque Discovery: On the Origins of Latino/Hispanic Religious Identity," a paper presented at *Re-constructing Time and Borders,* March 27, 1998. For a more thorough treatment of putative Taino identity in the Caribbean, see his "The Persistence of Religious Cosmovision in an Alien World," in *Enigmatic Powers,* 113–35.

13. Moraga, *The Last Generation,* 72.

14. Ibid., 76.

writes, signals "the end of a 500-year *historia sangrienta* that saw the near destruction of the Indigenous peoples of *Las Americas*. And from the ashes of destruction, a new era ... born: *El Sexto Sol: La época de la Conciencia Humana.*"[15]

What I find interesting in Moraga's essay is the way she so completely undermines the Aztec story about the earth goddess, Coatlicue giving birth to Huitzilopochtli, the sun and patron war god of the Aztecs. As the myth has come down to us:

> ... One day, when Coatlicue was sweeping, there fell on her some plumage, a ball of fine feathers. Immediately Coatlicue picked them up and put them in her bosom. When she finished sweeping, she looked for the feathers she had put in her bosom, but she found nothing there. At that moment Coatlicue was with Child.[16]

Coatlicue's daughter Coyolxauhqui, outraged and insulted by this dishonorable pregnancy, conspires with her brothers to murder her mother: "My brothers, she has dishonored us, we must kill our mother, the wicked woman who is now with child. Who gave her what she carries in her womb?" At the moment of attack, however, Huitzilopochtli springs out of Coatlicue's womb, fully caparisoned for battle, attacks Coyolxauhqui and dismembers her: The ancient text reads, "he cut off her head, and left it lying there on the slope of Coatepetl. The body of Coyolxauhqui went rolling down the hill, it fell to pieces, in different places fell her hands, her legs, her body." As a mythological description of the sunrise and the eclipse of the moon's powers, this story also served as a legitimation for Aztec imperialism under the patronage of the god Huitzilopochtli while the defeat of Coyolxauhqui and her allies served as a powerful reminder to tribute peoples of the awesome power of the Aztecs.[17] In her retelling of this story Moraga rewrites the plot. Her version finds Coyolxauhqui incensed that her mother is giving birth to a god

---

15. Ibid.

16. "The Birth of Huitzilopochtli, Patron God of the Aztecs," *Native Mesoamerica Spirituality*, ed. and trans. Miguel León-Portilla (New York: Paulist Press, 1980), 220.

17. See David Carrasco's explanation of the multiple meanings of this story in *Religions of Mesoamerica* (San Francisco: Harper & Row, 1990), 7–77; and "Myth, Cosmic Terror, and Templo Mayor," in *The Great Temple of Tenochtitlán: Center and Periphery in the Aztec World*, ed. Johanna Broda, David Carrasco, and Eduardo Matos Moctezuma (Berkeley: University of California Press, 1987), 132–37. An insightful and brief explanation of Coyolxauhqui's iconography and symbolism can be found in Esther Pasztory, *Aztec Art* (New York: Harry N. Abrams, 1983), 152–55.

of war; she decides to kill her mother "rather than submit to a world where war would become God."[18] In her analysis, Moraga observes:

> Here mother and daughter are pitted against each other and daughter must kill male-defined motherhood in order to save the culture from misogyny, war, and greed. But *el hijo* comes to the defense of patriarchal motherhood, kills *la mujer rebelde,* and female power is eclipsed by the rising light of the Sun/Son.... Huitzilopochtli is not my god. And although I revere his mother, Coatlicue, *Dios de la muerte y La Vida,* I do not pray to her. I pray to the daughter, *La Hija Rebelde.*[19]

Moraga ignores the transgression of sexual morality of the "original" story ("she has dishonored us...the wicked woman who is now with child"), interpreting it as a "*machista* myth" where the as-yet unborn male child is privileged over the sister. "In my own art, I am writing that wound." She explains:

> That moment when brother is born and sister is mutilated by his envy. He possesses the mother, holds her captive, because she cannot refuse any of her children, even her enemy son.... This *machista* myth is enacted every day of our lives, every day that the sun (Huitzilopochtli) rises from the horizon and the moon (Coyolxauhqui) is obliterated by his light.[20]

Thus, cowering at the top of a pyramid watching a reversal of this primordial patriarchal myth, Moraga finds the promise of a new epoch, the Sixth Sun. "I am not the church-goer that my mother is, but the same faithfulness drives me to write," she confesses. That is, she is searching in her writing "for Coyolxauhqui amid all the disfigured female characters and the broken men that surround them in my plays and poems. I search for a whole woman I can shape with my own Chicana tongue and hand."[21] "She who has been banished, the mutilated sister who transforms herself into the moon. She is *la fuerza femenina,* our attempt to pick up the fragments of our dismembered womanhood and reconstitute ourselves."[22]

---

18. Moraga, *The Last Generation,* 73.
19. Ibid.
20. Ibid., 73.
21. Ibid., 76.
22. Ibid., 74.

Like the enigmatic Page One of the Codex Fejervary-Mayer, which contains an image encompassing time, space, and divination, Moraga's text forces modern Chicano(a) consciousness to return full circle to a place that is *before* the imposition and separation of Western time and cartography. Her rewriting of myths and the insistence that we are the "last generation" of Chicano/as reveals that indeed we are undergoing the convulsions that signal the end of the *Quinto Sol*. She declares, "Amid the fires of the [1992] Los Angeles Rebellion, on the eve of the fading *Quinto Sol* and a rising new *época,* I paint in scribe colors — the black of this ink, and the red of those fires — my own Chicano codex. I offer it as a closing prayer for the last generation."[23] Throwing off the conventions of her cultural Christianity, received academic wisdom about the meaning of Mesoamerican cultures, and the pull to assimilation, she snatches the texts of Chicano(a) religions and spirituality away from the hands of the experts and asserts that, "The Chicano codex is a portrait of our daily lives. Images of spam next to a stack of store-bought tortillas. *Chavalitos* working in the family *panadería.* We are a codex of *lotería* and boxing matches. We pick *nopales,* graduate from college, are elected County Supervisor. We low-ride in East Los, bumper to bumper in minitrucks."[24] At the dawn of the new era of human consciousness, "Our Olmeca third eye begins to glisten in the slowly rising light."[25]

CONCLUSIONS

In this essay I have focused on religious innovators as examples of how Chicano(a) visionaries wrestle with the quandary of identities "between" ideas, cultures, religious systems, generations, nations, and even time frames. Innovators like Moraga and Arguelles are, however, hardly new to solving the predicament of Mexican Americanity. We know well the insistence of distinctively mestizo/*neplanta* forms of spirituality that have periodically burst out of the supposed dualisms of sacred/profane, Catholic/Protestant, *lo Indio/lo Español.* But even, and perhaps especially, in the life of communities of Mexican descent we can trace the importance and centrality of religious life — irrespective of orthodoxies or *neplanta* predicaments — back to the dramatic struggles of entire communities.

23. Ibid., 184.
24. Ibid., 192.
25. Ibid.

Historical records of 1875 show that the Mexican community in
Brownsville, Texas, was determined to keep a group of exiled Mexican
Sisters of Charity in their midst but were unable to convince the local
bishop to allow them to stay. When the bishop arranged rail passage
for the sisters to leave Brownsville, the local community showed up at
the train station. When the train arrived, they pulled a railroad car off
its track and away from the rails to make their point.[26] And again in
1939, the women of the San Diego Nuestra Señora de Guadalupe parish, unhappy with the removal of Spanish-speaking priests by the Anglo
bishop, stripped bare the furnishings and household items of the parish
house. When the new Anglo priest arrived to find an empty house, it
was determined that community members had taken back the furniture
and household items because they had been "gifts" and "loans" to the
previous occupant, the Spanish-speaking priest, and not "the Church."[27]

Whether we are speaking of individuals or whole communities of
faith, it is clear that what constitutes Latino(a) "religion" goes far beyond mass and sacrament, text or ritual. But how do we, or should we,
talk about, contain, or even understand the transformations and explorations of how "traditions" provide new or alternative meanings in the
neplanta spaces and processes that mark the experiences of Chicano/as,
and other U.S. Latino/as? Clearly, Chicano(a) religious transformations
and innovations into the next century will continue working through the
predicaments of *neplanta* "between things": between traditions, between
the institution and the vernacular practices of domestic space, between
the schematizations of academics and the "messiness" of everyday life,
and between the relationship between humanity and the sacred —
between two Americas.

In their return to indigenous texts Moraga, Arguelles, and others require Chicano(a) consciousness to move forward but also back to the
time before European imposition. And in the taking-up of such texts (al-
beit interpolated by generations of scholars and other "outsiders") — a
"leap of faith" into the fulfillment of an Indigenous past — they attempt
to resolve the discomfort of *neplantism* by "rescuing" the Indian from
the lopsided dialectic between brown and white. Arguelles, however, is
confident in the felicitous convergence of mestizo ideas, pre-Columbian

26. Carmen Tafolla, "The Church in Texas," in *Fronteras: A History of the Latin American Church in the USA since 1513* (San Antonio: Mexican American Cultural Center, 1983), 191.

27. Alberto López Pulido, "Nuestra Señora de Guadalupe: The Mexican Catholic Experience in San Diego," *Journal of San Diego History* 37, no. 4 (1991): 249.

Mayan calendrics, and modern science. Moraga, on the other hand, offers a flesh-and-blood alternative spirituality in the face of modernity
and postmodernity. She creates a counter-discourse, an antisyncretism,
that may or may not depend on or at least admit to the European half of
the dialogue for her pretensions to universal meaning from the periphery
of Bay Area Chicana lesbian *indigenismo*.

Given Enrique Dussel's critique and suspicion of universalizing discourses masquerading as though Indian America does not exist (in his
book of essays *The Underside of Modernity*), I do not believe that it
is mere coincidence that as examples of Chicano(a) religious thinkers,
both José Arguelles and Cherríe Moraga deny the structures and texts
of Christianity in favor of indigenous ones.[28] In these ancient and epic
spaces there is room to move and breathe new life and interpretations
into ancient stories and knowledges away from the censoring pens of
"scholars" and theological authority. And in so doing, they pay homage
to a world that — despite the corrosive powers of the modern and postmodern predicaments — has managed to survive and can still declare,
after more than five hundred years, "do not be astonished; we are still
neplanta."[29]

---

28. Enrique Dussel, "Modernity, Eurocentrism, and Trans-Modernity: In Dialogue with
Charles Taylor," in *The Underside of Modernity: Apel, Ricoeur, Rorty, Taylor, and the Philosophy of Liberation,* ed. and trans. Eduardo Mendieta (Atlantic Highlands, N.J.: Humanities
Press, 1995), 129–59. I reject Alan Neely's comment that Arguelles and Moraga do not fall
into the category of "thinkers" but are appropriately "uliterary" or within the realm of "imagination." I would argue that dissident and singular voices like Arguelles and Moraga represent
types of "subjugated knowledges" in insurrection, as defined by Foucault. Given Maduro's
observations about the need to go beyond orthodox religiosity, systems, and ideas, those of
Arguelles and Moraga cannot be held to "orthodox" standards of what constitutes religious
thought (regardless of content or applicability). Consult Alan Neely, response to panel, "Re-
Constructing Borders: Latin American and U.S. Latino(a) Religious Identities," *Reconstructing
Time and Borders,* March 28, 1998.
29. My thought regarding the idea of *neplanta* religion continues to experience evolution
and is being further developed in a book-length manuscript that I am currently preparing for
publication by Indiana University Press.

Index

accompaniment, theology of, 115
action, creative dimensions of, 151
Acts of the Martyrs, 40n.15, 45, 48–49
aesthetic experience, 147–48, 157n.58
aesthetic form, 136
aesthetic-praxic realm, 158
aesthetic praxis, 159
aesthetics
 focus on suffering, 197
 theological attraction for, 191–94
 wisdom of, 196
aesthetic theology, challenge of evil and
 suffering to, 8
Africa, bringing story together with
 Bible, 27
Ahlstrom, Sydney E., 57–62
Albanese, Catherine L. 63
America: Religions and Religion
 (Albanese), 63
Americans
 characterization of, 84–85
 Others for, 87
 protecting from feminized influence,
 88
 related characteristics, 85–86
*America's Religions: Traditions and
 Cultures* (Williams), 63
ambiguity, 188
Anglada, David, 210–11
Anzaldúa, Gloria, 75, 242, 243
apartheid, 29–30
Apocryphal Acts, 45
Aquino, María Pilar, 55, 121, 135
Arguedas, José María, 122
Arguelles, José, 240–42, 248–49
Aristotle, 145–46
assigned readings, 21

assimilation, 177
Atkinson, Clarissa W., 45–46
Augustine, 36n.3
autobiographical paragraphs, 21

Baird, Robert, 57
Barajas, Teresa, 232–33
Basso, Teresa, 221–22, 223, 224
beauty. *See also* tragic beauty
 divine, 192–93
 encounter with, 127–28
 at forefront of von Balthasar's
 theology, 130–31
 hunger for, 193
being, literature and arts revealing
 nature of, 133
Bernstein, Richard, 157n.59
Beveridge, Albert, 85
Bhabha, Homi, 50, 80, 184
Bible
 focus on as literary, ideological,
 rhetorical, 14–15
 influence of social identity factors on
 reading of, 24
 liberating, 24, 26
 read-across strategy, 15
 teaching in diverse world, 5–6
Bible-lacking people, 92–93
biblical hermeneutics, postcolonial
 studies from within, 102
biblical studies
 assumptions challenged, 33
 examining assumptions regarding, 28
 identity in, 15
 teaching in age of diversity and
 globalization, 13
Bingemer, María Clara, 135

251

black experience
  element of traditional religious
    historiography, 60, 61
  excluded from military and mission
    work in Puerto Rico, 85
black theology, 162n.71
black/white paradigm
  deconstructing, 72
  excluding Latino/as from U.S.
    religious paradigm, 73, 75
Boff, Leonardo, 149
Bolton, Herbert Eugene, 75
border crossing deaths, 182–86
borderlands, 74–76
Borderlands/La Frontera (Anzaldúa),
  242
Bowden, Henry Warner, 58, 60
Boyarin, Daniel, 16–17
Boyer, Paul, 66–67
Brauer, Jerald C., 58, 59
Brown: The Last Discovery of America
  (Rodriguez), 198
Browne, Tess, 222

cacerolazos, 172
Caminemos con Jesús: Toward a
  Hispanic/Latino Theology of
  Accompaniment (Goizueta), 140,
  144–49
Canavarro, Marie de Souza de, 242
Caribbean culture, 213–14
Carrion, Adolfo, 210–11
Casserella, Peter, 154
Castañeda, Margarita, 228
Catholicism
  aesthetic celebration, 196
  missionaries' exclusion from true
    Christianity, 92
  as patriarchy, 226–27
  peripheral location of, 51
Cervantes, Miguel de, 124
chaos
  darkness of, 81n.6
  imposing control over perception of,
    94–95

Chicano(a) consciousness, reclaiming,
  248–49
Chicano(a) culture, 243–44
Chicano(a) spirituality, 239–40
Chicano codex, 247
A Chicano Theology (Guerrero), 140–
  43
Christian aesthetics, in von Balthasar's
  Glory of the Lord, 132
Christianity and Culture (Elizondo),
  105
church writings, early, 36
climate, linked to racial evolution, 87
Cofer, Judith Ortiz, 126
Colin, Ernesto, 123, 124–26
collaborative theology. See teología de
  conjunto
colonial discourses, 50–51, 53
colonial identity, denying dependence
  on the Other, 80
colonialism
  disjointedness of, 86
  enforcer of unequal and unjust
    relations, 52–53
  rewriting Puerto Rico's history, 88
colonial phases, 91n.48
colonization, mission's relation to in
  Puerto Rico, 83–84
communicative action, 145n.20
competitiveness, 17n.12
Concilio Latino-Americano de Iglesias
  Cristianas, 206
Cone, James H., 122
Congregation of the Sisters of Charity
  of the Incarnate Word (C.C.V.I.),
  18
constructive theology, 108
contextuality, 30
contextualization, 15–19
contextual theology, 120
creativity
  of action, 151
  metaphors of, 152–53
criollo, 175
critical Marxists, 154–55

critical social theory, 157–58
cultural memory, 101–2
cultural resistance, 139, 149
cultural subjugation, 111
cultural symbols, 141, 143
cultural theorizing, advancing mode of, 107
culture
   increased interest in concept and theorization of, 104
   related to identity, 110–11
   as theoretical category, 109–10
   turn to in Hispanic/Latino(a) theology, 106–8
   varieties of views of, 110

Daniels, David, 59, 68–69
decolonial imaginary, 57
decolonial processes, 54
decolonizing, 77
De La Torre, Miguel A., 23, 24–27
Delgado, Teresa, 123, 126–27
deprivation, theory of, 201
desire, primacy of, 135–36
Dewey, John, 151n.40
Díaz-Stevens, Ana María, 123–24, 226–27, 236–37
Didache, 41n.18
difference, facilitating solidarity of, 116
dignidad, 102
Dirlik, Arif, 55
dis-covery, 54–56, 64–65, 77–78
diversity
   openness to, 34
   promoting in readings, 23
Divine Hiddenness, 190–91
Divine reality
   intellectualization of, 170
   substantivization of, 168
dominant culture, resistance of, 212–15
dominant theologies, misconstruing liberation theologies, 168
Dube, Musa W., 27, 29–33
Durán, Diego, 238–39
Dussel, Enrique, 53, 249

ecclesiology, from barrio context, 102
ego formation, 80
Elías, Rosamaría, 222
Eliot, T. S., 192
Elizondo, Virgilio, 101, 104–5, 140n.3, 150, 226
En la lucha (Isasi-Díaz), 231
erasure, politics of, 16
Espín, Orlando, 128n.26, 154, 197
Espinoza, Carmelita, 221
ethics, relationship with aesthetics, 128
ethics of interpretation, 33
ethnic identity, 16, 20
ethnicity, focus on European immigrants, 70
ethnographic accounts, 114
Europe
   center of modern colonial system, 51
   self-located at center of World History, 53
Eusebius, 44
evil, confronting, 181–82, 186
Exhortation to Martyrdom (Origen), 44
existential-empirical tension, 170–74
expression, 151–52
extrachurch, 8–9

Fanon, Frantz, 50–51, 56–57n.22
Félix, Efraín, 209–10
female imagery, in colonizing, 87
feminine images, for body and land, 80–81
feminism, including in U.S. religious paradigm, 73
feminization, in portrayal of Puerto Ricans, 88–89
Ferré, Rosario, 126
Feuerbach, Ludwig, 201n.1
Filipino Americans, 238n.1
Filosofía, teología, literatura: Aportes cubanos en los últimos 50 años, 123
Fishbane, Michael, 186n.5
Fitzpatrick, Joseph, 207
Flores, María Carolina, 235

forgetfulness, potential for, 184
Fornet-Betancourt, Raúl, 123
Foucault, Michel, 62n.41
Freud, Sigmund, 201n.1
Friedman, Susan, 115
frontier thesis, 74
fundamentalists, 25

Gadamer, Hans-Georg, 169
Galilean Journey: The Mexican-American Promise (Elizondo),
    140–41n.3
Gallardo, Gloria, 219, 225
García-Rivera, Alejandro, 128–29, 130,
    154, 197
Gebara, Ivone, 136
gendered representations, 81
gender ideologies, 80–81
gender issues, black/white paradigm
    guiding work in, 72
gender relations, egalitarianism of Jesus
    movement excluded, 45
general history, 62n.41
globalization, 172, 177
    effect on identity, 16
    effect on liberation theologies, 171
    encouraging differences within, 29
    resistance to, 30
The Glory of the Lord (von Balthasar),
    130–31, 132
God
    as Other, 169
    treated in Hispanic/Latino(a)
        theologies, 109
Goizueta, Roberto, 114, 128, 129–30,
    134–35, 153–54
    on day-to-day survival, 157–58
    explaining mediation between aes-
        thetic praxis and ethical-political
        action, 155
    wisdom of aesthetics, 196–97
González, Justo, 114
Gospels, compared to *Iliad,* 188
Gramsci, Antonio, 154
Greider, Brett, 122

grounding, 164, 171
Guerrero, Andrés, 140–43
Gutiérrez, Gustavo, 120–21, 122, 183,
    186, 191, 226

Haas, Alois M., 131n.38
Hall, Stuart, 15n.6, 52–53
Harmonic Convergence, 241
Hatch, Roger D., 65, 69
Herder, Johann Gottfried, 151
Hermanas. *See* Las Hermanas
Hernández, Karen, 203–4
"hiddenness from God" tradition, 189
hierarchalism, 32
hierarchical dyads, 81
Hispanic, 1n.1
Hispanic/Latino(a) cultural production,
    incorporating into theologies,
    104–10
Hispanic/Latino(a) religious experience,
    recovering, 1–2
Hispanic/Latino(a) theology, 101–4
    aesthetics central to, 129
    anthologies devoted to, 4
    articulating accents of integral
        liberation theology, 149–50
    aspiring to transformative social
        relevance, 117–18
    as body of work, 143n.13
    caught between theological traditions,
        163–64, 165, 169, 171–74
    characteristics of, 118
    cultural focus, 6–7
    focus on identity, 110–13
    as *Fuenteovejuna theology,* 114
    incorporating culture, 104–10
    interdisciplinary approach to, 5
    lack of involvement with
        socioeconomic issues, 112–13
    and "liberation," ambiguous use of, 7
    need to critique social structures of
        domination, 157
    need to engage Marxist roots, 161
    need to understand emphasis on
        cultural resistance, 153

Hispanic/Latino(a) theology *(continued)*
  overlooking economic metaphors,
    152–53
  recognition increasing, 2
  as theology of liberation, 105
  tragic beauty in, 196–97
  treatment of God in, 109
  three waves of in United States, 2–3
  uniqueness of, 103–4
*Hispanic Women: Prophetic Voice in the
  Church* (Isasi-Díaz and Tarango),
    114, 218, 230
historical connectedness, 35
historical Jesus study, 102
historical writing, revision of, 50
historiography, challenges to, 54. *See
  also* U.S. religious historiography
history
  fictive character of, 56
  myths of dominant discourses, 56
*History of Christianity in the United
  States and Canada, A,* (Noll), 60
hospitality, 184–85
human action, end in itself, 145
Humane Borders, 183
humanities, change in theoretical
    foundations of, 104

identity
  in biblical studies, 15
  in Christ Jesus, 17
  cultural advantages related to, 21
  disclosure of, 22–23, 33
  discussion related to justice, 112
  essentialist notion of, 17
  exercises about, 21–22
  Hispanic/Latino(a) theology focus on,
    110–13
  introductory topic for biblical
    criticism, 19
  self-identification, 16
  students', 20–22
  teacher's, 19–20
  of text, 22–23
Iglesias, María, 222, 223

imaginary, 81
imitatio Christi, 43, 44
inculturation from above, 31
inculturation from below, 31
inculturation hermeneutics, 28–29,
    30–31
Informes, 235
integral liberation, 7, 140, 149–50, 153
intellectual assimilation, 164, 170–74
intercultural criticism, 14, 34
  contextualization, 15–19
  dimensions of interpretative process,
    14–15
  emphasizing reading across texts,
    readers, and interpretations, 17
  pedagogic strategies, 19–23
  understanding through literature,
    23–33
Irigaray, Luce, 82n.8
Isasi-Díaz, Ada María, 105, 114,
    160–61n.68, 218, 230, 236

Jesus
  member of marginalized culture, 25,
    27
  mestizo identity of, 112
Joas, Hans, 151
John of the Cross, 132
joint theology. See *teología de conjunto*
Joyce, James, 193, 194

Kabbalah, 200
Kay, Jeffrey Ames, 133
Keller, Catherine, 81n.6

La Raza, 221
labor
  creative dimension of, 153
  labor, role in perception of theology,
    167–68
Laboy, Wilfredo, 211–12
Lacan, Jacques, 80
laity, theology of, 132
Las Casas, Bartolomé de, 183–94,
    196–97

Las Hermanas, 8
  activism of, 217–18
  addressing lack of ethnic repre-
    sentation in church hierarchy,
    224–26
  addressing social issues, 225, 226
  alliances of, 227
  attempts to marginalize, 226
  doing theology, 218–19, 231
  early growth of, 222
  empowering nature of, 232–33
  four-part methodology, 231–32
  lack of early focus on feminist
    agendas, 227–28
  later focus on issues affecting
    grassroots Latinas, 228
  legacy of, 237
  limiting membership to native Spanish
    speakers, 221–22
  membership extended to Latin laity,
    223–24
  mission of, 223
  reduced membership, 235
  ritualizing among, 233–35
  role as voice of dissension, 236
  sense of the divine, 229–30
  sociohistorical context, 219–28
  spirituality of transformative struggle,
    229–37
Last Generation, The, (Moraga), 243
Latina feminism, 160–61n.68
Latina theology, as communal process,
  114
latinidad, 152
Latino(a) cultural identity, 105
Latino(a) experience, neglected in U.S.
  society, 2
Latino(a) Pentecostalism, 8, 202
  dangers of overgeneralizing, 202–3
  growth of, 206–8
  leadership development in, 208–9
  Puerto Rican roots, 207
  social issues, approach to, 203
  vehicle for dealing with social issues,
    204–5

Latino(a) Protestant churches, history
  of, 35–36
Latino(a) religious history, 76
Latino/as
  history in U.S., 106
  left out of U.S. religious historical
    discourses, 73
  provided space for new epistemology,
    78
  surrendering heritage, 39
Latino(a) theology. See His-
    panic/Latino(a) theology
Latino/Latina/Latino(a), 1n.1
Leadership Conference of Women
  Religious, 219–20
liberalism, fundamental problem of,
  177–78
liberation
  ambiguous use of term, 7
  as creative act, 151
  eclipse of, 169
  geopolitical dimension of, 29. See also
    globalization
  implicit, 155, 156–57
  linked with salvation, 24
  links with economics, 139
  meaning in Latino(a) context, 138–39
  role in Hispanic/Latino(a) theology,
    162
  top-down process, 142–43
liberation hermeneutics, 24
liberationist worldview, 172–73
liberation process, totalitarian affinities
  in, 156
liberation theology, 120
  absorbed into center, 170
  distinguishing types of, 139
  exploring marginalized voices, 121,
    122
  misunderstood, 168
  representations of Christ crucified,
    183
  theological self-understanding, 166–
    67
  using Marx as departure point, 154

liberative action, clarifying, 161
Limón, Graciela, 124, 125–26
literature
    characterizing as theological, 136–37
    human expression of divine Glory,
        133
    offering vision of the future, 126–27
    and theological methodology, 124,
        134
    as theological resource, 119–20
    as theological source and voice, 7
    understanding as theology, 120
    using to combat isolation of theology,
        125
    vehicle for unearthing Latin American
        intellectual heritage, 122
    von Balthasar's use of, 131
Literature and Theology at Century's
    End (Salyer), 119
Location of Culture, The (Bhabha),
    50
Long, Charles H., 72
Lugo, Juan, 207
Luther, Martin, 189–90

MacDermot, Violet, 42
Machado, Daisy, 73, 75, 76
Macías, Rosa Martha Zárate, 217
male power, trinity of, 97
manifest destiny, 74, 77
marginalized readings, 24
margins, locating God at, 24–25
Márquez, Gabriel García, 124
Martin, David, 213–14
Martin, Shane, 123, 124–26
Marty, Martin E., 73n.69
Martyrdom of Perpetua and Felicitas,
    46
martyrs
    prophetic figures, 41–42
    purpose of testimonies about, 37
    subversive nature of, 43–44, 46–48
    visions of, 37–38
    visions as communal property, 41–43
    writings about, 36

Martyrs, The: A Study in Social Control
    (Riddle), 42
Marx, Karl, 142, 145–47, 152, 153,
    201n.1
masculinity, aspect of American
    colonialism, 84–85
Matsuoka, Fumitaka, 119
Mayan Factor, 240
Mayan Factor, The (Aguelles), 241
McKinzie, Steve, 63, 65
McLean, Robert, 89, 95
Mejido, Manuel J., 128n.28, 144n.15
Memmi, Albert, 56–57n.22
memoria rota, 78
Mesoamerican myth, Moraga
    undermining, 244–47
mestizaje, 102, 105, 112, 125, 126, 148,
    164–65, 172, 174–78
    fragmentation, 177–78
    fundamental choice of, 176–77
    history of, 175–76
Mexican American Women's National
    Association, 236
Mexican Sisters of Charity, 248
Mignolo, Walter, 53–54, 78, 81n.7, 91
migration, 182–86, 198–99
Miles, Margaret, 128n.26
missionaries
    characterizing subjects by colors,
        89–91
    depiction of Puerto Rico, 87
    portrayal of Puerto Ricans as Others,
        88–89
    postinvasion experience in Puerto
        Rico, 6
missionary work, in Puerto Rico, 82–84
modernity
    discourse of, 55
    Eurocentric understanding of, 51n.5
    impetus behind traditional and
        colonial historiography, 51
    the "West" and, 51–54
modern theology, self-assessment,
    165–66
Mohr, Nicholasa, 126

Moore, R. Laurence, 63
Moraga, Cherrie, 240, 243–47, 249
Mujeres Activas en Letras y Cambio
    Social, 236
Mujeres Grandes, 235
mujerista theology, 218, 230
Murphy, Joseph, 214

narrative form, in analysis of U.S.
    religious history, 62
negative instrumentalization, 155n.54
neoliberalism, 171, 172–73, 177
neo-Pentecostalism, 201n.1
neplanta religion, 8–9, 238–49
*New Directions in American Religious
    History,* 65–67
new internationalism, 184
new socialism, 141–42, 152
Nietzsche, Friedrich, 194
Noll, Mark, 60, 61, 68
nonperson, center of theological
    reflection, 121
Nuestra Señora de Guadalupe (San
    Diego), 248

Oakes, Edward, 131
objectivity, 25–26
Odell, Edward, 95
Olazabal, Francisco, 206
oppression
    memory of, 158
    paradigm of, 121–22
    sources of, 106
    subversion of, 6
ordinary readers, 30–31
Orientalism (Said), 56–57n.22
Origen, 44–45
Ortega, Gregoria, 219, 225
Other
    boundary with Christian, 92
    Catholics as, 92–93
    need for portrayal in colonial
        discourse, 86
    Puerto Rican portrayed as, 88
    seeing God in, 190

Other (*continued*)
    stereotype, 81
    within U.S. Protestant-Puritan
        tradition, 61
    within U.S. religious historiography,
        71
*Our Country: Its Possible Future and
    Its Present Crisis* (Strong), 84

PADRES (Priests Associated for Re-
    ligious, Educational, and Social
    Rights), 225–26
Paul, vision of, 47–48
pedagogy
    nontraditional practices, 17
    strategies, 19–23
Pedraja, Luis, 114
Pentecostal beliefs, dangers of
    overgeneralization, 202–3
Pentecostal movement, history of,
    206–8
Pérez, Emma, 57, 76
Pérez, Luis, 212
personal disclosure, 22–23
philosophers, source of theological
    reflection, 187
poiesis, 145–47, 148–49
political resistance, in Pentecostalism,
    202–3
politics of erasure, 16
popular religion, 105, 112, 152–53,
    157, 174
    importance of, 160
    subordinate to *mestizaje,* 178
Porto Alegre, 172
Porto Rico. *See* Puerto Rico
postcolonial discourses, 54–55, 56–57
postcolonial migration, 184
postcolonial perspective, 18–19
postcolonial studies, origins of, 56–
    57n.22
postcolonial theory, approach to Puerto
    Rico, 79
positivism, 25–26

postmodernism, 173, 177–78
postmodern theologies, 169
praxis
  as creative act, 160
  Latina, 232
  quality of action, 156–57
  reinterpretation of, 144–47, 148–49
production, as metaphor of creativity, 152
prophets
  change in perception of, 43
  true vs. false, 41n.18
  unwelcome messengers, 43
Protestant churches, eagerness for missionary activity in Puerto Rico, 82
Protestantism, positioning of, 93
Protestant-Puritan perspective, 70
  effect of revisions within, 71
  responses to voices from outside, 71–72
  tradition of, 59, 60, 61
Puerto Ricans
  missionary influence on, 212–13
  Pentecostalism's influence on, 213–14
  receptors of Spanish culture, 91
Puerto Rican theology, 101–2n.1, 126–27
Puerto Rico
  condition in 1898, 81–82
  missionaries' depiction of, 87
  naming of, 81–82
  Other in, 87
  portrayed awaiting American order, 88, 94
  redemption linked to conquest, 95–96
  relationship between occupation and mission, 83
  revised creation story for, 79
  role in Latino(a) Pentecostalism, 207
Puritanism, central role in U.S. religious history, 60

Quintero-Rivera, Angel, 205–6

race
  black/white issue only in U.S., 69
  Puerto Rican portrayal within, 89–90
  racial/ethnic paradigm, replacing, 77
  racial/ethnic pluralism, lack of emphasis on, 69
Ramos, Efrén Rivera, 87n.33
rational, superiority over irrational, 53
raza de bronce, 176
raza cósmica, 140, 175–76
raza theology, 226
Readers, 64
Reading the Bible in the Global Village (Dube), 23, 27–33
"Reading the Bible in the Global Village: Issues and Challenges from African Readings" (Upkong), 28–29
Reading the Bible from the Margins (De La Torre), 23, 24–27
reading strategies, 23
  comparative analysis, 31–33
  geopolitical dimension, 32
  reading-across strategy, 17, 23, 27–33
  reading-with strategy, 17, 23, 24–27
rebellion, in Pentecostalism, 202–3
Recinos, Harold J., 139n.2
Recognizing the Latino Resurgence in U.S. Religion (Díaz-Stevens and Stevens-Arroyo), 1
Reformed Church in America, 212
religious diversity, 63
religious historiography, alternative methodology for, 6
Religious History of the American People, A, (Ahlstrom), 57–62
Religious Outsiders and the Making of Americans (Moore), 63
religious pluralism
  Ahlstrom's narrative as apologia for, 59–62
  increasing plural nature of, 63
resistance, 140, 141–43
Retelling U.S. Religious History (Tweed), 64–65
revisionist theory of praxis, 160–61

revolution, 149, 152
revolutionary social action, 140, 141–43
Riddle, Donald W., 42
ritualizing, among Las Hermanas,
    233–35
Rivera-Pagán, Luis N., 122
Rodríguez, Edmundo, 225
Rodríguez, Rebecca, 204
Rodriguez, Richard, 198
Roman Catholicism, 36, 91–92
Roman Catholics (U.S.), little interest in
    Puerto Rican immigrants, 215
Roosevelt, Theodore, 85, 89n.40
Rorty, Richard, 173
Rosado, Leonecia ("Mama Leo"), 204
Ruiz, Vicki, 227

Sabato, Ernesto, 122
sacred, presence in all aspects of daily
    life, 214
Said, Edward W., 56–57n.22, 79
salvation history, 168
Salyer, George, 119
Sandoval, Chela, 54
Santería, 214
Santiago, Esmeralda, 126
Santiago-Valle, Kevin, 205
scholastic epistemocentrism, 173–74
Segovia, Fernando, 102–3
Sobrino, Jon, 153–54
social change, foundation for, 116
social-cultural transformation, 28–29
social movements, 205–6
social transformation, 149, 152
Southwest U.S.
    as borderlands, 74–76
    religious historiography's view of, 74,
    75
Spain
    northern Europe's displacement of as
        center of colonial system, 51
    stereotypical image of, 91
Spanish American Bible Institute, 207
Steiner, George, 157n.58
Stephen (deacon), 46–47

Stevens-Arroyo, Anthony, 244n.12
storytelling, 123–24
Stout, Harry S., 67–68, 70
Strong, Josiah, 84
students, identities of, 20–22
subjugated knowledge, 249n.29
subversion, 43–44
subversive dimension, 38
suffering, 194–95
    aesthetics facing, 197
    attempts to categorize events of,
        188–89
    memory of, 155, 158–59
symbolic order, 104
The Symbolism of Evil (Ricoeur), 181

Tañón, Ricardo, 208–9
Tarango, Yolanda, 105, 114, 218, 220,
    227–28, 229, 230, 237
Taylor, R. M., 67–68
teacher, disclosing identity in biblical
    studies, 20
teaching
    contextualization of, 14
    politics of, 33
    recognizing context of, 17–18
teología de conjunto, 3, 7, 104, 114–18
Texas revolution, 56
text, identity of, 22–23
theologians
    responsibilities of, 108
    using literature as resource, 119
theological aesthetics, 126, 127–30, 132
theological inquiry, through cultural
    means, 124–25
theological knowledge, sociology of,
    170
theological logos, perception of, 165–68
theology
    combating isolation of through
        literature, 125
    as critically oriented science, 165,
        166, 167, 169
    form and content separated, 129–30

theology (*continued*)
  as historical-hermeneutic science,
    165–66, 167, 169
  uniting form and content, 134–35
  varied understandings of, 7
theology of the cross, 190
theopoetics, 134, 159
total history, 61–62
Tracy, David, 160–61, 188–89, 190–91
tragedy, 187
tragic beauty, 181–82, 191, 194–97
transformative struggle, 218, 229–37
Turner, Victor, 143
Tweed, Thomas A., 64–65
two-party system, 73n.69

U.S. religious historiography
  black/white paradigm constructed
    within, 70
  class issues in, 72–73
  as colonial enterprise, 57–63, 77
  three-party system, 70
  unchallenged, 64–68
  view of Southwest, 74, 75–76
U.S. religious history
  collections, increased production of,
    64
  critique of, 68–69
  micronarratives and case studies in,
    63–64, 67
  new approaches to, 63–69
  regional approach to, 64
universal history, 61–62
universalism, oppressiveness of, 16
University of the Incarnate Word, 18
Upkong, Justin S., 28–29, 30–31

Vasconcelos, José, 144, 147–49, 196
Vásquez, Enedina Cásarez, 235
Vásquez, Sylvia, 230–31
Viladesau, Richard, 128n.25
"Villagizing, Globalizing, and Biblical
  Studies" (Dube), 28
la Virgen de Guadalupe, 140, 142–43,
  152

visions, 37–38
  as communal property, 41–43
  consciousness vs. trance, 46–47n.37
  effect of, 48
  historical overview of subversive
    dimensions of, 43–48
  inspiration for grassroots theology,
    38–39
  modern function of, 39–40
  subject of address, 40–41
  subversive nature of, 46–48
von Balthasar, Hans Urs, 129, 130–33,
  192–93

Weber, David J., 56
Weil, Simone, 187–88, 192, 195
Weinrich, William, 42n.21, 46–47n.37
West, Cornel, 162n.71
West, the
  as historical construct, 52
  as proof of redemptive work of U.S.
    government, 95
  "the West and the Rest," 52
  writing history of colonized, 53
White, Hayden, 62
Wilder, Amos Niven, 134
Williams, Peter W., 63
Wilson, James, 85
Winner, Lauren F., 64, 66
Wittgenstein, Ludwig, 169
women
  overlooked in inculturation
    hermeneutics, 31
  role in Latino(a) Pentecostalism,
    203–4
  stereotypical images, 81
  theology of liberation, 102
writing assignments, 21–22

Ybarra, María de Jesús, 220, 224

Zapata, Dominga, 222
Zárate, Rosa Martha, 233, 234, 236
Žižek, Slavoj, 173
Zubiri, Xavier, 168